Return this book on or before the
Latest Date stamped below.

14

A Guide to
ILLIAC PROGRAMMING

by
L. D. FOSDICK

DIGITAL COMPUTER LABORATORY

UNIVERSITY OF ILLINOIS

URBANA, ILLINOIS

1961

PREFACE TO 1961 EDITION

These notes were originally entitled "Lecture Notes for Mathematics 385". Since this course has been discontinued and replaced by other courses, it seemed appropriate to use a new name for this edition.

The present edition, entitled "A Guide to ILLIAC Programming", contains the same material as the original edition with minor exceptions: in a few places changes were necessary to bring old information up to date; some additional descriptions of the commonly used subroutines have been included; the codes for the post-mortem routines have been removed, but the descriptions of how to use them have been retained. A number of typographical errors have been removed.

The organization of this edition is different than the old one. The formal text is at the front and all appendices are at the back, rather than at the end of individual chapters. The page numbering is sequential throughout, in place of the chaotic scheme that existed in the old edition.

The burden of preparing this new edition has been borne in large measure by my wife, to whom I here express my grateful thanks.

PREFACE

These notes were used during the spring semester and summer session of 1958. A number of errors in the original set of notes has been corrected. Some of the chapters have been modified slightly in order to make the discussion more complete or to clarify certain points. Some parts of these notes, particularly the appendices, are taken directly from the Illiac programming manual, from reports, and library subroutines issued by the Digital Computer Laboratory.

The author wishes to thank members of the staff of the Digital Computer Laboratory and students in the last two semesters in Mathematics 385 for helpful comments and criticisms offered on the original set of notes.

Finally, the author wishes to thank Miss Mary Lou Wells for the excellent job she did in typing the manuscript.

CONTENTS

UNIVERSITY OF ILLINOIS

DIGITAL COMPUTER

CHAPTER 1

BIBLIOGRAPHY - DIGITAL AND ANALOGUE REPRESENTATIONS

The object of these notes is to guide the reader in the use of the
electronic, high-speed, digital computer known as the ILLIAC, which was
constructed at the University of Illinois and put into operation in 1952.
These notes can be used by a beginner, who has had no previous experience
with high-speed computing equipment, and they will serve as a reference
manual for the experienced user; in the latter capacity they replace the
"ILLIAC Programming Manual".

Unfortunately there are no good texts available dealing with the
general aspects of the usage of high-speed computing machines. Various parts
of this subject in which you may be especially interested are probably treated
in the literature listed below.[*]

The following four references deal particularly with the logical
design and circuitry of computers.

(1) "Preliminary Discussion of the Logical Design of an Electronic
Computing Instrument", A. W. Burks, H. H. Goldstine and J. von Neumann.
This is a classic paper documenting the ideas entering into the
design of a class of computing machines sometimes called "Institute
Machines" or "von Neumann Machines". The ILLIAC belongs to this class.
The paper appears as a report issued by the Institute for Advanced
Study, dated June 28, 1946.

(2) "High-Speed Computing Devices", Engineering Research Associates,
McGraw-Hill, 1950. This is one of the earlier books in the field
and is becoming out-of-date. Chapter 14 contains a discussion of
storage units, including a readable discussion of the electrostatic
storage unit.

(3) "Automatic Digital Calculators", A. D. Booth and K. H. V. Booth,
Butterworths Scientific Publications, 1953.

---

[*] Additional literature references are given in Appendix 1.

(4) "Arithmetic Operations in Digital Computers", R. K. Richards, D. van Nostrand Company, Inc., 1955.

The following well written book deals with a variety of aspects of computing machinery, analogue and digital. Although it is somewhat old it contains interesting historical information.

(5) "Calculating Instruments and Machines", D. R. Hartree, University of Illinois Press, 1949.

The following references are devoted primarily to programming.

(6) "The Preparation of Programs for an Electronic Digital Computer", M. V. Wilkes, D. J. Wheeler and S. Gill, Addison-Wesley Press, Boston, 1951. This book is specialized in that it primarily concerns programming for the EDSAC (the Cambridge University Computer) however it illustrates good programming techniques and has been written by experts in the field.

(7) "Digital Computer Programming", D. D. McCracken, John Wiley and Sons, Inc., 1957.

The following reference on numerical analysis contains an extensive bibliography on numerical methods.

(8) "Principles of Numerical Analysis", A. S. Householder, McGraw-Hill, 1953.

The list of references in the above book was brought up to date recently in the following publication.

(9) A. S. Householder, Journal of the ACM, vol. 3, 85 (1956).

The following book contains a more or less popular account of automatic computing with some amusing anecdotes.

(10) "Faster Than Thought", B. V. Bowden, Sir Isaac Pitman and Sons, Ltd., 1953.

Some of the periodicals of particular interest are the following:

(11) Journal of the Association for Computing Machinery,

(12) Mathematical Tables and Other Aids to Computation (MTAC),

(13) IBM Journal of Research and Development.

Another periodical of a less technical nature is

(14) Computers and Automation.

An extensive survey of domestic electronic computing systems containing specifications and photographs will be found in

(15) "A Third Survey of Domestic Electronic Digital Computing Systems", M. H. Weik, BRL Report No. 1115, March 1961, Aberdeen Proving Ground, Maryland.

The above list is presented to acquaint you with various information sources in the field which you may desire to look into in the future. The original description of ILLIAC programming is contained in

(16) "ILLIAC Programming Manual".

The present notes may be used in place of this manual which is now out of date.

Calculating instruments or machines use analogue or digital schemes for the representation of numbers. Some calculating machines use the two schemes in combination but this is not the usual custom.

Representation of numbers by <u>continuously</u> varying physical quantities such as voltage, current or angular position of a wheel is called an analogue representation. The accuracy of such systems is limited by the precision with which measurements of these quantities can be made. For most practical cases this limit is about three decimal figures. Large analogue computing machines tend to be specialized in that they are built to handle a rather limited class of problems. Thus, these machines are generally limited in accuracy and the range of problems which they can handle. However, because of their special-ization they are sometimes faster for the class of problems they are designed

to handle than a general purpose digital computer. These computers find a
frequent application in situations where the data presented to it are in an
analogue form; for example, the data coming from wind tunnel tests is
frequently analyzed with analogue computing devices. More common examples
of analogue computing instruments are slide rules and differential analyzers.

Representation of numbers by <u>discrete</u> states of physical quantities
which again may be voltage, current, or angular position of a wheel is called
a digital representation. The familiar desk calculator uses a digital
representation of numbers. Each "wheel" in the desk calculator has ten discrete
positions and thus can precisely represent the ten decimal digits 0, 1, ..., 9.
Each wheel represents a distinct digital position. A set of three such wheels
can represent the three digit decimal numbers 000, 001, 002, ..., 999. Unlike
the analogue computer, the accuracy here is limited only by the number of
"wheels" we desire to use. In principle an arbitrarily high degree of accuracy
can be attained with a digital computer.* The ILLIAC is a digital machine, its
digits being binary (two discrete states) rather than decimal, which represents
numbers to an accuracy equivalent to about twelve decimal places.

With the exception of certain of the input and output equipment the
ILLIAC is wholly electronic. Thus, the representation of numbers is by discrete
voltage states and the sequence of logical operations that the ILLIAC performs
is controlled by electronic switches, called flip-flops, the basic element of
which is the vacuum tube or transistor. The flip-flop is an electronic circuit
capable of two stable states; it conserves its last state until new information
is presented to it. The flip-flop circuit contains at least two vacuum tubes or
transistors. A discussion of these circuits and their application can be found
in reference 4. The absence of mechanical movement permits the attainment of
very high speeds of operation. The time required to change the state of a flip-
flop in the ILLIAC is about 1 microsecond (μs) = 10^{-6} seconds.[+]

---

* It should be pointed out however, that as the number of "wheels" increases
the execution time for the elementary arithmetic operations also increases.

[+] Flip-flop circuits currently being developed at the University of Illinois
Digital Computer Laboratory have switching times of about 15×10^{-9} seconds.

The times required to execute various arithmetic operations by the ILLIAC are listed below. Each arithmetic operation is of course comprised of many switching operations.

OPERATION	EXECUTION TIME
Add	90 μ s.
Subtract	90 μ s.
Multiply	700 μ s.
Divide	800 μ s.

UNIVERSITY OF ILLINOIS
DIGITAL COMPUTER
CHAPTER 2

PARTS OF A GENERAL PURPOSE COMPUTER

It should be fairly clear that a device capable of doing arithmetic at the high speed indicated earlier for the ILLIAC cannot be operated efficiently if used like a desk calculator. Requiring the user to enter each number or operand into the machine by hand via a set of keys would result in virtually no change in the overall time to do a set of computations. Further, if the user must write down, or otherwise manually record, the intermediate and final results of each arithmetic operation, then the speed advantage gained by doing the arithmetic itself at high-speed is almost completely lost. In order to make efficient use of such a machine it is evident that the sequencing and control of arithmetic operations and the recording of results must proceed at speeds at least comparable to the arithmetic operation speed. Consequently the present computing machines are designed to meet these requirements by having the above functions performed automatically without human intervention.

For the reasons cited above the ILLIAC and other modern high-speed computers consist of a CONTROL unit which controls the execution of the sequence of operations in a computation, a STORAGE unit where numbers can be "written" and "read" at high speed, and an ARITHMETIC unit where the arithmetic operations are executed. In addition there is an INPUT-OUTPUT unit which permits information to be communicated to the computer and permits information to be communicated to the outside world from the computer.

The ILLIAC is described as a general purpose computer to distinguish it from a class of computers called special purpose computers designed to do computations on a very limited set of problems. The general purpose computer is designed to obey automatically very simple and basic operations; addition, subtraction, multiplication, division and a variety of strictly logical operations. The computer can be instructed to obey any desired sequence of these elementary operations, hence it is possible to solve an almost

unlimited range of problems, storage space and computation time being the
only limitations.

The STORAGE unit of the computer holds information necessary to the
computations, thus it holds both numbers and the sequence of operations in
an appropriately coded form. This information is contained in blocks called
"words". A single word may represent a number or an instruction to the
control unit to perform one of the elementary operations. Actually in the
ILLIAC there are two such instructions in every word. A word used to represent
a number in the ILLIAC has about 12 decimal digits of significance. In the
ILLIAC the storage unit provides space for 1,024 words. Reference to a word
in the memory is made by specifying which of the 1,024 "locations" it occupies;
for convenient reference the locations are numbered 0, 1, 2, ..., 1,023.
"Address" is frequently used synonymously with "location".

It is a feature of the ILLIAC in common with many other computers
that words representing numbers are not distinguishable from words representing
instructions and all portions of storage are available for either instructions or
numbers. The inclusion of this feature in a computing machine was suggested by
von Neumann and results in a more efficient use of expensive storage space.

The ILLIAC storage unit is described as a random access storage. This
implies that the time required to gain access to any location for reading or
writing is independent of the location; the access time is about 18.6 μ s.
We will discuss the physical nature of the storage unit later, and say only
now that it is an electrostatic storage device known as a Williams tube
memory.

The CONTROL unit contains as one of its basic parts a counter which
keeps track of the location in storage holding the next instruction word in
the sequence of instructions to be obeyed. The instructions are stored in a
linear sequence in the memory so by advancing the control counter by units of
one the control is provided with the proper sequence of instructions. The
control "decodes" the instruction word and causes the computer to execute the
operation specified by it. There exist instructions for setting the control
counter to any desired address thus permitting alterations in the sequencing

of instructions. It is in fact possible to thus alter the sequencing if and only if a specifiable number is positive. In this sense the ILLIAC can make "decisions" during the course of a computation.

In the ARITHMETIC unit the operations of addition, subtraction, multiplication, division and certain logical operations are performed. There are three "registers" in the arithmetic unit, accumulator register (A), quotient register (Q), and number register (R^3), which temporarily hold words brought from the memory preceeding the execution of arithmetic operations on them. Results of arithmetic operations are also held in these registers, and certain instructions cause the results to then be returned to the storage unit. The function of these registers is analogous to the function of the three registers of a desk calculator.

The INPUT-OUTPUT unit is responsible for all communication between the user and the computer. At the outset of a computation the user places the instructions and necessary numbers into the storage unit via the input unit. In the ILLIAC this consists of punching the information on teletype tape and placing the tape in a photoelectric device which then "reads" the tape. Information can be transmitted from the computer in several different ways; most commonly the information is punched onto teletype tape; it can be transmitted directly to a teleprinter --- this is slower and consequently not frequently used; or the results may be presented graphically as a plot on a cathode ray tube display to which a camera is attached for photographic recording.

It is sometimes necessary to have more storage space than the 1,024 words provided by the Williams Memory (WM) unit, consequently an auxiliary storage unit, a magnetic drum, with a 12,800 word capacity is available. The access time for the drum is considerably greater (average is about 9,000 μ s.) and consequently it is used only when the (WM) capacity is exceeded.

A machine of this type clearly places quite different and greater demands on the user, than those placed on the user of a desk calculator. The primary difference is that all of the individual logical steps involved in solving the problem must be completely specified in advance of doing the problem.

The user must therefore anticipate in advance all of the possible outcomes of each operation and make the appropriate provisions. The user is inhibited, although not completely, from approaching the high-speed computer with just a hazy notion of every step in the calculation as he might do with a desk calculator. Furthermore it is not easy to approach a computation with the philosophy - "I will see how the numbers go and then figure out what to do"; cases arise when it is virtually impossible to do otherwise but in general such an attitude should be discouraged.

The process of laying out the set of logical operations to be performed in a computation is known as programming or coding. Most people prefer to reserve the term code to refer to the specific set of operations, comprising a computation, written according to the prescription required by a particular computer. The term program refers more generally to the set of logical operations, without reference to the detailed form in which they are to be presented to the computer. The words program and code will be used in this sense here.

UNIVERSITY OF ILLINOIS
DIGITAL COMPUTER
CHAPTER 3

THE BINARY NUMBER SYSTEM

The ILLIAC along with most other high-speed computers uses the binary (base 2) number representation rather than the more familiar decimal (base 10) number representation. The use of the binary system was strongly advocated by Burks, Goldstine and von Neumann (see Reference 1, Chapter 5). There are several reasons for advocating the binary system. Binary arithmetic is simple and the elementary operations can be performed at high speed. A computing machine is essentially a logical device containing many "yes - no" decision making elements and because homogeneity implies simplicity it is natural to desire a "yes - no" scheme for number representation. The binary system tends to provide a greater reliability since the unit elements are restricted to only two stable states; these states being the two states of the flip-flop. Reliable decimal schemes really are basically binary and use a binary coded decimal representation which is wasteful of the information storage capacity of the computer. Actually the only argument that can be advanced in favor of the decimal system is simply that we are familiar with it. This, however, is not really a strong argument since the computer can be given the task of performing the necessary conversions between the two number systems, permitting the user to enter all numbers into the computer as decimal numbers and to obtain all answers as decimal numbers. Nevertheless, intelligent use of a binary machine does demand an understanding of the binary number system and binary arithmetic. By way of introduction to the binary number system and binary arithmetic let us discuss briefly some schemes for number representation.

In a desk calculator a number is represented as the angular positions of a set of wheels. Each wheel has ten allowed positions representing the digits 0 through 9 and each wheel corresponds to a distinct digit position. There is a wheel for the units place, the tens place, the hundreds place and so on. In a high-speed computer, as mentioned earlier, the representation of a number is realized electronically. We will not be concerned with the physical details of this scheme of representation but in order to have some appreciation of the logical ideas that are involved let us consider such a representation in a schematic way. To represent decimal digits we could, for example, have a device capable of having ten distinct states by the presence of a current in one of ten wires. Such a device is indicated schematically below. In this figure the switch is set to the output wire labeled 7, and thus by the presence

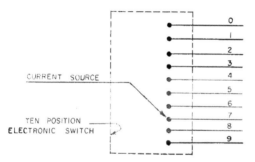

of a current in this wire the digit 7 is represented. With a set of such devices we could represent the various digital positions; for example three such units could represent the decimal numbers 000 through 999.

The scheme outlined above, although adequate for the representation of numbers, is actually very wasteful. Let us fix our attention on the ten output wires. To each wire we can assign two distinct states according as it does or does not carry a current. Since each of the ten wires has two possible states it is clear that there are $2^{10} = 1,024$ possible states for the ten wires (here we remove the restriction that only one wire at a time may carry a current). Thus, in principle the decimal numbers 0000 through 1023 could be represented on the ten wires, each number corresponding to a particular one of the 1,024 states; thus we obtain a considerable improvement in capacity over the first scheme. A device of this type leads us quite naturally to use the binary system.

The base or radix of the binary number system is two and each digit can have only two possible values 0 or 1. Each digital position corresponds to a distinct power of two; thus, there is the units place, the twos' place, the four's place, etc. More precisely, a four place binary number is represented by an ordered sequence of four digits, $a_3\, a_2\, a_1\, a_0$, where a_i can be either 0 or 1 and the number, n, so represented is

$$n = 2^3 \times a_3 + 2^2 \times a_2 + 2^1 \times a_1 + 2^0 \times a_0 .$$

where it has been assumed that the binary point is located just to the right of a_0. If the binary point is placed between digits a_1 and a_2, then the number, n', so represented is

$$n' = 2^1 \times a_3 + 2^0 \times a_2 + 2^{-1} \times a_1 + 2^{-2} \times a_0 .$$

To illustrate the representation of numbers in the binary system the integers zero through fifteen are listed below in the decimal system and the binary system.

Decimal	Binary
0	0000
1	0001
2	0010
3	0011
4	0100
5	0101
6	0110
7	0111
8	1000
9	1001
10	1010
11	1011
12	1100
13	1101
14	1110
15	1111

The elementary rules for binary arithmetic are exceedingly simple. The binary addition table is

$$0 + 0 = 0 ,$$
$$1 + 0 = 0 + 1 = 1 ,$$
$$1 + 1 = 10 .$$

The multiplication table is

$$0 \times 0 = 0 ,$$
$$1 \times 0 = 0 \times 1 = 0 ,$$
$$1 \times 1 = 1 .$$

To assist in a familiarization with binary arithmetic some examples are given below executed according to methods familiar in decimal arithmetic. The equivalent decimal arithmetic is performed alongside each example. In the examples of addition and subtraction below arrows are used to indicate carrys and borrows (↰ carry, ↱ borrow).

```
  ↰↰↰
  101101           4 5
+ 111100          + 6 0
  1101001          1 0 5


  ↱↱   ↱
  110010            5 0
- 011001           - 2 5
  011001            2 5
```

Multiplication in the binary system is especially simple. Examples follow:

```
     1 0 0 1 1          1 9
     0 1 1 0 1          1 3
     1 0 0 1 1          5 7
   1 0 0 1 1 0          1 9
 1 0 0 1 1              2 4 7
 1 1 1 1 0 1 1 1
```

```
    0 1 1 0 0            1 2
    1 0 1 1 1            2 3
    0 1 1 0 0            3 6
  0 1 1 0 0            2 4
  0 1 1 0 0            2 7 6
0 1 1 0 0 0
1 0 0 0 1 0 1 0 0
```

Notice that in binary multiplication the product is formed by the following
prescription. Examine the least significant digit of the multiplier: if it
is zero write zero for the partial product; if it is one write the multiplicand
for the partial product. In either case move the multiplicand one digital
position to the left. Examine the next-most significant digit of the multiplier:
if it is zero leave the partial product unchanged; if it is one add the shifted
multiplicand to the partial product. In either case move the multiplicand one
more digital position to the left. Continue in this manner until all of the
digits of the multiplier have been so examined. The small number of simple
rules involved in this process indicates the relative ease with which a
device can be designed for doing this automatically.

Examples of binary division follow.

```
        1 1 1                      7
 1 0 1 )1 0 0 1 0 1        5 ) 3 7
        1 0 1                     3 5
        1 0 0 0                    2
          1 0 1
          0 1 1 1
            1 0 1
            1 0
```

```
        1 0 0 0 0                   1 6
 1 1 1 )1 1 1 0 1 1 0        7 )1 1 8
        1 1 1                      7
        0 0 1 1 0                  4 8
                                   4 2
                                    6
```

The convenience of the binary number system should now be apparent. In the device mentioned earlier one can regard each output wire as representing a distinct digital position in the binary number system. As a convention we might take the presence of a current as the representation of the digit 1 and the absence of a current as the representation of the digit 0.

It is natural at this point to inquire why it is that we do not construct our device so that each wire has more than just two possible states and thereby increase its information capacity. For example if each wire has three allowed states (for example, corresponding to currents i = 0, i', 2i') then the set of ten wires would have 3^{10} = 59,049 distinct states. Note that here the natural number system would be the ternary (base 3) system. Such a scheme is entirely possible and in fact is used in some computing equipment. However, the simple binary on-off scheme is much more common. The binary system is still favored for the same reasons advanced earlier in favoring it over the decimal system though it is true that the simplicity of the ternary system reduces the strength of these reasons. Further, a simple and reliable tristable element is not yet available.

A single binary digit's worth of information is called a bit. The information capacity of a 10 digit binary number is described as 10 bits. More generally a bit is an information unit and one describes quantitatively the information capacity of any scheme by the number of bits required to describe uniquely all possible "messages" (words, numbers, etc.) of the scheme. For example a single decimal digit has ten possible states (messages). It would take more than 3 bits to represent a decimal digit since with 3 bits one can uniquely distinguish just 2^3 = 8 states. On the other hand 4 bits is more than enough since with 4 bits 2^4 = 16 states are distinguished. Regarding the number of states of the decimal integer expressible in the form 2^p, p not necessarily an integer, we see that the information capacity of the decimal integer is p = $\log_2$ 10 = 3.32 bits. Correspondingly, the information capacity of a letter of the alphabet is $\log_2$ 26 = 4.70 bits. Of course a binary computer contains only an integral number of binary digits, consequently a decimal digit requires four bits in the computer for its representation. Correspondingly, in order to represent the letters of the alphabet by binary numbers in the computer one would need five binary digits for the representation.

UNIVERSITY OF ILLINOIS

DIGITAL COMPUTER

CHAPTER 4

NEGATIVE NUMBER REPRESENTATION

Let us now consider the representation of negative numbers. The
customary scheme of using a symbol (1 bit of information) preceeding the
absolute value of a number to represent positive and negative numbers turns
out to be not quite so convenient in a digital computer. A natural scheme
for computers is the representation of negative numbers by complementation*.

The complement of a number x with respect to a base b is simply
b - x; this is also called "the b's complement of x". Thus, the 10's complement of 6 is 10 - 6 = 4; the 3's complement of 7 is -4, etc. Representation
of negative numbers by complementation means that each negative number x is
represented by the b's complement of $|x|$ (vertical bars mean absolute magnitude)
where b is a suitably chosen base. Such a scheme turns out to be convenient
because electronic circuits which affect complementation are relatively easy
to construct and one can then bypass the problem of constructing the relatively
complicated subtracting circuits (in which provision to "borrow" must be made)
because subtraction is then achieved by complementation followed by addition
(since $x - y \equiv x - (-y)$. The use of this scheme in a base 10 number system is
illustrated below.

We fix our attention on a range of numbers restricted to
$-5.000 \leq x < + 5.000$. The negative numbers -0.001, -0.002, ..., -5.000 can be
represented in an unambiguous way as follows: write the negative number x as
$x^* = 10 + x$. The negative numbers are thus represented by 9.999, 9.998, ...,
5.000. This is the 10's complement representation. A few examples will
demonstrate that this representation is consistent with respect to the usual
properties of negative numbers. Below are shown, side by side, examples of

---

* Some computers nevertheless use a sign and absolute magnitude representation,
e.g. IBM 704.

additions and subtractions with negative numbers represented on the left by 10's complement and on the right by sign and absolute magnitude. It is assumed in this arithmetic that carrys to the left of the most significant digit are "lost" just as they would be in a desk calculator with four wheels.

10's COMPLEMENT		SIGN AND ABSOLUTE MAGNITUDE	
	1.000		1.000
(+)	9.000	(+)	-1.000
	0.000		0.000
	3.015		3.015
(+)	7.884	(+)	-2.116
	0.899		0.899
	6.500		-3.500
(-)	7.600	(-)	-2.400
	8.900		-1.100

The arithmetic in the left column where the left-most carry is lost so that there is a return to zero after counting up to 9.999 is called modular arithmetic and in this instance it is arithmetic modulo 10 (mod 10). This is the natural arithmetic of computers where the number of digits is fixed. In this arithmetic one equates numbers A and B modulo C, i.e.

$$A = B \qquad (\text{mod } C)$$

if, when A and B are expressed as

$$A = N C + A'$$
$$B = M C + B'$$

with A' and B' less than C and N and M integral, then

$$A' = B' \quad .$$

Thus,

1 0 = 0,	(mod 10)
1 1 = 1,	(mod 10)
1 2 = 2,	(mod 10)
3 = 1,	(mod 2)

etc.

Using the ideas just introduced notice that both the representation of negative and positive numbers is included when the rule for obtaining the representation of x $(-5.000 \leq x < +5.000)$ is stated simply as

$$x^* = 10 + x \qquad (\text{mod } 10)$$

Demonstration that this representation is consistent with respect to addition is very simple. We must show that if

$$x_i + x_j = x_k$$

and if

$x_i^* = x_i + 10$	(mod 10)
$x_j^* = x_j + 10$	(mod 10)
$x_k^* = x_k + 10$	(mod 10)

then

$x_i^* + x_j^* = x_k^*$	(mod 10)

To do this form

$$x_i^* + x_j^* = x_i + x_j + 10 + 10 \qquad \text{(mod 10)}$$

$$= x_k + 10 + 10 \qquad \text{(mod 10)}$$

$$= x_k^* + 10 \qquad \text{(mod 10)}$$

$$= x_k^* \qquad \text{(mod 10)}$$

as was to be shown.

Now consider the representation of negative binary numbers by comple-mentation. Consider binary numbers x in the range $-1 \le x < 1$. The representation for these numbers will be

$$x^* = 2 + x \qquad \text{(mod 2)} ,$$

The range on x* is

$$0 \le x^* < 2 .$$

This representation is illustrated in the table below where we consider six digit binary numbers.

x (DECIMAL)	x^*	
	POSITIVE x	NEGATIVE x
0.75	0 . 1 1 0 0 0	1 . 0 1 0 0 0
0.50	0 . 1 0 0 0 0	1 . 1 0 0 0 0
0.25	0 . 0 1 0 0 0	1 . 1 1 0 0 0
0.125	0 . 0 0 1 0 0	1 . 1 1 1 0 0
0.96875 ($\frac{31}{32}$)	0 . 1 1 1 1 1	1 . 0 0 0 0 1
1.0	1 . 0 0 0 0 0	1 . 0 0 0 0 0

Notice that the leading digit of negative numbers is always 1 and that the leading digit of positive numbers is always zero (except for 1.0 which is discussed below); that this must always be so is immediately inferred from the rule x* = 2 + x modulo 2. Thus, with a 2's complement representation of negative numbers, positive and negative numbers can be discriminated just as easily as with a sign and absolute magnitude representation. In each case just a test of one bit is required. The decimal numbers +1.0 and -1.0 lead to an ambiguity since they are both represented by 1.00000. To maintain consistency with the rule that the leading digit is 1 for negative numbers only, it is the practice to take 1.00000 as the binary 2's complement representation of -1.

It is sometimes helpful to think of this number system in the following way. Let the range of x* be mapped onto the circumference of a circle as shown by the 3 digit binary numbers on the outside of the circle below. As x* is increased by counting we proceed clockwise around the circle. The positive and negative numbers represented by x* are shown on the interior of the circle.

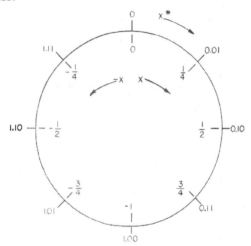

It is convenient to generate -x by a slightly different prescription than forming 2-x in the straightforward way. This prescription requires that the digitwise complement of x be taken (i.e., replace each 1 by 0 and each 0 by 1) then add 1 into the least significant digit. The result is just the 2's complement of x [+]. This logical procedure for constructing the 2's complement of x is used by the ILLIAC. (It should be easy to infer from this that circuits to affect complementation are not very complex, as pointed out at the beginning of this chapter.)

[+] The proof of this result follows immediately from the fact that
$$2_D = 1.11 \ldots 11_B + 0.000 \ldots 01_B$$

UNIVERSITY OF ILLINOIS
DIGITAL COMPUTER
CHAPTER 5

ILLIAC WORDS AS NUMBERS AND INSTRUCTIONS,
AND BINARY-DECIMAL CONVERSION

Earlier it was pointed out that information in the ILLIAC is handled in blocks called words. An ILLIAC word is composed of 40 binary digits:

$$w = w_0 \, w_1 \, w_2 \, w_3 \, \cdots \, w_{39} \, ,$$

where $w_i = 0, 1$ for $i = 0, 1, \ldots, 39$. This is a typical word length for present day computers but the trend in new computers is toward longer words.

ILLIAC is described as a parallel machine. This means that operations, arithmetic or logical, performed on a word are carried out simultaneously on all digits of the word. Thus when a word is transferred from the storage unit to a register in the arithmetic unit all digits are transferred simultaneously. When two words are added all digits are added simultaneously. In some computers these operations are performed serially, the computers being called serial computers. They have the advantage of requiring less equipment but they are slower than a parallel machine with equivalent equipment. Some computers are hybrids, operating partially in the parallel mode and partially in the serial mode.

The ILLIAC word may be used to represent fractions in the interval $-1 \leq x < 1$ just as we described fractions earlier in the six bit example. Specifically the binary point is located between bits w_0 and w_1 with

$$x^* = 2 + x \qquad (\mathrm{mod} \ 2)$$

$$x^* = w_0 \, 2^0 + w_1 \, 2^{-1} + w_2 \, 2^{-2} + \ldots + w_{39} \, 2^{-39}$$

and we note that

$$x = -2 + x^* \quad (\mathrm{mod} \ 2)$$

so

$$x = -w_0 + w_1 \, 2^{-1} + w_2 \, 2^{-2} + \ldots + w_{39} \, 2^{-39}$$

Since $w_0 = 0$ if x is positive and $w_0 = 1$ if x is negative, w_0 is called the sign digit. The use of the asterisk to denote ILLIAC representation of numbers will be adopted throughout the remainder of these notes.

The assignment of the location of the binary point is completely arbitrary. All arithmetic performed by the ILLIAC on a word is independent of the location of the binary point, just as it is in a desk calculator. Thus w might equally well represent $y = 2^p x$, then

$$y^* = 2^{p+1} + y \qquad (\text{mod } 2^{p+1})$$

$$y^* = \sum_{i=0}^{39} w_i \, 2^{p-i}$$

The assignment of a value to p is strictly up to the programmer.

Although the placement of the binary point is arbitrary it is convenient to treat numbers as either fractions or integers, thus "placing" the binary point between bit positions w_0 and w_1 (fractions) or immediately to the right of bit position w_{39} (integers). The maximum and minimum magnitude integers and fractions, excluding zero, which may be represented are listed below.

	+ FRACTIONS	- FRACTIONS	+ INTEGERS	- INTEGERS
Max	$1 - 2^{-39}$	-1	$2^{39} - 1$	-2^{39}
Min	2^{-39}	-2^{-39}	1	-1

In the decimal system

$$2^{-39} = 1.818\ 989\ 403\ 545\ 856\ 475\ 830\ 078\ 125 \times 10^{-12}$$
$$2^{39} = 5.497\ 558\ 138\ 88 \times 10^{11}$$

With a binary computer it becomes necessary to convert numbers from the binary system to the decimal system and vice versa. Schemes for doing this are discussed below. First let us consider the conversion of a binary fraction to a decimal fraction. The number x is represented as a fraction (we temporarily neglect sign) by

$$x = \sum_{i=1}^{39} w_i 2^{-i} \qquad\qquad (w_i = 0, 1) .$$

Alternatively x can be represented in the decimal with N digits by

$$x = \sum_{i=1}^{N} w_i{'} 10^{-i} \qquad\qquad (w_i{'} = 0, 1, 2, \ldots, 9).$$

The binary to decimal conversion requires that we generate the set of digits $\left\{w_i{'}\right\}$ from the given set $\left\{w_i\right\}$. We have the equality

$$\sum_{i=1}^{N} w_i{'} 10^{-i} = \sum_{i=1}^{39} w_i 2^{-i} .$$

Multiply both sides of this equation by 10 to obtain

$$\sum_{i=1}^{N} w_i{'} 10^{1-i} = 10 \times \sum_{i=1}^{39} w_i 2^{-i}$$

The integer part of the quantity on the left, namely $w_1{'}$, must be equal to the integer part of the quantity on the right; i.e.

$$w_1{'} = \text{integer part of } 10 \times \sum_{i=1}^{39} w_i 2^{-i} .$$

The first decimal digit of the fraction has thus been obtained. The fractional parts must also be equal

$$\sum_{i=2}^{N} w_i{'} 10^{1-i} = \text{fractional part of } 10 \times \sum_{i=1}^{39} w_i 2^{-i} .$$

Multiplication by 10 again yields the next decimal digit $w_2{'}$ as the integer part of the resulting expression on the right. Proceeding in this fashion, successively multiplying by 10, the decimal digits of a fraction represented in the binary system are obtained. An example, using six fractional bits for simplicity, is worked out below.

```
           x = 0.1 0 1 1 1 0
      10  x : 0.1 0 1 1 1 0
        D          1 0 1 0
             1 0 1 1 1 0 0
         1 0 1 1 1 0 0
         1 1 1.0 0 1 1 0 0        w₁' = 7
                   1 0 1 0
               0 0 1 1 0 0 0
         0 0 1 1 0 0 0
         0 0 1.1 1 1 0 0 0        w₂' = 1
                   1 0 1 0
               1 1 1 0 0 0 0
         1 1 1 0 0 0 0
   1 0 0 0.1 1 0 0 0 0            w₃' = 8
                   1 0 1 0
               1 1 0 0 0 0 0
         1 1 0 0 0 0 0
         1 1 1.1 0 0 0 0 0        w₄' = 7
                   1 0 1 0
               1 0 0 0 0 0 0
         1 0 0 0 0 0 0
         1 0 1.0 0 0 0 0 0        w₅' = 5
```

$w_1' = 7$

$w_2' = 1$

$w_3' = 8$

$w_4' = 7$

$w_5' = 5$

Hence x = 0.71875   (decimal).

    Conversion from decimal to binary is effected in a completely analogous
way. The binary digits are here obtained from successive multiplication of the
decimal fraction by 2.

    When negative numbers are involved it is simplest to convert first to
sign and absolute magnitude representation.

    Next we consider integer conversion. Let x be represented as a p digit
binary integer

$$x = \sum_{i=1}^{p} w_{p-i} \, 2^{p-i} , \qquad (w_{p-i} = 0,1)$$

x can also be represented as a q digit decimal integer

$$x = \sum_{i=1}^{q} w'_{q-i} \, 10^{q-i} , \qquad (w'_{q-i} = 0, 1, \ldots, 9) .$$

Suppose that we are given the binary integer, i.e. the number set w_{p-i}, and that we wish to obtain the decimal integer, i.e. the number set w'_{q-i}. We have

$$\sum_{i=1}^{q} w'_{q-i} \, 10^{q-i} = \sum_{i=1}^{p} w_{p-i} \, 2^{p-i} .$$

Now divide each side by 10. This will give an integer quotient plus a remainder. The remainder is obviously w_0', i.e.

$$w_0' = \text{remainder} \;\; \frac{1}{10} \sum_{i=1}^{p} w_{p-i} \, 2^{p-i} .$$

The next digit, w_1', can be obtained by dividing the quotient obtained above again by 10, the remainder being just w_1'. Repetition of this process until the quotient is zero generates all the digits of the decimal integer.

Conversion of a decimal integer to a binary integer is done in an analogous fashion. An example follows. We wish to convert the decimal integer 2,963 into a binary integer.

$$
\begin{array}{lll}
2\ \underline{|\ 2{,}963} & & \\
2\ \underline{|\ 1{,}481} & +\tfrac{1}{2} & w_0 = 1 \\
2\ \underline{|\ 740} & +\tfrac{1}{2} & w_1 = 1 \\
2\ \underline{|\ 370} & & w_2 = 0 \\
2\ \underline{|\ 185} & & w_3 = 0 \\
2\ \underline{|\ 92} & +\tfrac{1}{2} & w_4 = 1 \\
2\ \underline{|\ 46} & & w_5 = 0 \\
2\ \underline{|\ 23} & & w_6 = 0 \\
2\ \underline{|\ 11} & +\tfrac{1}{2} & w_7 = 1 \\
2\ \underline{|\ 5} & +\tfrac{1}{2} & w_8 = 1 \\
2\ \underline{|\ 2} & +\tfrac{1}{2} & w_9 = 1 \\
2\ \underline{|\ 1} & & w_{10} = 0 \\
0 & +\tfrac{1}{2} & w_{11} = 1 \\
\end{array}
$$

Hence $x = 101110010011$ (binary)

     An alternative scheme for integer conversion consists of first converting the integer to a fraction and then obtaining the digits by successive multiplications as described above for fraction conversion. For example, if x is the p digit binary integer representation of a q digit decimal integer, then form $\dfrac{x}{10^q}$, a binary fraction. The most significant decimal digit is obtained by forming $10\left(\dfrac{x}{10^q}\right)$ and taking the integer part. If the remaining fractional part is again multiplied by 10 the next digit is obtained, etc. Care must be exercised in applying this method because of the possible error generated by the division.

     The techniques described above for the conversion of numbers from the decimal system into the binary system and vice versa are commonly employed in computer programs but they are usually not the most convenient ones for hand computations. For hand computations it will usually be found most convenient to

use the "Table of Powers of 2" in Appendix 2, p. 249, when converting
binary numbers to decimal numbers. This conversion is achieved by simply summing
the decimal equivalents of the appropriate powers of 2. One can also use the table
to convert from decimal to binary, though it is not as convenient for this purpose.
Supposing x is the <u>positive</u> number to be converted, the table is inspected for the
power, p, of 2 such that $2^p \leq x$ and $2^{p+1} > x$ to obtain the most significant binary
digit of x. The next digit is found by repeating the process for $x - 2^p$ and so on
for successive binary digits of x.

It is inconvenient to have to write out explicitly all 40 bits of an
ILLIAC word. For this reason another number system, a base 16 number system,
is used; it is called the sexadecimal number system[1]. Each digit of a sexadecimal number obviously contains 4 bits of information. The sexadecimal number
system uses the characters 0, 1, 2, 3, 4, 5, 6, 7, 8, 9 to represent the numbers
zero through nine. To represent the numbers ten through fifteen, new characters
must be introduced and these are K, S, N, J, F and L, respectively. Using the
sexadecimal number system it clearly takes just 10 characters to specify an
ILLIAC word. An example is given below.

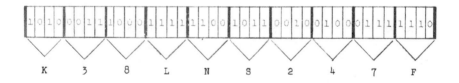

The groups of four bits which have been indicated by the heavy lines are called
tetrads. The binary word is thus written relatively simply as

K38LNS247F

Since we are dealing now with three number systems the subscripts B, S and D will

---

[1] Sometimes also called the hexadecimal number system.

be used to identify numbers as binary, sexadecimal or decimal if the base is
not already clear from the context. A table which is helpful for number
conversion between the sexadecimal and decimal number systems is
in Appendix 3, p. 250. The numbers within the boxes of this table are
decimal integers, the corresponding sexadecimal integer is given by the
sexadecimal characters which label the row and column of the box; the most
significant sexadecimal characters being given by the row label on the left
if the decimal number is in a box lying in the left half of the matrix (i.e.
to the left of the heavy verticle line) or by the row label on the right if
the decimal number is in a box lying in the right half of the matrix; the least
significant sexadecimal character is given by the column label. To illustrate,
the decimal number 750, which lies in the left half of the matrix is represented
sexadecimally as 2FF; the decimal number 470, which lies in the right half of
the matrix is represented sexadecimally as 1J6. This table covers decimal integers
in the range 0 to 1,023. This table is used especially for converting the address
digits of an order from sexadecimal to decimal or vice versa.

In addition to numbers the 40 bit ILLIAC words are also used to specify
the orders or instructions to be executed. There are two instructions in each
ILLIAC word: the left-hand (LH) order comprising the first five tetrads of the
word; and the right-hand (RH) order comprising the second five tetrads of the
word. The first two tetrads of every instruction are called the function digits.
They completely identify the instruction type: multiply, divide, add, etc.
The last ten bits of the remaining three tetrads of each instruction are called
the address digits. In most cases they refer to a location in the storage
holding one of the operands for the operation specified by the function digits.
Since there are just $2^{10} = 1024$ word locations in the ILLIAC storage unit the
10 bit address just permits reference to every word in storage. The remaining
two bits of the instruction are not used and in fact may contain any bit
configuration without effect on the instruction.
Thus, if

$$w = w_0 \ w_1 \ w_2 \ \cdots \ w_{39} \ ,$$

then for the LH order $w_0 w_1 \cdots w_7$ are the function digits, $w_{10} w_{11} \cdots w_{19}$
are the address digits and $w_8 w_9$ are not used. For the RH order $w_{20} w_{21} \cdots w_{27}$
are the function digits, $w_{30} w_{31} \cdots w_{39}$ are the address digits and $w_{28} w_{29}$ are
not used.

Let us review briefly now the logical sequence of events taking place in
the execution of a set of orders in the ILLIAC. The words containing the order
pairs are placed in the storage unit. The control counter is set to the location
in storage (address) of the word holding the first order to be obeyed. An
indicator is set telling which order LH or RH is to be obeyed. The specified
word is brought into the instruction register. The control counter is now
advanced by one to designate the address of the next order pair. Assuming
that the indicator has been set so that the first order to be obeyed is the LH
order, the LH order of the order pair in the instruction register is executed,
then the RH order of this order pair is executed. The next order pair at the
storage address indicated by the control counter is now brought into the instruction
register, the control counter is again advanced by one and so on. This process
continues until a transfer order is encountered, or until an order to stop the
computer is encountered. A transfer order causes the control counter to be
reset to the value specified by the address digits of the transfer order. Thus,
it is possible to alter the sequencing of the instructions. Later we will
discuss in detail the ILLIAC order code but before doing this we will examine
the operation of the ILLIAC arithmetic unit.

UNIVERSITY OF ILLINOIS
DIGITAL COMPUTER
CHAPTER 6

ADDITION AND SUBTRACTION

Having discussed the representation of numbers in the ILLIAC we now
discuss the operation of the arithmetic unit.

A block diagram of the arithmetic unit and connections to the memory
is shown below. The paths along which numbers may be transferred are indicated

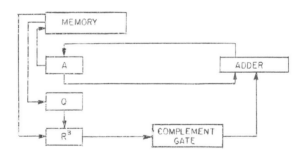

Figure 6-1

Block diagram of the arithmetic unit showing
connections with the Williams Memory.

by the lines. These lines actually represent a set of wires, one wire for each
binary digit of an ILLIAC word, thus permitting the digits of a word to be
transferred between these parts of the arithmetic unit simultaneously, i.e. in
parallel fashion.

To facilitate the subsequent discussion it will be convenient to use the following notation:

A   :   the accumulator register

A_i :   the ith (i = 0, 1, ..., 39) digital position of A.

Q   :   the quotient register

Q_i :   the ith (i = 0, 1, ..., 39) digital position of Q.

R^3 :   the number rigister

a   :   the contents of A

a_i :   the contents of A_i

q   :   the contents of Q

q_i :   the contents of Q_i

r^3 :   the contents of R^3

'   :   if an operation changes a, a_i, q, q_j, the new value is designated by the superscript ', thus the operation of multiplying a by 2 is written

$$a' = 2a$$

In general, capital letters indicate locations for holding digits and small letters represent the contents of these locations.

Let us first note the links between the memory and the arithmetic unit. There is just one entry into the memory and that is via the accumulator register. On the other hand words may be read from the memory into either the quotient register or the number register.

Addition in the ILLIAC always takes one operand, the augend, from A and the other operand, the addend, from R^3: the addend coming originally from Q or the memory. The sum is always placed in A.

As the addend is brought from R^3 to one of the adder inputs it passes first through the complement gate. In addition the complement gate is not activated and consequently it has no effect on numbers transmitted through it. (We will see later that the complement gate is used in the subtraction process). In the adder the sum of the two inputs is formed, the result is transmitted to A completing the addition operation.

The ILLIAC addition instruction may cause A to be cleared to zero before the addition takes place; this is called a "clear add" instruction. If A is not initially cleared the instruction is called a "hold add" instruction. The addition instruction takes the addend from R^3, but the addend is actually first taken from a memory location M, specified by the address of the instruction, and placed in R^3 before the sum is performed, or the addend is first taken from Q into R^3.

The preceeding remarks are summarized below. The steps comprising the add instructions are indicated. The ILLIAC order representation, two sexadecimal function digits followed by an address M, appears in the parentheses.

    A. Clear add   (L5 M)

        (1) $a' = 0$
        (2) $r^{3'} = m$
        (3) $a' = a + r^3$
        The net effect is
            $a' = m$

    B. Clear add   (S5 M)

        (1) $a' = 0$
        (2) $r^{3'} = q$
        (3) $a' = a + r^3$
        The net effect is
            $a' = q$

    C. Hold add   (L4 M)

        (1) $r^{3'} = m$
        (2) $a' = a + r^3$
        The net effect is
            $a' = a + m$

D. Hold add   (S4 M)

   (1) $r^{3'} = q$

   (2) $a' = a + r^3$

   The net effect is

   $a' = a + q$

   Four subtraction instructions correspond to the above. When a
subtraction is executed the complement gate is activated and takes the digitwise
complement of the number transmitted through it. Also a circuit is activated
to add 1 into the least significant digit of the adder. This appears as a
carry digit from the non-existent 2^{-40} position. It will be observed that these
operations have the effect of taking the 2's complement of the number brought
from R^3. The nature of these instructions is listed below.

E. Clear subtract   (L1 M)

   (1) $a' = 0$

   (2) $r^{3'} = m$

   (3) $a' = a + \underbrace{(2 - 2^{-39} - r^3)}_{\substack{\text{digitwise comple-}\\\text{ment from comple-}\\\text{ment gate}}} + \underbrace{2^{-39}}_{\substack{\text{carry insertion}\\\text{into right-most}\\\text{position of adder.}}}$

   The net effect is

   (4) $a' = -m$ (remember in the machine -m is represented
                    by 2-m)

F. Clear subtract   (S1 M)

   (1) $a' = 0$

   (2) $r^{3'} = q$

   (3) $a' = a + (2 - 2^{-39} - r^3) + 2^{-39}$

   The net effect is

   (4) $a' = -q$

G. Hold subtract   (LO M)

(1) $r^{3'} = m$

(2) $a' = a + (2 - 2^{-39} - r^3) + 2^{-39}$

The net effect is

$a' = a - m$

H. Hold subtract   (SO M)

(1) $r^{3'} = q$

(2) $a' = a + (2 - 2^{-39} - r^3) + 2^{-39}$

The net effect is

$a' = a - q$

The above outlines should give some insight into the nature of the elementary operations of addition and subtraction performed by the ILLIAC. The execution of all instructions will not be outlined in detail as above but the logic involved should be reasonably apparent from the above introduction to addition and subtraction. Other operations of addition and subtraction involve the manipulation of absolute magnitudes. A list of these operations follows.

$a' = a + |m|$

$a' = a - |m|$

$a' = a + |q|$

$a' = a - |q|$

These operations may be performed with or without initial clearing of A. These operations can easily be performed by testing m_0 (the sign digit) and activating or inhibiting, accordingly, the complement gate and carry insertion circuit to yield the above sums and differences.

UNIVERSITY OF ILLINOIS
DIGITAL COMPUTER
CHAPTER 7

SHIFTING

Registers A and Q are called shifting registers because it is possible to translate their contents to the right or to the left according to the following rules. Let

$$a = a_0\ a_1\ a_2\ \cdots\ a_{39} \qquad\qquad (6\text{-}1)$$

$$q = q_0\ q_1\ q_2\ \cdots\ q_{39}$$

then after one right shift

$$a' = a_0\ a_0\ a_1\ a_2\ \cdots\ a_{38} \qquad\qquad (6\text{-}2)$$

$$q' = q_0\ a_{39}\ q_1\ q_2\ \cdots\ q_{38}\quad .$$

In the right shift notice that

(1) $a'_i = a_{i-1}$, $q'_i = q_{i-1}$

except   (2) $q'_1 = a_{39}$

(3) $a'_0 = a_0$

(4) $q'_0 = q_0$

(5) q_{39} is lost.

A left shift of (6-1) yields

$$a' = a_1 \, a_2 \, \cdots \, a_{39} \, q_1 \qquad\qquad (6\text{-}3)$$

$$q' = q_0 \, q_2 \, \cdots \, q_{39} \, 0 \quad .$$

In the left shift notice that

(1) $a'_i = a_{i+1}$, $q'_i = q_{i+1}$

<u>except</u> (2) $a'_{39} = q_1$

(3) $q'_{39} = \text{zero}$

(4) $q'_0 = q_0$

(5) a_0 is lost.

Thus in the shift operation A and Q are connected (this connection is not indicated in Figure 6-1) in the sense that digits may be transferred between A_{39} and Q_1. The position Q_0 does not take part in the shifting. The transfer of bits in the shift operations is illustrated in the figures below.

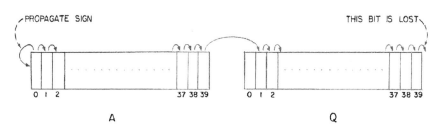

Figure 7-1

Illustration of the transfer of bits
when <u>1 right shift</u> is executed.

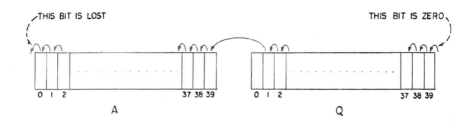

THIS BIT IS LOST

THIS BIT IS ZERO

A

Q

Figure 7-2

Illustration of the transfer of bits
when 1 left shift is executed.

One can regard a and q as representing a single number, a being the
most significant part and q being the least significant part, namely,

$$aq = a_0 \times 2^0 + a_1 \times 2^{-1} + \ldots + a_{39} \times 2^{-39} \tag{6-4}$$

$$+ q_1 \times 2^{-40} + q_2 \times 2^{-41} + \ldots + q_{39} \times 2^{-78} .$$

Now if aq is positive and less than 1/2 (i.e. $a_0 = a_1 = 0$) then it is obvious
that a right shift yields

$$|aq' = \frac{1}{2} aq \tag{6-5}$$

and a left shift yields

$$aq' = 2 aq . \tag{6-6}$$

These relations remain true even if aq is negative provided that
$|aq| < \frac{1}{2}$ (i.e. $a_0 = a_1 = 1$). Let aq be the ILLIAC representation of a
number x

$$aq = x^* = 2 + x . \qquad (\text{mod } 2) \tag{6-7}$$

Consider a right shift when $a_0 = 1$; that is, x negative.

$$aq' = \frac{1}{2} x* + 1 = 1 + \frac{x}{2} + 1 \qquad \text{(mod 2)} \qquad (6\text{-}8)$$

from $a_0' = a_0$

$$= 2 + \frac{x}{2} \,. \qquad \text{(mod 2)}$$

But $2 + \frac{x}{2}$ is the representation for $\frac{x}{2}$, thus

$$aq' = \left(\frac{x}{2} \right)^* \qquad (6\text{-}9)$$

It is seen that the condition $a_0' = a_0$ insures that negative numbers are correctly halved by a right shift. Now consider a left shift when $a_0 = a_1 = 1$

$$aq' = 2x* - 2 = 4 + 2x - 2 \qquad \text{(mod 2)} \qquad (6\text{-}10)$$

Because a_0 is lost

$$= 2 + 2x \,. \qquad \text{(mod 2)}$$

(The -2 could be omitted since we are doing arithmetic mod 2.) But $2 + 2x$ is just the representation for $2x$, thus

$$aq' = (2x)^* \,. \qquad (6\text{-}11)$$

One important detail in the above remarks concerning the right shift has been overlooked. In a right shift q_{39} is lost and if $q_{39} = 1$ it is clear that we do not have precisely

$$(aq)' = \left(\frac{x}{2} \right)^*$$

but

$$(aq)' = \left(\frac{x}{2} - 2^{-79} \right)^* \,.$$

An error of 2^{-79} has thus been generated. If $q_{39} = 0$ no error is generated by the right shift.

Our considerations have been restricted to $|x| < \frac{1}{2}$ to guarantee that a left shift will always yield a number that does not exceed scale; we can permit $x = -\frac{1}{2}$ without exceeding scale with one left shift. The violation of this condition is a common source of overflow error.

It should be mentioned here that an ILLIAC shifting register is physically composed of two registers, designated in the case of A as $\underline{A}$ (A lower) and $\overline{A}$ (A upper). $\overline{A}$ temporarily holds $\underline{a}$ during the shifting operation, thus the left shift consists of the logical events

(1) $\overline{a}'_i = a_{-i}$

(2) $a'_{-i-1} = \overline{a}_i.$

The flow of digits is indicated schematically below. A right shift is achieved

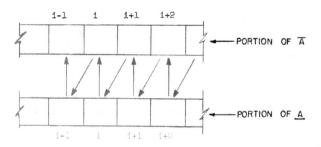

Figure 7-3

Showing the flow of digits in a
left shift operation.

in a corresponding fashion. The necessity for this arises from the difficulty
encountered when one tries to transfer information into a position already
holding information which itself must be transferred. There are of course
other ways of handling this problem but this is one of the most common. Unless
specifically noted otherwise we will always mean A when we refer simply to A.
The above remarks apply to Q as well.

UNIVERSITY OF ILLINOIS
DIGITAL COMPUTER
CHAPTER 8

MULTIPLICATION

The operations of multiplication and division are composed of a
sequence of addition and shift operations. Multiplication, being somewhat
simpler, will be discussed first.

The multiply instruction always assumes the multiplier to be in Q
and the multiplicand to be taken from location M in the memory. The
location M is specified in the address portion of the multiply instruction.
Before the multiplication process is initiated m is brought into R^3. The
product at the completion of the multiplication operation appears in AQ as
a double length number. Notice that provision for a double length number
is necessary for maximum accuracy since two 39 digit numbers (omit sign) yield
a 78 digit product.

We consider first the formation of the product xy where x is called
the multiplier and y the multiplicand, and both are positive. The logical steps
follow: 1. x is in Q, and we assume A is clear
         2. Bring y from the memory into R^3
         3. Sense Q_{39} (i.e. sense x_{39})
         4. If $x_{39} = 1$ form $a' = a + r^3$ (i.e. $a + y$)
         5. If $x_{39} = 0$ proceed to step 6
         6. Execute one right shift of AQ
         7. Sense Q_{39} (i.e. sense x_{38})
         8. If $x_{38} = 1$ form $a' = a + r^3$
         9. If $x_{38} = 0$ proceed to step 10
        10. Execute one right shift of AQ and so on until all digits
             $x_{39}, x_{38}, \ldots x_1$ have been sensed. The product then resides
             in AQ.

Referring back to the example written out in Chapter 3 it is seen that the above process corresponds exactly with the conventional process carried out there. To further illustrate this process the successive stages of AQ for an example (the second one executed in Chapter 3) are shown below. We assume 6 bit registers for simplicity.

	A	Q	R^3
	0.0 0 0 0 0	0.1 0 1 1 1	0.0 1 1 0 0
Sum and Shift	0.0 0 1 1 0	0.0 1 0 1 1	
Sum and Shift	0.0 1 0 0 1	0.0 0 1 0 1	
Sum and Shift	0.0 1 0 1 0	0.1 0 0 1 0	
Shift	0.0 0 1 0 1	0.0 1 0 0 1	
Sum and Shift	0.0 1 0 0 0	0.1 0 1 0 0	

The product in AQ is 0.0 1 0 0 0 1 0 1 0 0. It is possible for overflow to occur at an intermediate stage of this process, just before a shift, and since a 1 in a_0 will propagate with a right shift a special provision is made to inhibit the propagation in this instance.

Multiplication involving a negative multiplier is somewhat more complicated. Suppose $x < 0$ and $y > 0$, then

$$y* = y$$
$$x* = 2 + x .$$

The number x* is in the quotient register at the outset of the multiplication operation, and the digits of this number are successively shifted into Q_{39} and tested during multiplication except for the sign digit of x* (because the digit in Q_0 is not affected in a shift operation). Hence the product that is actually formed by the machine is

$$(x* - 1) \; y* = (1 + x) \; y = y + xy \tag{8-1}$$

The desired result is, of course,

$$(xy)* = 2 + xy \qquad (\text{mod } 2) \tag{8-2}$$

The result shown in Equation (8-1) can easily be corrected to obtain the correct result by simply subtracting y:

$$(x* - 1) \; y* + (-y)* = (1 + x) \; y + 2 - y$$
$$= y + xy + 2 - y$$
$$= 2 + xy$$

Consequently, to insure a correct product, the sign digit of Q, Q_0, is sensed after the 39 step shifting and adding process described above is complete and if $q_0 = 1$, then the multiplicand (i.e. y) is subtracted from the "product" to obtain the correct product; if $q_0 = 0$ no correction is necessary. It is to be understood that the sensing of Q_0 and correction of the product, if necessary, takes place automatically as a part of the multiplication order.

After Q_0 is sensed its contents are set to zero (i.e. $q'_0 = 0$). This step is necessary to give the correct algebraic representation to the least significant part of the product. The double precision number, N, expressed in terms of the contents of A and Q at the completion of the multiplication is

$$N = a + 2^{-39} \; q \tag{8-3}$$

where

$$a = -a_0 + \sum_{i=1}^{39} a_i \; 2^{-i}$$

$$q = -q_0 + \sum_{i=1}^{39} q_i \; 2^{-i} \; .$$

It is important to recognize that q_0 must be zero for Equation (8-3) to be correct; e.g. the double precision number -2^{-78} is correctly represented in a and q when

$$a_0 = a_1 = a_2 = \ldots = a_{39} = 1$$

$$q_0 = 0, \; q_1 = q_2 = \ldots = q_{39} = 1$$

for then

$$a + 2^{-39} q = -2^{-39} + 2^{-39} \cdot (1 - 2^{-39}) = -2^{-78} \; .$$

There are a number of variations of the basic multiply instruction, for example ILLIAC will perform

$$\left.\begin{aligned} (aq)' &= q \, m + 2^{-39} \, a \\ (aq)' &= q(-m) + 2^{-39} \, a \\ (aq)' &= q \, |m| + 2^{-39} \, a \end{aligned}\right\}$$

with A initially not cleared, cleared to zero, or set equal to 1/2 as desired.

In connection with multiplication, a common coding error is to forget that the multiplier is to be placed in Q _not_ in A at the outset of a multiplication.

UNIVERSITY OF ILLINOIS
DIGITAL COMPUTER
CHAPTER 9

DIVISION

For positive divisor and dividend, the ILLIAC division process is analogous to elementary long division. At the outset of the division process the dividend, call it x, is in AQ, and is thus treated as a double length number. This feature provides consistency with the precision of the double length product obtained from a multiplication. The divisor, call it y, is brought from the memory, the location being specified by the address of the divide instruction, and placed in R^3. Division then proceeds according to the following rules:

(1) Form $a - r^3$ in the adder (i.e. [most significant part of x]-y)

(2) $q'_{39} = 0$ if $a - r^3 < 0$, or

$q'_{39} = 1$ and $a' = a - r^3$ if $a - r^3 \geq 0$;

$a - r^3$ is called the partial remainder ;

(3) $(aq)' = 2(aq)$ and $q'_0 = q_1$, i.e. a left shift with q_1 shifting into q_0 as well as a_{39} ;

(4) Form $a - r^3$ and so on until 39 such tests and shifts have been executed ;

(5) $q'_{39} = 1$; hence, when the shifting is completed a one resides in Q_{39}*.

At the completion of (5) above the rounded quotient resides in Q and a quantity called the residue resides in A. Step 5 provides the rounding. The first digit entered into q_{39}, step 2, is the sign digit of the quotient. Since q_1 shifts into q_0 it is seen that on the last shift the sign digit will enter q_0. When divisor or dividend or both are negative the rules are similar.

---

* This one is actually placed in Q_{39} at the outset of the division process. The quotient digits generated in step (2) above are placed in $\bar{Q}_{39}$ and get gated into Q on the left shift operation in step (3). The contents of $\underline{Q}_{39}$ are held to 1 during the shifting process.

To further illustrate the division process we will follow the states of A and Q and the tentative partial remainder in a sample problem (the first division problem of Chapter 3). The registers are shortened for simplicity.

	A	Q	Tentative Partial Remainder	R^3
	0.1 0 0	0.1 0 1		0.1 0 1
			1.1 1 1	
$q_3 = 0$ and shift	1.0 0 1	1.0 0 0		
			0.1 0 0	
$q_3 = 1$ and shift	1.0 0 0	0.0 1 0		
			0.0 1 1	
$q_3 = 1$ and shift	0.1 1 0	0.1 1 0		
round	0.1 1 0	0.1 1 1		

An important difficulty encountered in division is that unlike addition, subtraction and multiplication, it produces a result that in general cannot be held in a register of finite length. The quotient is therefore rounded to provide a more accurate result than would be obtained by a simple truncation at the 39th digit of the quotient. This rounding scheme is discussed in Chapter 26. The fact that the remainder is not directly available on completion of the division, but must be generated from the residue somewhat complicates this operation.

The relationship between the dividend x the divisor y, the quotient z and the remainder r is

$$x = y z + r \ . \tag{9-1}$$

ILLIAC division yields a quotient z', the "machine quotient", and a corresponding remainder r' satisfying the relation

$$x = y z' + r' \ . \tag{9-2}$$

In general $z' \neq z$ and $r' \neq r$. z' is in fact related to z according to

$$z' = z + 2^{-39} (1 - z_{39})(1 - 2 y_0) \quad . \tag{9-3}$$

From which we see that $z' = z$ _if_ the true quotient has least significant digit 1, $z_{39} = 1$. If $z_{39} = 0$ then z' is in error ϵ ($= z - z'$) by $+2^{-39}$ or -2^{-39} according as the divisor was positive or negative. Now consider the remainder. We represent the residue, the number in A at the completion of the ILLIAC division, by r_{es}. We have for r' (see Eq. 9-2)

$$r' = 2^{-39} (r_{es} + (2 z_0 - 1) y)$$
$$+ 2^{-78} (x_{78} - z_0) \quad .$$

Thus, except for a possible error of 2^{-78}

$$r' \cong 2^{-39} (r_{es} - y) \quad \text{for positive quotient}$$
$$r' \cong 2^{-39} (r_{es} + y) \quad \text{for negative quotient}$$

When the dividend exceeds the divisor in magnitude, or when their magnitudes are equal, the results described above do not apply. The special situations that result are listed below.

	Quotient
$\lvert\text{dividend}\rvert > \lvert\text{divisor}\rvert$	$\div$ hangup*
$\lvert\text{dividend}\rvert = \lvert\text{divisor}\rvert$ and	
dividend +	$\div$ hangup*
dividend -, divisor +	$-1 + 2^{-39}$
dividend -, divisor -	$1 - 2^{-39}$

* ILLIAC stops with the divisor in R^3.

If the divisor is -1, the ILLIAC generates a quotient which is the digitwise complement of the dividend except for the quotient roundoff.

The programmer must exercise caution in scaling his problem to avoid the generation of a $\div$ hangup. Some computing machines do not stop under the above conditions but set an indicator when an improper division has taken place. A special instruction tests the state of the indicator and thus permits the programmer to rescale the numbers and do a proper division automatically; the IBM 704 has this feature. It remains, however, generally more efficient to scale properly at the outset to prevent such a situation from arising.

Aside from improper scaling leading to a $\div$ hangup, one of the most common coding errors in connection with division is to forget that the quotient is in Q not A. Another common error is to forget that the dividend is in AQ not just in A alone.

UNIVERSITY OF ILLINOIS
DIGITAL COMPUTER
CHAPTER 10

THE ILLIAC ORDER CODE - I

In Chapter 5 the structure of the ILLIAC instruction word was discussed. The significance of the digits will now be examined in more detail. A 40 digit register is drawn below showing the significance of the digital positions for an order pair.

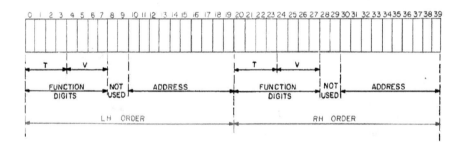

The function digits are grouped into two tetrads; the first is called T and specifies the order type; the second is called V and specifies the one of the possible variants of the order type. T has sixteen possible values, 2^4. These values with the order type they specify are listed below.

T	Order Type
O	Left shift
1	Right shift
2	Unconditional transfer
3	Conditional transfer
4	Store from A register
5	Memory to Q register
6	Divide
7	Multiply
8	Input or output
9	Special input or output
K	Increment add from Q
S	Add from Q
N	Not used
J	Extract
F	Increment add
L	Add

LIST OF ORDER TYPES

There are also sixteen possible values for V but not all are used. The individual binary digits of V have in many cases, but not all, a unique significance independent of the other digits of V and T. This feature is a considerable help to the memorization of the order code. The various effects of V will be illustrated in the following examples.

In this chapter and the five succeeding chapters the use of various ILLIAC orders will be illustrated by a number of examples*. In these examples the address will always be written as a decimal integer, it being understood that in the machine this number is a binary number. The function digits T and V will always be written as sexadecimal characters. Parentheses will indicate the contents of a memory location; (100) denotes the word in memory location 100_D, (101) denotes the contents of location 101_D, etc. It will be assumed that the order pairs are stored sequentially beginning at memory location 10_D.

* The complete order code is in Appendix 4, pp. 251-270.

Examples of the use of order types 4 and L.

Example: $(102)' = (100) + (101)$; i.e. add the number at location 100 to the number at location 101 and place the sum in location 102. The sequence of instructions, written as order pairs is listed below. The WM location of the order pair is in the left-most column.

WM	Order Pair	Comments
10	L5 100	$a' = 0$, $a' = a + (100)$
	L4 101	$a' = a + (101)$
11	40 102	$(102)' = a$
	0F 000	STOP

The least significant V digit, V_1, causes A to be cleared or not according as $V_1 = 1$, $V_1 = 0$. This clearing is always done first before the remainder of the operations of the instruction are executed: this property of V_1 is true for all order types. Thus in the LH order at 10 the variant digit $V = 5$, having $V_1 = 1$, causes $a' = 0$ first. This is a clear-add order. Notice that the RH order at 10 has $V_1 = 0$ so the contents of A are not initially cleared. The L4 order thus achieves the sum $(100) + (101)$ with the result residing in the A register. The L4 order is a hold-add order.

In an L order the state of V_4 ($V = V_8 \ V_4 \ V_2 \ V_1$) indicates whether or not the number brought from the R^3 register into the adder is to be complemented as it passes through the complement gate and a carry added into the least significant digit in the adder (see Chapter 6). Thus, if $V_4 = 0$ the number from R^3 is subtracted from the contents of A, and if $V_4 = 1$ the number from R^3 is added to the contents of A. Above we see that $V_4 = 1$ for both L orders to specify that the desired additions are to be performed.

The LH order at 11 is a store order. It places the contents of the accumulator into the WM at location 102. We might notice here that if V_1 were equal to 1 in this order, then A would be cleared first and then the contents of A would be placed in the WM at 102; the net effect being to put zero in A and WM location 102.

The last order at the RH position of location 11 is an order causing the ILLIAC to stop. Any order in which $V_8 = 1$ and $V_1 = 0$ independent of the state of the other digits of T and V causes ILLIAC to stop; in this case we note V = F so $V_8 = 1$ and $V_1 = 0$.

A read from the memory for an operand does not change the state of the location consulted. In the example above locations 100 and 101 are unchanged when the addends are read from them. (The store order (40) does change location 102 but not A.) This also applies to the reading of the instructions by the control unit. In the above example the control unit must read locations 10 and 11 which hold the orders it must execute. This reading does not change the state of these locations. In fact if after the STOP (OF 000), the control counter was reset to ten and ILLIAC was restarted these very same orders would be executed again and would give exactly the same result as before.

Example 2: $(102)' = (100) - (101)$. The instructions are listed below.

WM	Order pair	Comments
10	L5 100	$a' = 0, a' = a + (100)$
	L0 201	$a' = a - (101)$
11	40 102	$(102)' = a$
	OF 000	STOP

Here just V_4 of the RH order at 10 is changed from 1 to 0. Otherwise the instructions are just as they were in example 1. $V_4 = 0$ causes the subtraction to be executed. It is perhaps obvious but nevertheless take particular notice of the effect that a change of one binary digit has in this computation. One cannot emphasize too strongly the need for writing every order with great care, since the slightest error can completely change an instruction. The ILLIAC does not execute what you "meant" but what you "wrote".

This same calculation can be done with a slightly different sequence of instructions. This alternate scheme is shown below.

WM	Order Pair	Comments
10	L1 101	a' = 0, a' = a - (101)
	L4 100	a' = a + (100)
11	40 102	(102)' = a
	OF 000	STOP

In the LH order at 10 V_1 = 1 causing A to be cleared first; V_4 = 0 causing the subtraction a - (101), the net effect being to put - (101) into A. The hold-add instruction at the RH of 10 has the effect of placing (100) - (101) in A.

Example 3: $(102)' = (100) + |(101)|$; the vertical bars denote absolute magnitude. The instructions are listed below.

WM	Order Pair	Comments
10	L5 100	a' = 0, a' = a + (100)
	L6 101	a' = a + |(101)|
11	40 102	(102)' = a
	OF 000	STOP

In the L order the variant digit V_2 specifies whether or not the absolute magnitude of the number from R^3 is to be added to the contents of A. If V_2 = 1 the absolute magnitude is added to a; if V_2 = 0 a normal addition is performed. The adding of the absolute magnitude of a number is effected by simply testing the sign digit of the number in R^3 and then setting the gates for an addition or subtraction according as the outcome of this test yields 0 or 1 for the sign digit of the number in R^3. Because of this technique for producing the absolute magnitude of a number it should be noted that the absolute magnitude of the machine representation of -1, namely 1.00 ... 0, is -1. This is a peculiar situation which can cause difficulty if overlooked.

Example 4: $(102)' = (100) - |(101)|$. The instructions are listed below.

WM	Order Pair	Comments
10	L5 100	$a' = 0$, $a' = a + (100)$
	L2 101	$a' = a - |(101)|$
11	40 102	$(102)' = a$
	OF 000	STOP

The RH order at 10 has $V_4 = 0$ to cause a subtraction and $V_2 = 1$ to cause the absolute magnitude of the operand to be used. An alternate sequence of instructions producing the same result is given below.

WM	Order Pair	Comments
10	L3 101	$a' = 0$, $a' = a - |(101)|$
	L4 100	$a' = a + (100)$
11	40 102	$(102)' = a$
	OF 000	STOP

The negative of the absolute magnitude of (101) is here brought into A with the LH order at 10; $V_1 = 1$ causes the initial clearing of A.

Example 5: $(102)' = \frac{1}{2} + (100) - (101)$. Just as $V_1 = 1$ causes A to be initially set to zero it is also possible, via the variant digit, to set $A = \frac{1}{2}$ initially. This is effected by setting $V_8 = 1$ and $V_1 = 1$. The sequence of instructions below illustrates the use of this feature in doing the above computation.

WM	Order Pair	Comments
10	LJ 100	$a' = \frac{1}{2}$, $a' = a + (100)$
	L0 101	$a' = a - (101)$
11	40 102	$(102)' = a$
	OF 000	STOP

The variant digit J in the LH order at 10 has $V_8 = V_1 = 1$ and thus initially causes $\frac{1}{2}$ to be put into A; $V_4 = 1$ signifying addition. The ability to thus preset the accumulator to $\frac{1}{2}$, which now seems unimportant will later be seen to be quite useful.

Example 6: We have discussed two forms of the store order, namely 40 and 41. The store order can also be used to effect a partial substitution; the left or right address digits of the accumulator may be placed in the corresponding position of a word in the memory leaving the remainder of the word in the memory unchanged. This type of order is used most commonly to change the address of orders in a code. An example is given below.

Suppose that in some part of a program we want to form the sum $z = x + y$, where the memory location of the number x and the memory location of the number y have themselves been computed by the program. Let us assume that the computed memory location of x has been placed in the LH address digits of the word at 215; thus it is stored as the fraction $(x\text{-address}) \cdot 2^{-19}$. Let us assume that the computed memory location of y has been placed in the RH address digits of the word at 230; thus it is stored as an integer or alternatively as a fraction $(y\text{-address}) \cdot 2^{-39}$. The instructions below will produce $z = x + y$ at location 100. Square brackets indicate that an address is altered by the program and if the word at location L caused the alteration we write "by L" in the comments column alongside the altered address.

WM	Order Pair	Comments
10	15 215	a' = (215)
	46 12	Plant LH add. at 12
11	15 230	a' = (230)
	42 12	Plant RH add. at 12
12	15 [000]	By 10; a' = x
	14 [000]	By 11; a' = x + y
13	40 100	(100)' = x + y = z
	0F 000	STOP

The 46 instruction at RH of 10 puts the address of x into the address digits of the instruction at LH of 12. Variant digit V_2 = 1 identifies the 46 order as a _partial_ store order. Variant digit V_4 = 1 identifies the 46 order as a _left-hand address_ store order. The 42 instruction at RH of 11 puts the address of y into the address digits of the instruction at RH of 12. Again, variant digit V_2 = 1 identifies the 42 order as a _partial_ store order. Variant digit V_4 = 0 identifies the 42 order as a _right-hand address_ store order. Thus, we see that at the time of execution of the orders at 12 these orders have been given the desired addresses.

We have assumed in the above example that the x address and y address are held "clean" in the left and right address positions of the words at 215 and 230; "clean" here means that all other bits in the word are zero with the exception of these addresses. This simplifying assumption was completely unnecessary since the partial store orders affect _only_ the 10 address digits, left or right according as V_4 = 1 or V_4 = 0, respectively. It is important to recognize that the two unused digits are _not_ affected by the partial store order. Neglection of this fact is the source of a common coding blunder.

In a 4 order V_1 = 1 causes an initial clearing of A. Thus a 43 order first clears A and then puts the right address digits of A into the right address digits of the specified memory position. It is thus possible to clear just the address portion of a word.

The order 42 m, if located at the LH order position of m itself, will alter the address of the RH order at location m _in the memory_. But at the time of execution of the 42 m order the RH order at m is already in the instruction register and is unaffected by the 42 order. Consequently in the order pair

p-1	
p	42 p
	L5 [0]
p+1	

the 42 p order will _not_ change the address of the next order to be obeyed, namely the L5 [0] order, although it will change the word at location p in the memory in the usual way. Overlooking this is a not uncommon source of headaches.

UNIVERSITY OF ILLINOIS
DIGITAL COMPUTER
CHAPTER 11

THE ILLIAC ORDER CODE - II

Examples of the use of order types 2 and 3. Type digits 2 and 3
signify transfer orders. The type 2 order is called an unconditional transfer
order and the type 3 order is called a conditional transfer order. The word
"jump" is frequently used synonymously with transfer. The use of the unconditional transfer order is illustrated in two examples below.

Example 1: Let us suppose that at location 10 we have a block of
orders to perform x + y = z; x is at 100, y at 101, and z is to be stored at
102. Further let us suppose that following this calculation we want to perform
u + v = w; u is at 103, v is at 104, and w is to be stored at 105. We assume
that the instructions to do this latter calculation are stored in a block at 20.
Using the notation of Chapter 10 we have to perform,

$$(102)' = (100) + (101)$$
$$(105)' = (103) + (104)$$

WM	Order Pairs	Comments
10	L5 100	a' = x
	L4 101	a' = x + y = z
11	40 102	(102)' = z
	26 20	Jump to 20
20	L5 103	from 11, a' = u
	L4 104	a' = u + v = w
21	40 105	(105)' = w
	OF 000	STOP

After execution of the 40 order at 11 the unconditional transfer order causes the control counter to be reset to 20. The V_4 digit is 1 in the 26 order indicating that the next order is to be taken from the <u>left side</u> of the word at 20. Notice that like the store order (T = 4) V_4 = 1 refers to an operation involving the left half of a word, and V_4 = 0 (22 is a jump to the <u>right side</u> of a word) refers to an operation involving the right half of a word. It is customary to write "from m" in the comments column (see word at 20) opposite the word to which the transfer has been made, with m being the location of the transfer instruction.

Example 2: An example of the use of the 22 instruction is given below where it is assumed that the block of orders executing u + v = w begins at the <u>right side</u> of 20.

WM	Order Pair	Comments
10	L5 100	a' = x
	L4 101	a' = x + y = z
11	40 102	(102)' = z
	22 20	Jump to 20
20	-- ---	
	L5 103	from 11, a' = u
21	L4 104	a' = u + v = w
	40 105	(105)' = w
22	OF 000	STOP
	-- ---	

Here the 22 order at 11 causes the jump to the right side of 20.

Every program worthy of a high-speed digital computer has at least one "loop" in it and frequently it contains many "loops". A loop is a set of orders which are executed more than once, commonly with modification of some of the orders. Thus, to perform

$$z = \sum_{i=1}^{n} x_i \qquad\qquad (11\text{-}1)$$

one uses a loop containing one add order (and certain other orders) which is executed repetitively just n times. The necessity for enabling a high-speed computing machine to execute such a loop is immediately evident when we consider the alternative way of computing this sum by simply writing explicitly every add order into the code when n is 4,000. It would be impossible to get all of the orders in the memory at one time. Furthermore, the time needed to write out each add order could just as well be taken up in executing the sum on an adding machine. Finally, let us observe that the time required to execute 2048 instructions, the maximum that can be held in the ILLIAC memory, is about 0.3 seconds (assuming 150 μ sec. per instruction) while the time taken to read 2048 orders into ILLIAC is at least 34 seconds; consequently, without loops a considerable portion of time would be consumed in a long program in the relatively slow process of reading new instructions into the memory.

One can recognize immediately two necessary properties of the loop for the calculation of the sum (11-1). First, on each pass through the loop a new addend x_i is required; therefore it will be necessary to alter the address of the add order on each pass through the loop. Second, the program must somehow automatically determine when the required number of passes through the loop has been achieved, and then arrange to stop executing the loop and proceed to a new set of orders. The second feature of the loop, the end test, requires as a necessary part the conditional transfer order which is perhaps the most valuable single order in the computer since it does make the loop possible. Examples of the use of the conditional transfer order are given below.

Example 3: First we consider a set of instructions to perform the sum (11-1) above, assuming n = 100 and that the x_i's are stored in a block at 201 (x_1 in 201, x_2 in 202, etc.) and the sum z is to be stored at 500. We further assume that the x's are suitably scaled so that the sum is in machine range. To perform the sum we use the iterative scheme

$$z_0 = 0$$
$$z_i = x_i + z_{i-1}$$
$$z_{100} = z$$

The program for this calculation follows.

WM	Order Pair	Comments
10	41 500	partial sum = 0
	L5 [201]	by 15, from 15; $\sigma' = x_1, x_2 \ldots x_1$
11	L4 500	$\sigma' = x_i + z_{i-1} = z_i$
	40 500	
12	L5 10	Modify address
	L4 16	
13	42 10	$(10)' = (10) - 2^{-39}$
	L5 17	step the counter
14	L0 16	
	40 17	$(17)' = (17) - 2^{-39}$
15	32 10	transfer when $(17) \geq 0$
	0F 000	Stop. Here when $(17) = -1 \times 2^{-39}$
16	00 000	$= 1 \times 2^{-39}$
	00 001	
17	00 000	by 14; $= 99 \times 2^{-39}$
	00 99	end counter (C_{end})

A "flow chart" of the logical operations for this calculation is given below.

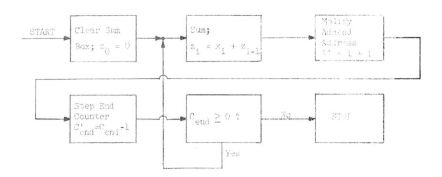

The order at LH of 10 clears the memory location in which the sum
is to be located; it executes $z_0 = 0$. The following three orders execute the
actual summation; they do $z_i = x_i + z_{i-1}$. Next, beginning at the LH of 12 are
three orders which modify the address at RH of 10, namely the addend address,
so that on the next pass through the loop the next addend, x_{i+1}, will be summed.
Notice that in this modification the order pair is treated just as a number,
the effect of adding 1×2^{-39} to this number being simply to advance the
address of the RH order by 1. The modified address is placed back in the
memory via the 42 order. A 40 order could just as well have been used for this
purpose; however, for reasons which will become clear later it is best to use
the partial substitution order for this purpose. Following the address modification orders there is a set of orders used to count the number of passes
through the loop and test for the end. For this purpose location 17 is used
as a "counter". On the very first entry the counter is equal to 99×2^{-39}.
This counter is reduced by 1×2^{-39} on each pass through the loop. The conditional
transfer is executed as a transfer to RH of 10 so long as the counter remains
positive (including zero) and it will not be so executed as soon as the counter

becomes negative. After 99 passes through the loop the counter will be equal
to zero, the transfer will be executed and one more pass, the 100th, will be
made after which the counter is reduced to -1×2^{-39}. At this point, since
the counter is negative, the transfer is not executed and the next order is
taken from RH of 15. Thus 100 passes have been made through the loop and the
desired sum is in location 500 when the OF order is encountered. $V_4 = 0$ on
the conditional transfer order prescribes a transfer to the right side of the
location specified by the address, just as with a type 2 order. In fact, all
V digits have the same significance for type 2 and type 3 orders.

The flow chart above which illustrates the logical sequence or "flow"
of events in a pictorial fashion should be self explanatory. Many programmers
find these charts to be helpful in laying out the logic of a program. For
complex programs they are almost essential prerequisites to writing the code.

Example 4: There are many sets of orders which could be used to
achieve the same result as above. An alternative code is given below.

WM	Order Pair	Comments
10	41 500	partial sum = 0
	L5 [201]	by 15, from 14; $a' = x_1, x_2 \cdots x_{i}C$
11	L4 500	$a' = x_i + z_{i-1} = z_i$
	40 500	$(500)' = z_i$
12	L5 10	modify address
	L4 16	
13	42 10	
	L0 17	end test
14	36 15	transfer if end
	22 10	here if not end
15	OF 000	from 14, Stop
	-- ---	
16	00 000	by 12
	00 001	
17	41 500	end constant
	L5 301	by 13

The difference between this code and the previous code is the manner in which the test for the end is carried out. Here the order pair at 10 is itself used as a counter. Notice that this order pair represents a positive number which increases in units of 1×2^{-39} with each pass through the loop. After 100 passes through the loop, including the 100th address advance, the order pair at 10 will be precisely 41 500 L5 301. Now in this code the maximum value of location 10 is subtracted from the current value of location 10 on each pass through the loop to see if the maximum value has been achieved. If it has not been achieved, then the result in the accumulator will be negative and the conditional transfer will not cause a transfer; instead, the 22 order at RH of 14 will be executed for a new pass through the loop. but when 10 contains 41 500 L5 301, then the subtraction will yield zero, a positive number, in the accumulator and the transfer to the OF order will be executed to terminate the loop. In this code a half-word has been wasted, namely RH of 15.

Example 5: The code below shows still another slightly different scheme for computing the above sum.

WM	Order Pair	Comments
10	41 500	partial sum = 0
	15 [201]	by 15,from 14; a' = $x_1,x_2 \cdots x_{100}$
11	14 500	a' = x_i + z_{i-1} = z_i
	40 500	500' = b_i
12	15 10	modify address
	14 15	
13	42 10	
	16 16	end test
14	36 15	transfer if end
	22 10	here if not end
15	0F 000	from 14; by 12; STOP
	00 1	
16	41 500	end constant
	15 301	by 13

Here the word at 15 is used to effect the unit increment of the right
address at 10. However since 15 contains the non zero digit F in the left order
the increment of 10 will cause F to be added to the variant digit of the left
order at 10. The partial substitution order (LH of 13) insures against this
alteration of the variant digit being put into the memory; this would not be
the case if a 40 order had been used instead of a 42 order. It is clear that a
different end constant than that used in the previous example must be used here.
In the present case the accumulator will contain

$$a = 4L\ 500 \qquad L5\ 301$$

$$\boxed{1 + F}$$

after the 100th address advance; consequently the end constant used here (see
location 16) will just give zero on the subtraction (RH of 13), a negative
result always being obtained before the 100th pass.

The variant digit $V_2 = 0$ will cause the ILLIAC to stop before a
transfer is executed with either the type 2 or type 3 order. The operation of
the ILLIAC can be resumed with the setting of a switch called the black switch
on the control panel of the ILLIAC.

When $V_1 = 1$ for either the type 2 or type 3 order the accumulator
will be cleared. The accumulator is cleared before the sign digit of the
accumulator is tested in the type 3 order and consequently $V_1 = 1$ will always
cause the transfer to be executed in a type 3 order.

UNIVERSITY OF ILLINOIS

DIGITAL COMPUTER

CHAPTER 12

THE ILLIAC ORDER CODE - III

Examples of the use of order types 0, 1 and F. The shift instructions, types 0 and 1, are used for multiplying by powers of 2 and also for strictly logical operations. Examples of each use are given below. The increment add order, type F, is used primarily for counting and incrementing addresses. It can be used to replace the L5, L4 combination used previously as will be seen in the following examples.

Example 1: Let us suppose that a list of numbers x_i ($i = 1, 2, \ldots, 50$) is stored in a block at 200 and another list of numbers y_i ($i = 1, 2, \ldots, 50$) is stored in a block at 250. It is desired to compute a third list $z_i = x_i + \frac{1}{4} y_i$ ($i = 1, 2, \ldots, 50$) and store it in a block at 300. The flow chart and code follow.

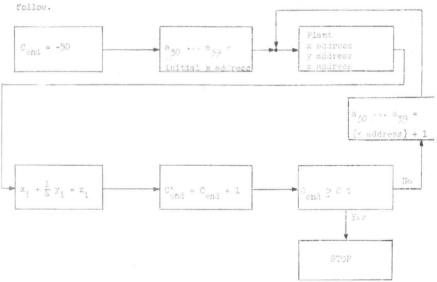

WM	Order Pair	Comments
10	L1 20	Set initial value
	40 21	of end counter to -50
11	L5 19	From 18
	42 15	Plant x address
12	L4 20	
	42 14	Plant y address
13	L4 20	
	00 20	
14	46 16	Plant z address
	L5 [0]	By 12; $e' = y_i$
15	10 2	$\frac{1}{4} y_i$
	L4 [0]	by 11; $\frac{1}{4} y_i + x_i = z_i$
16	40 [0]	by 14; store z_i
	F5 21	$C'_{end} = C_{end} + 1$
17	40 21	
	36 19	Jump if done
18	F5 15	
	22 11	Jump to compute next z
19	0F 000	From 17; STOP
	00 200	By 11
20	00 000	By 10, 12, 13
	00 50	
21	[00 000	By 10, 16, 17:C_{end}
	00 000]	

The "working part" of this code, that is the part which does the actual arithmetic computation of z, is composed of the orders in the RH of 14 to the LH of 16. The remainder of the code is devoted to "bookkeeping", or "housekeeping" as it is sometimes called. In the working part of this code it is seen that a right shift of two places is used to multiply y_i by $1/4$. (Similarly a left shift of two places would have effected a multiplication by 4.) The left shift is also used in the housekeeping orders, RH of 13, to position the address of z_i. When the z_i address is computed it is held in A as a RH address, it must then be shifted to the LH address position since the z_i reference is made by a LH order (LH of 16).

This example also illustrates the use of the increment add order, type F. At location 16 the F order is used to increase the end counter; it advances the end counter by 1×2^{-39} (or integer 1) on each pass through the loop. At location 18 the F order is used to advance the x address on each pass through the loop. The other addresses are generated by adding 50 to the x address, to form the y address, and then adding 50 to the y address to form the z address.

The modified addresses in the loop and the counter are "preset", that is at the very beginning the initial value of the end counter, the x address, y address and z address are stored in the proper positions in the code. In the earlier examples it was always assumed that the addresses which were modified in a loop were stored in the memory with their correct initial address. However it is generally good coding practice to preset such addresses as in the above example. One reason for this is that frequently the loop is part of a larger program and is to be used again at some later point in the program. Presetting the addresses will always guarantee that the loop will always have the right starting addresses on entry into the loop no matter how often the loop has already been used. It is of course possible to "post-set" the addresses; i.e. store them in the memory with their correct initial value and then reset them to their initial value upon exit from the loop. This procedure is susceptible to coding blunders, one reason being that there is frequently more than one exit possible from a loop and one forgets sometimes to post-set addresses on all possible exits.

In this example one should also notice the efficient use that is made of the address planting orders. They are used both in the presetting part of the routine and in the address-advance part.

Another illustration of the use of the shift order, a strictly logical use, is given below where the sum of the digits in a word is computed.

Example 2: Let us suppose the word w in location 100 is

$$w = w_0 \; w_1 \; w_2 \; \cdots \; w_{39} \qquad\qquad (w_i = 0, 1)$$

and the following sum is to be computed,

$$\sum_{i=1}^{39} w_i = S \; ;$$

thus, we desire the sum of the digits of w excluding the sign digit. The sum is to be stored in location 200. The flow chart and code appear below.

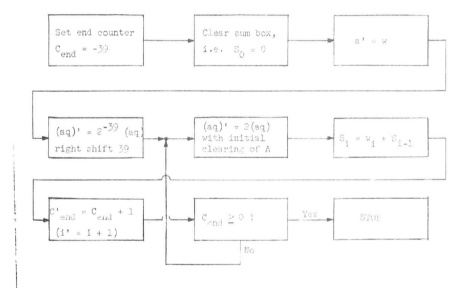

WM	Order Pair	Comments
10	L1 17	Set end counter
	40 18	$C_{end} = -39$
11	41 200	Clear sum box
	L5 100	a' = w
12	10 39	w into Q
	01 1	From 15; a' = $w_i \times 2^{-39}$
13	L4 200	$S_i = w_i + S_{i-1}$
	40 200	
14	F5 18	$C'_{end} = C_{end} + 1$
	40 18	
15	36 16	Jump if done
	22 12	return for next iteration
16	0F 000	From 15; STOP
	-- ---	Waste
17	00 000	End constant
	00 039	By 10
18	[00 000	By 10, 14; C_{end}
	00 000]	

The order at LH of 12 moves the digits w_1 w_2 ... w_{39} into Q_1 Q_2 ... Q_{39}. At the completion of this shift A will contain all 0's or all 1's depending on whether w was positive or negative, since a 1 in the sign position propagates on a right shift. (See Chapter 7, page 36, item (3) of the right shift description.) The order at RH of 12 clears A, since $V_1 = 1$, and then shifts a binary digit from Q_1 into A_{39}. Notice that this initial clearing of A before the shift is essential for proper operation of the code.

In connection with the shift orders a property which is frequently forgotten is the fact that the address of the shift order is always interpreted modulo 64. The maximum number of places that aq can be shifted by a single shift order is 63. If a shift of more places is desired, then two shift orders must be used. In the preceeding example we could alter the word at 12 to read

10 103

01 129

without affecting the answer.

An address of $64 \times n$ $(n = 0, 1, 2 \ldots)$ on a shift order will cause the ILLIAC to stop. This condition is called a zero left shift or zero right shift hangup, and is probably the most common type of unexpected machine stop. This property of the ILLIAC is a very desirable safety feature for the coder. The locations of the WM which are not to be used in a program normally contain zero (the memory is "cleared to zero" as a part of the normal starting procedure). A common coding blunder is to transfer to an incorrect memory position and we see that such a blunder will cause ILLIAC to stop immediately on a zero left shift if the transfer is to a location containing zero. This prevents the possibility of proceeding to do a series of nonsense computations after the erroneous transfer and thereby increase the difficulty of an error diagnosis.

The increment add order is a frequent source of confusion when $V_4 = 0$ ("increment subtract"). At least part of this confusion is removed if one considers the logic involved in the execution of a type F order. The F order is a simple modification of the L order, the modification being simply this: if the variant digit indicates addition, then do not complement the number brought from R^3 into the adder but do insert the carry into the least significant digit of the adder; if the variant digit indicates subtraction, then complement the number as it passes through the complement gate but do not insert the carry into the least significant digit of the adder. Recall that the carry is inserted into the least significant digit of the adder when a subtract instruction (L1, L0) is executed in order to correctly form the 2's complement after digitwise complementation in the complement gate (see Chapter 6). We see therefore that F5 and F4 have the effect of incrementing the number brought from R^3 by 1×2^{-39}.

It is frequently erroneously assumed that Fl and FO correspondingly decrease the number by 1×2^{-39} -- <u>this</u> <u>is</u> <u>not</u> <u>so</u> as one can clearly see from the above discussion. Fl and FO will in fact cause the digitwise complement of the number m in memory to be added to a: thus FO M does a' = a -m -2^{-39}.

UNIVERSITY OF ILLINOIS
DIGITAL COMPUTER
CHAPTER 13

THE ILLIAC ORDER CODE - IV

Examples of the use of order types 5, 7 and S. Below, several examples of the use of the multiply instruction, type 7, are given. The type 5 instruction (read a number from the WM into Q) normally accompanies the multiply instruction since the multiplier must be placed in Q before multiplication. Notice that a shift instruction is, in general, not suitable for this purpose since the sign digit will not be transferred into Q_0 by shifting.

The S order is identical to the L order except that it takes the addend from Q rather than from the memory. It sometimes occurs with the type 7 order as a means for transmitting the least significant part of a product into A.

Example 1: Suppose that we wish to compute

$$z = c(bx + y)$$

where the fractions c, b, x, y are in locations 100, 101, 102, 103, respectively, and z is to be stored in location 200. It is assumed that all numbers are scaled so that overflow will not occur. The flow chart and code follow.

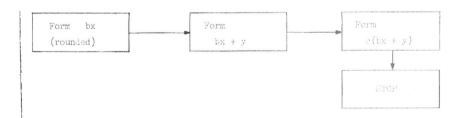

WM	Order Pair	Comments
10	50 102	$q' = x$
	7J 101	$a' = bx$ (rounded)
11	L4 103	$a' = bx + y$
	40 000	Temporary store
12	50 000	$q' = bx + y$
	7J 100	$a' = c(bx + y)$ (rounded)
13	40 200	Store $z = c(bx + y)$
	0F 000	STOP

The 50 order at LH of 10 places the multiplier in Q in preparation for the multiplication. The variant digit on the multiplication order is J, producing a rounded product in A. Let us now consider how the rounding of the product is brought about. Since variant digit J implies $V_8 = V_1 = 1$, the fraction 1/2 will be placed in the accumulator before multiplication is initiated. From our earlier consideration of the multiplication process (Chapter 8, see the example on page 43) we observe that the initial contents of A are always added into the product such that the number actually formed by an ILLIAC multiplication is

$$(aq)' = q \times r^3 + a \times 2^{-39} ;$$

i.e. the initial contents of A are added into the least significant part of the product. Now observe that if $a = 1/2$ the above relation becomes

$$(aq)' = q \times r^3 + 2^{-40}$$

It is easy to see that this yields a rounded product in A: if the least significant part of the unrounded product, digital positions 2^{-40}, 2^{-41}, ... 2^{-78}, is greater than or equal to 2^{-40} then the above procedure will cause the most significant part of the product to be incremented by 2^{-39}; if the least significant part of the unrounded product is less than 2^{-40}, then the above procedure will have no effect on the most significant part of the product.

The variant digit J also implies $V_4 = 1$. This variation causes the contents of R^3 to be added successively to the contents of A, or not added depending on the multiplier digits; i.e. the process would be just as outlined on page 42. When $V_4 = 0$ the contents of R^3 are subtracted from the contents of A rather than added so that a negative product is formed; i.e. $- m \cdot q + 2^{-39} a = (aq)'$. Notice that this effect is analogous with the effect that this variant digit has with the type L order. In a similar fashion the V_2 digit causes multiplication by the absolute magnitude of the number in R^3 when $V_2 = 1$.

In the RH order at 11 the partially formed result is temporarily stored in order to properly place it into Q for the next multiplication via a 50 order. Had the number $bx + y$ been positive, a right shift of 39 places would have served this purpose, but had $bx + y$ been negative this shifting would not produce the correct multiplier in Q. It is certain that $q_0 = 0$ when the order at RH of 11 is executed because the previous multiplication will have produced a zero in Q_0; multiplication always produces $q_0 = 0$.

In this example we come upon, for the first time, a thing called temporary store. In most programs it is necessary to have a portion of the memory designated as "temporary storage" wherein numbers are held for a few fleeting moments during the course of the calculation as in this example. It is very common to use locations 0, 1, 2 etc. for this purpose.

Example 2: In this example a code for the evaluation of a polynomial will be considered. The polynomial is

$$y = b_n x^n + b_{n-1} x^{n-1} + \ldots + b_1 x + b_0 .$$

and it is to be evaluated by the iterative scheme

$$y_{i+1} = y_i x + b_{n-i} \qquad (i = 1, 2, \ldots, n)$$

with $y_1 = b_n$. Combining the steps of this procedure it is clear that y is expressed in the form

$$y = \left[\cdots \left(\left((b_n x + b_{n-1}) x + b_{n-2} \right) x + b_{n-3} \right) x + \cdots + b_0 \right]$$

which is readily seen to be identical to the above expression for the polynomial when the indicated multiplications are executed. There are of course a number of logical schemes one could use for the evaluation of the polynomial. The above iterative scheme is selected because it is possible to code this logic into a relatively simple loop. Actually, this is not the only reason for selecting this scheme; the other reason is based on an error analysis. A discussion of errors is given in chapters 25, 26, and 27.

The flow chart and code follow. As before it will be assumed that the numbers have been appropriately scaled so that no overflow problems arise. For definiteness let us take $n = 12$, and assume that the coefficients b_{12}, b_{11}, b_{10}, $\ldots$, b_0 are stored as fractions in a block at 500 (i.e. b_{12} is in 500, b_{11} in 501, b_{10} in 502, etc.), and that x is a fraction stored in location 100, and finally that the result, y, is to be stored at 200.

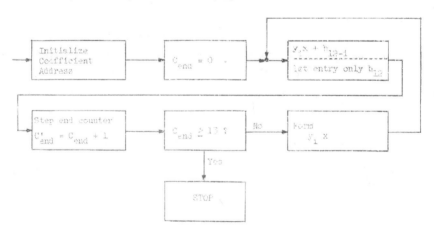

WM	Order Pair	Comments
10	15 17 42 11	Plant address of 1st coefficient, b_{12}
11	41 18 L4 [0]	Clear end counter By 10, 14, 15: $a' = a + b_{12-i}$ From 16
12	40 200 F5 18	Store y_{i+1}
13	40 18 L0 19	$C'_{end} = C_{end} + 1$ $C_{end} - 13$
14	36 17 F5 11	Transfer if END ($C_{end} = 13$) Advance coefficient address.
15	42 11 50 200	$q' = y_i$
16	7J 100 22 11	$y_i \cdot x$
17	0F 000 00 500	From 14; STOP By 10
18	[00 000 00 000]	By 11, 12, 13: END counter
19	00 000 00 13	By 13: END constant

The first three orders in this code do the initialization or pre-setting of the polynomial coefficient address and the counter which is to keep track of the number of iterations. Notice that the code has been written so as to permit the hold add order at RH of 11 to serve two purposes. When this order is first executed it sets up the initial condition for the iteration process; that is, it makes $y_1 = b_{12}$. This results from the fact that the 41 order clears A just before this hold add order is <u>first</u> executed. On subsequent executions of this hold add order A holds $y_1 \cdot x$, as a result of the 7J order at 16, and the hold add order forms $y_1 \cdot x + b_{12-i}$ in A. The 22 order following the 7J order does not affect A or Q.

It should be observed that by simply changing the end constant at 19 one can use this code to evaluate polynomials of arbitrary degree, <u>including</u> <u>zero degree polynomials</u>. The relationship between the end constant and the degree of the polynomial, n, is (treating all numbers as integers)

END Constant = n + 1 .

The above may seem like a trivial observation and it may appear unnecessary to write the program to handle the unusual special case of $n = 0$; however, it will be found by painful experience that many codes which are supposed to handle "all" cases fail in the limiting case. To avoid such possible future difficulty the coder should try to make codes applicable even in the limiting or extreme cases within, of course, the bounds of common sense.

A common coding error in writing loops is to give an incorrect value to the end constant such that a loop which is supposed to be executed just k times is actually executed k-1 times or k+1 times. A good check on the formula for computing the end constant is to consider what happens when just 1 or 2 passes through the loop are desired. To check the above formula for the end constant it is suggested that you consider the operation of this code when n = 0 and when n = 1.

It sometimes occurs that either or both of the operands in a multiplication are represented in the machine as integers. Such cases require special attention. It is always simplest in these considerations to regard all ILLIAC numbers as having the binary point at the extreme left; thus, the integer x is represented in the machine as $x \cdot 2^{-39}$. Suppose we are to form the product of the <u>integer</u> x and the <u>fraction</u> y. The product formed by the ILLIAC is $x \cdot y \cdot 2^{-39}$. Thus the product, treated as a double length number in AQ, is "scaled" by 2^{-39} just as the integer x was scaled by 2^{-39}. When speaking of a number in this form it is common to call the portion of the number residing in A "the integer part", and the portion residing in Q "the fractional part". Multiplication of two integers $x \cdot 2^{-39}$ by $y \cdot 2^{-39}$ yields a product in AQ of $xy \cdot 2^{-78}$. The product is thus scaled by 2^{-78}. In this case the least significant digit of the integer product resides in Q_{39}. When doing multiplication involving both integers and fractions it is frequently desired to retain both the fractional and integral parts of products. In such cases unrounded multiplications are necessary.

Example 3: In this example we consider the code for computing

$$z = e(bx + cy + d)$$

where it is assumed that e, b, c and d are integers stored in memory locations 100, 101, 102, and 103, respectively; x and y are fractions stored in locations 104 and 105; z is to be computed to a precision of 78 binary digits; the integer part of z is to be stored at 106 and the fractional part of z is to be stored at 107. The code follows.

WM	Order Pair	Comments
10	50 104	q' = x
	75 101	(aq)' = bx
11	40 106	(106)' = int. (bx)
	S5 000	a' = frac. (bx)
12	50 105	q' = y
	74 102	(aq)' = cy + frac. (bx)
13	L4 106	a' = int. (bx + cy)
	L4 103	a' = int. (bx + cy + d)
14	40 106	(106)' = int. (bx + cy + d)
	75 100	(aq)' = e · frac. (bx + cy + d)
15	40 000	Temp. store int. part.
	S5 000	
16	40 107	(107)' = frac. e(bx + cy + d)
	L5 000	a' = int. (e · frac. (bx + cy + d)

(Continued on page 80)

WM	Order Pair	Comments
17	50 106	$q' = int. (bx + cy + d)$
	74 100	$q' = int. e(bx + cy + d)$
18	00 59	$a' = int. e(bx + cy + d)$
	40 106	$(106)' = int. e(bx + cy + d)$
19	OF 000	STOP
	-- ---	

At the RH of 10 the multiplication order first clears A, since $V_1 = 1$, and then produces the product bx as a double length number in AQ. The integer part of the product resides in A and is stored at 106. The fractional part of the product resides in Q and is brought into A via the S5 order. The fractional part of bx is retained in A for the execution of the next product cy. When cy is formed it is done with a hold multiply order, 74, in which the fractional part of bx becomes added to the fractional part of cy; remember, the order 74 m produces $(aq)' = q \times m + 2^{-39} a$. Following this multiplication the integer part of bx + cy + d is assimilated into location 106. The fractional part of bx + cy + d remains in Q and the product e. frac (bx + cy + d) is formed. The integral part of this product is temporarily stored so that the fractional part of $z = e(bx + cy + d)$ which is in Q may be transmitted to memory location 106. Finally the integer multiplication, e. int (bx + cy + d), is executed with a hold multiply order so that the integer part of (e. frac. (bx + cy + d)), which was temporarily stored at zero and then returned to A, will be added into this product.

This is the first time an example using the S order has been considered; however, the order type should not need special discussion because of its close similarity to the L order which has already been extensively discussed by examples. Since the operand is taken from Q in an S order the address of an S order is irrelevant and indeed may have any value without affecting the operation of the S order. Because of this feature of the S order its address digits are frequently used for storing constants; for example, the initial address of an order in a loop which is to have its address modified is frequently stored in the address digits of an S order.

It should be observed in this example that the S order rather than a shift order must be used for transferring the least significant part of the product from Q into A. A shift order would not guarantee proper treatment of the sign of the least significant part. Notice however in the order at location 18 a shift must be used to get the product of the two integers into A with proper sign.

UNIVERSITY OF ILLINOIS
DIGITAL COMPUTER
CHAPTER 14

THE ILLIAC ORDER CODE - V

Examples of the use of order types 6 and J. In this chapter we will consider examples using the divide order, type 6, and the extract order, type J.

Recall from the discussion in Chapter 9 that the dividend in ILLIAC division is assumed to be in AQ. Consequently before a divide order there must be given orders for proper placement of the dividend; for this one might use the sequence L5, 50. ILLIAC division produces a rounded quotient in Q and a residue (Chapter 9, page 48) in A. It was seen in Chapter 9 that rounding of the quotient was effected by "stuffing" a 1 into the least significant digital position of the quotient.

The extract order, type J, is perhaps most easily remembered by noting that it produces the digitwise (or logical) product of the contents of Q and a number in location m of the memory; the location is specified in the address of the J order. Representing the digital positions by the conventional subscript notation, the effect of the J order is described precisely by the relation

$$q_i' = q_i \times m_i \cdot (i = 0, 1, \ldots, 39)$$

Thus, the resultant digit in Q_i is 1 if and only if q_i and m_i are 1. The type J order is commonly used for extracting portions of words.

Example 1: In this example the function

$$w = \frac{x + y}{z}$$

will be computed. It is assumed that the fractions x, y, z are properly scaled so that $|x + y| < |z|$. Suppose x, y and z are in locations 100, 101, 102 and the quotient w is to be placed in location 103. The code follows.

WM	Order Pair	Comments
10	L5 100	a' = x
	L4 101	a' = x + y
11	50 14	q' = 0. Set least sig. part of dividend = 0.
	66 102	$q' = \frac{x+y}{2}$, a' = residue
12	S5 000	$a' = \frac{x+y}{2}$
	40 103	$(103)' = \frac{x+y}{2}$
13	0F 000	STOP
	00 000	
14	00 000	By 11; constant zero
	00 000	to clear Q

      This code is quite simple and its operation should be self-evident.
Two points are worthy of special attention. Notice that Q is cleared by the LH
order at 11 just before the division. This operation guarantees that the least
significant part of the dividend is indeed zero. If this is not done, then the
contents of Q, which in general will be some arbitrary number left there by an
earlier sequence of orders, will be treated as the least significant part of x + y
and consequently will cause the quotient to be slightly in error. The clearing
of Q could have been effected by the order 11 39 (a' = 0 right shift 39 places)
which would have been more efficient of memory space since in the above example
a word identically equal to zero (the word at 14) is needed in addition to the
50 order. However the right shift order would require a longer execution time
(624 μ sec. as opposed to 55 μ sec. for the 50 order). The choice of which
scheme to use will be dictated by the problem at hand. Frequently the constant
zero is available anyway for the above purpose because it is commonly needed by
many parts of a given program. The second point to notice is that in transmitting
the quotient to the memory it must be first brought from Q into A (the S order at
LH of 12) and then to the memory. There is no instruction which provides for

writing into the memory directly from Q. One could use a shift to transmit the quotient into A, though it would be slower, and have a properly signed result. This may seem odd since q_0 does not take part in the shifting operation but let us recall a peculiarity of ILLIAC division; in step 3 on page 46 (Chapter 9) it should be noted that the digit shifted into Q_0 is also shifted into A_{39}, consequently after the last step in the division process the sign digit of the quotient resides in A_{39} as well as in Q_0.

Example 2: In this example let us again consider a calculation of

$$w = \frac{x+y}{z}$$

but this time it will not be assumed that $|x + y| < |z|$. Here we require the code to properly scale the sum $x + y$ so that this condition is satisfied. This is to be achieved by shifting $x + y$ to the right s times, and thus scaling $x + y$ by 2^{-s}, where s is understood to be the minimum number of shifts required. Again suppose that x, y and z are in locations 100, 101, 102 and the scaled quotient $w \cdot 2^{-s}$ is to be placed in location 103. The scaling parameter, s, is to be placed in location 104. The flow chart and code follow.

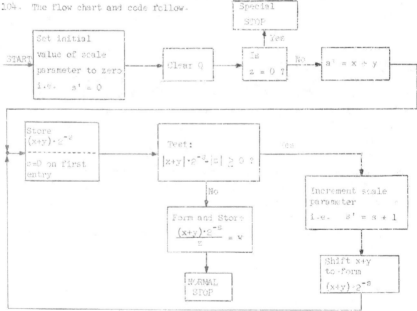

WM	Order Pair	Comments
10	41 104	n' = 0
	50 104	q' = 0
11	L2 102	a' = -|z|
	32 17	Jump if z = 0
12	L5 100	a' = x
	14 101	a' = x + y
13	40 000	from 20; temp store $(x+y) \cdot 2^{-s}$
	L7 000	a' = $\|x+y\| \cdot 2^{-s}$
14	L2 102	a' = $\|x+y\| \cdot 2^{-s} - \|z\|$
	36 18	Jump to scale
15	L5 000	here when $\|x+y\| \cdot 2^{-s} < \|z\|$
	66 102	q' = ($(x+y) \cdot 2^{-s}$)÷z = w
16	85 000	a' = w
	40 103	(10x)' = w
17	0F 000	Normal Stop
	0F 001	from 11; Special Stop; z = 0
18	F5 104	from 14
	40 104	s' = s + 1
19	L5 000	a' = (x + y)·2^{-s}
	10 1	
20	26 13	Jump to test again

The operation of this code is fairly straightforward. Notice that absolute value operations are used in making the test for numerator less, in magnitude, than denominator. Observe that a test for $|z| \equiv 0$ is made. This technique of testing for zero is standard, and is based on the characteristic of ILLIAC that $-|x|$ is positive if, and only if, $x \equiv 0$; in particular $-|0| \equiv 0$. That this is to be expected in ILLIAC is evident from the remarks made earlier in

Example 3 of Chapter 10. It is absolutely essential that this test be made. If
the test is omitted and z happens to be zero, then the program will go into a loop
that will not end until the computer is turned off since the condition
$|x+y| - |z| < 0$, which is necessary for emergence from the scaling loop, can never
be satisfied. This program executes a transfer to a STOP order when the condition
$z \equiv 0$ is found. This is a different STOP order than the one that is encountered
when the program does not find $z \equiv 0$ and does compute a quotient. The special stop
order is a signal to the user that the situation $z \equiv 0$ has occurred. It is not
necessary, of course, to stop the machine at all in this circumstance. Most likely
the programmer will have some special thing to do when this situation arises (for
example write the quotient as the largest possible number which can be represented)
and will make provision in the code to transfer to a routine for executing this
whenever it is found that $z \equiv 0$.

Another feature of this code which should be noticed is that the least
significant digits of x+y, which become shifted into Q as a result of the scaling,
are not lost and do indeed properly appear in the dividend at the time of
execution of the 66 order.

Certain problems arise in the division of integers which require some
attention here. The division round-off is one problem; clearly all integer
quotients will be odd integers because the division round-off guarantees that
the last binary digit will be a 1. The nature of the ILLIAC division process
itself causes the error in the quotient to be dependent on the sign of the divisor.
Integer division in the case of positive divisor and positive dividend, however,
can be easily programmed. This is the situation one normally meets in practice.
When other sign combinations for divisor and dividend arise it is best to make
all the integers positive, do positive integer division, and then appropriately
adjust the sign of the quotient. When positive integers are divided
according to the procedure used in the following example, it can be
shown that the exact quotient and remainder are obtained.

Example 3: Suppose the quotient, z, and remainder r of $x \div y$ are to be computed where x and y are positive integers. x, y, z and r must satisfy

$$x = yz + r \quad .$$

We assume $x \cdot 2^{-39}$ and $y \cdot 2^{-39}$ are stored in locations 100 and 101, respectively. The quotient, $z \cdot 2^{-39}$, is to be stored in location 102 and the remainder, $r \cdot 2^{-39}$, is to be stored in location 103.

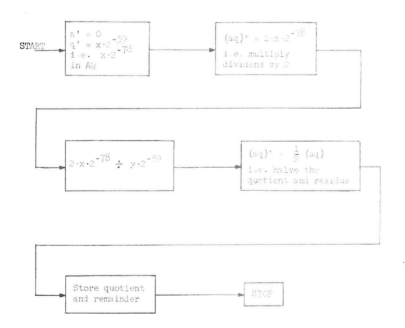

WM	Order Pair	Comments
10	51 100	$(aq)' = x \cdot 2^{-78}$
	00 1	$(aq)' = 2 \cdot x \cdot 2^{-78}$
11	66 101	$q' = 2 \cdot (z \cdot 2^{-39}) + 2^{-39}$
		$a' = 2 \cdot r \cdot 2^{-39}$
	10 1	$q' = z \cdot 2^{-39}$, $a' = r \cdot 2^{-39}$
12	40 103	Store remainder, $r \cdot 2^{-39}$
	S5 0	$a' = z \cdot 2^{-39}$
13	40 102	Store quotient, $z \cdot 2^{-39}$
	OF 0	STOP

Notice that the dividend is brought into Q with an initial clearing of A (LH order at 10). This is necessary for proper representation of $(aq)' = x \cdot 2^{-78}$. The right shift at RH of 11 causes the division round-off digit to be dropped from the right end of Q. Notice that one need not worry about a 1 entering Q from A_{39} with this shift because A_{39} holds the sign of the quotient which is guaranteed positive. After the right shift at RH of 11 the quantity in A is the correct remainder.

Now let us consider the use of the logical multiply or extract order, type J. The extract order arises in computations where data is "packed" into a word; an example of this type of computation is given below.

Example 4: Let us consider a problem in which one must store in the WM the coordinates (x, y and z) of a set of points in a three dimensional space. There are 500 points to be so represented and therefore there are not enough locations in the WM to use a separate one to hold each coordinate of all 500 points. However, suppose that the requirements on accuracy in this problem are of such a nature that no more than 13 bits for the representation of each coordinate are necessary. Then it is possible to "pack" the three coordinates of each point into a single word. Thus, representing a word in memory as

$$w = w_0 \, w_1 \, w_2 \, \cdots \, w_{39} \, ,$$

the digits w_1 to w_{39} may be divided into three groups of 13 bits wherein the 2's complement binary fractions x, y and z, the three coordinates of a point, are held; in particular

$$x = w_1 \, w_2 \, \cdots \, w_{13} \; ,$$
$$y = w_{14} \, w_{15} \, \cdots \, w_{26} \; ,$$
$$z = w_{27} \, w_{28} \, \cdots \, w_{39} \; .$$

In this representation the sign digits are w_1, w_{14} and w_{27} and the binary point is assumed to be located immediately to the right of the sign digit.

Let us suppose that the coordinates of those points which are contained in the "box"

$$-\frac{1}{4} \le x < \frac{1}{4} \; ,$$

$$0 \le y < 1 \; ,$$

$$-\frac{3}{8} \le z < \frac{1}{8} \; ,$$

are to be transformed according to the rules

$$x' = -x \; ,$$
$$y' = -y \; ,$$
$$z' = -z \; ,$$

where the new coordinate has been indicated by the primes. Points that are not inside the above box are to remain unchanged. The flow chart and code follow. It is assumed that the list of 500 words holding the coordinates x, y, z of each point (call them the point words) begins at location 200 in the WM.

90

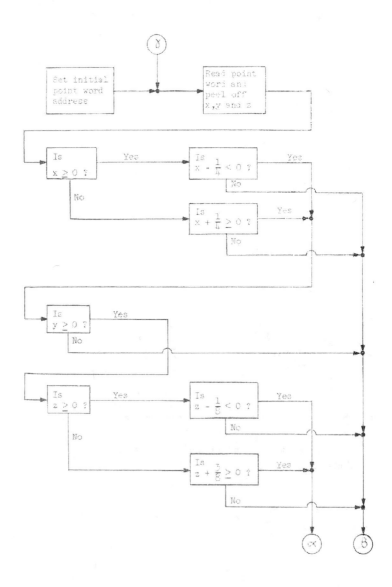

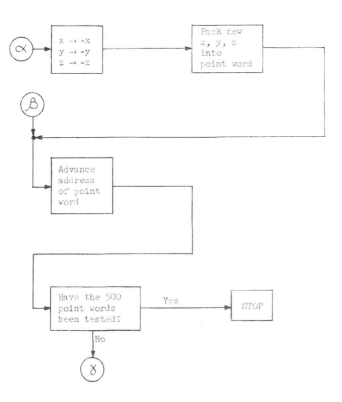

NOTICE: The round boxes containing Greek letters are used to indicate common points when it is inconvenient to join them by a line; e.g. the line leading to ⓐ on the first page of the flow chart is understood to be continued on the second page at the point marked ⓐ .

WM	Order Pair	Comments
10	L5 32	plant initial
	42 11	address of point word
11	42 34	from 37
	50 [0]	by 10, 35 q' = point word
12	01 13	a' = 0, shift x into A
	40 0	temp. store x
13	01 13	a' = 0, shift y into A
	40 1	temp. store y
14	01 40	shift z into A as
	40 2	fraction and temp. store
15	L5 0	
	00 27	position x as fraction
16	40 0	temp store x
	62 18	jump if $x \geq 0$
17	L4 38	$a' = x + \frac{3}{4}$; here if $x < 0$
	52 19	jump if $x \geq -\frac{1}{4}$
18	26 35	jump if $x < -\frac{1}{4}$
	L0 38	from 16 ; $a' = x - \frac{1}{4}$
19	36 35	jump if $x \geq \frac{1}{4}$
	15 1	from 17
20	00 27	position y as fraction
	40 1	temp. store y
21	36 22	jump if $y \geq 0$
	26 35	jump if $y < 0$
22	L5 2	from 21; $a' = z$
	38 24	jump if $z > 0$

(Continued on page 93)

WM	Order Pair	Comments
23	L4 39	$a' = z + \frac{3}{8}$
	32 25	Jump if $z \geq -\frac{3}{8}$
24	26 35	Jump if $z < -\frac{3}{8}$
	L0 40	from 22; $a' = z - \frac{1}{8}$
25	36 35	Jump if $z \geq \frac{1}{8}$
	L1 0	from 23; here if point is in the box
26	10 1	
	40 0	$(0)_1 \ (0)_2 \ \cdots \ (0)_{13} = -x$
27	L1 1	
	10 14	
28	40 1	$(1)_{14} \ (1)_{15} \ \cdots \ (1)_{26} = -y$
	L1 2	
29	10 27	
	40 2	$(2)_{27} \ (2)_{28} \ \cdots \ (2)_{39} = -z$
30	50 0	
	J0 41	extract x
31	S5 0	pack x into A
	50 1	
32	J0 42	extract y
	S4 200	pack y into A; address used by 10
33	50 2	
	J0 43	extract z
34	S4 0	pack z into A
		by 11, 36
	40 [0]	store new point word
35	F5 11	From 18, 19, 21, 24, 25
	42 11	advance point word address

(Continued on page 94)

WM	Order Pair	Comments
36	42 34	
	LO 44	end test
37	32 11	jump if not end
	OP 0	STOP.
38	20 0	constant $= \frac{1}{4}$
	00 0	by 17, 18
39	30 0	constant $= \frac{z}{8}$
	00 0	by 23
40	10 0	constant $= \frac{1}{8}$
	00 0	by 24
41	7L 4032	extractor for
	00 0	$w_1 \, w_2 \, \cdots \, w_{13}$; by 30
42	00 63	extractor for
	LF 0	$w_{14} \, w_{15} \, \cdots \, w_{26}$; by 32
43	00 0	extractor for
	01 4095	$w_{27} \, w_{28} \, \cdots \, w_{39}$; by 33
44	N2 34	end test
	50 700	constant

The first part of this code, namely the orders at RH of 11 to LH of 25, determine whether or not the word called into Q (the point word) by the order at RH of 11 represents a point that is in the box. First the x coordinate is examined to see if x satisfies the condition $-\frac{1}{4} \leq x < \frac{1}{4}$; if this condition is satisfied then the y coordinate is tested; if this condition is violated the point must fall outside of the box so a jump is made immediately to the part of the program which advances the address of the point word (address at RH of 11 and RH of 34) and tests for the end of the loop. The y and z coordinates are similarly tested. If, after testing all coordinates, it is found that the point does lie in the box then a sequence of orders beginning at RH of 25 executes the transformation $x \rightarrow -x$, $y \rightarrow -y$, $z \rightarrow -z$. The orders beginning at LH of 30 take the transformed coordinates and "pack" them into a new point word; this is where the J order enters. Consider the order pair at 30, the LH order places the word holding the new x into Q; specifically the digits of x are in locations $Q_1 Q_2 \cdots Q_{13}$. The remaining digits of Q are of no interest so far as x is concerned, but for the packing which is about to begin it is necessary that these remaining digits of Q be cleared to zero. This is done via the J order at RH of 30. The address of the J order is 41 and the word at 41 is 7L 4032 00 0, which expressed as a 40 digit binary number is

0111 1111 1111 1100 0000 0000 0000 0000 0000 0000

Thus digital positions 1, 2, ..., 13 are 1 and the remaining positions are zero. Recalling the rule cited earlier (page 82) for the construction of the logical product it is evident that the J order at RH of 30 will not change the state of $Q_1 Q_2 \cdots Q_{13}$ but all other digits of Q will be made zero. This result is transmitted to A by the S5 order at 31. Then the word holding y is brought into Q; specifically y is in $Q_{14} Q_{15} \cdots Q_{26}$. The J order effects a logical multiplication with the word at 42, which written in binary is

0000 0000 0000 0011 1111 1111 1110 0000 0000 0000 .

This logical multiplication leaves $Q_{14} Q_{15} \cdots Q_{26}$ unaffected but all other digits of Q are set to zero. The hold add from Q order at 32 then adds the y coordinate digits to the word in A which at present only holds the digits of x. Thus the digits of y are packed into A. Notice that the use of the J order is necessary otherwise this addition of the y digits into the accumulator could cause "hash" to be added to the digits of x. In a similar way the digits of z are extracted and packed into A. When the digits of z have been packed into A the new point word, the word now in A, is stored in the memory by the order at RH of 34.

In addition to illustrating the use of the J order there are several other new features illustrated here. The words at 38, 39 and 40 are used as constants, $\frac{1}{4}$, $\frac{3}{8}$, and $\frac{1}{8}$, respectively. That these words do indeed represent these fractions is evident when they are written out as a binary number:

Binary Point

at 38 we have $0\ 010\ 0000\ \ldots\ 0 = \frac{1}{4}$;

at 39 we have $0\ 011\ 0000\ \ldots\ 0 = \frac{3}{8}$;

at 40 we have $0\ 001\ 0000\ \ldots\ 0 = \frac{1}{8}$

The end test is somewhat different than the ones used earlier. Notice that the test constant can be regarded as the sum of two order pairs, namely

$$\begin{matrix} N2 & 34 \\ 50 & 700 \end{matrix} = \begin{matrix} 80 & 0 \\ 00 & 0 \end{matrix} + \begin{matrix} 42 & 34 \\ 50 & 700 \end{matrix} \quad .$$

This test constant is subtracted from the word at 11,

42 34
50 [x] ,

for the end test. Consider these order pairs as numbers and let us look at this subtraction.

42 34   N2 34
50 [x]   50 700   positive if x < 700
                          negative (= -1) if x = 700

$$= \begin{matrix} 42 & 34 \\ 50 & [x] \end{matrix} \begin{matrix} 42 & 34 \\ 50 & 700 \end{matrix} \begin{matrix} 80 & 000 \\ 00 & 000 \end{matrix}$$

negative if x < 700
zero if x = 700

The first two terms on the right side of the above equation yield a negative result so long as x < 700. This negative result has sign digit equal to 1 hence the subtraction of 80 000 00 000, the last term on the right, generates a

positive number as the final result for the right side of this equation.
Consequently the conditional transfer order at LH of 37 will cause a jump to
be executed so long as the right address (x in the above equations) at 11 is
less than 700. When this address becomes equal to 700 the jump is not executed
and the stop order at 37, OF 0, is reached.

The trick to the above form of the end test is the addition of sexadecimal 8 to the left digit of the end constant. Without this addition an extra
order is necessary, for the test would become

WM	Order Pair	Comments
35	F5 11	
	42 11	
36	42 34	
	LO 44	End test
37	36 38	jump to stop if end
	22 11	jump if not end
38	OF 0	from 37; STOP

where the end constant is

44	42 54	end constant
	50 700	

The addition of the sexadecimal 8 thus reverses the "sense" of the transfer:
the conditional transfer causes a jump so long as the end of the loop has not
been completed and the jump is not obeyed when the end of the loop is reached;
but when the sexadecimal 8 is not added to the end constant, the reverse is
true for then the conditional transfer causes a jump only when the end of the
loop has been reached.

UNIVERSITY OF ILLINOIS

DIGITAL COMPUTER

CHAPTER 15

THE ILLIAC ORDER CODE - VI

Examples of the use of order types 8 and 9. In this chapter we will consider the input-output orders; order types 8 and 9. Certain forms of the input-output orders, namely those connected with the use of the CRT display and the drum, will not be discussed here. In this chapter the operations involved in reading information from teletype tape and punching information onto teletype tape will be the primary concern.

With regard to output the 82 or 92 order will either punch the indicated character, or characters, onto teletype tape or they will print the characters directly via a teleprinter. The mode of output, punch or printer, is specified by a 96 order; if the address of the 96 order is 1 (i.e. if the order is 96 1F) then the output will be on the punch; if the address of the 96 order is 129 (i.e. if the order is 96 129F) then the output will be on the teleprinter.* Once the mode of output has been specified by a 96 order all succeeding output will appear on the unit designated until a new 96 order is executed. The mode of output can also be set manually; there is a set of toggle switches on the control panel of ILLIAC for this purpose. Since the punch operates at a considerably greater speed than the printer (the times are indicated below) it is customary to use the punch for output. The data on the punched tape may later be printed by putting the tape into the reader of a teleprinter.

Punch Speed - 60 characters/sec.

Printer (slow) Speed - 6 characters/sec.

Printer (high) Speed - 10 characters/sec.

---

* Another 96 order, 96 65F is used to connect the Cathode Ray Tube display unit to ILLIAC for output.

Let us now consider briefly the physical appearance of the teletype tape. The figure below shows a section of this tape. A hole in the tape is

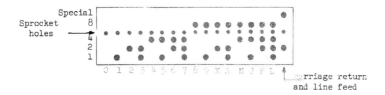

Figure 15-1

Sample of paper tape code.

indicated by a dot. One set of holes, the smaller ones, is used to control the movement of the tape by the various equipment which reads and punches this tape; these holes are called the sprocket holes. Associated with each sprocket hole, reading across the width of the tape, is a 5 digit binary number; three digital positions are below the sprocket hole and two are above. The weight assigned to each position is indicated by the numbers at the left end of the tape in this figure. The tape is "read" by sensing for the presence of a hole in each digital position; a hole represents the binary digit 1, no hole represents the binary digit 0. The tape reading equipment reads the 5 positions across the width of the tape simultaneously (i.e. in parallel) and the tape is mechanically advanced to read successive groups of five digits. The appearance of the sexadecimal numbers 0, 1, 2, ..., L when punched on the tape is indicated in the above figure. The firs four digital positions, having weight 1, 2, 4 and 8, are thought of as representing a single tetrad or sexadecimal character. The fifth digital position or "fifth hole-position" is regarded separately and does not truly have a weight of 16 as the fifth binary position ordinarily would have. The fifth-hole position is used to identify some letters of the alphabet, special symbols, and certain printing operations such as "carriage return and line feed[1]" (the punches for this are indicated in this figure). The complete tape code is given in Appendix 6, p. 272.

Let us now consider the orders which cause the ILLIAC to read information from the tape. The 80 and 81 orders are used for reading sexadecimal characters from the tape. They are identical except that the 81 order causes an initial clearing of A. The 80 order causes the execution of the following operations

(1) $(aq)' = 16(aq)$; i.e. left shift 4 places

(2) $a'_{36} \, a'_{37} \, a'_{38} \, a'_{39}$ = tetrad on tape

(3) repeat $n/4$ times, where n is the address of the 80 order; n should be a multiple of 4.

In the above, the tape is advanced on each repetition so that the next tetrad may be read. If the fifth-hole is punched the tetrad is ignored by this order.

Example 1. Below is given a very simple code which reads the tetrads on the tape of Figure 15-1. The tetrads will be read two at a time and the tetrad pairs will be stored in a block at location 200 of the WM. It is assumed that at the time the first instruction of the following code is to be executed the tape of Figure 15-1 is in the reader and in proper position for reading the first character, namely the character 0.

---

[1] This operation causes the teleprinter to move the carriage into position for printing a new line.

WM	Order Pair	Comments
10	L5 14 42 11	Set initial block address
11	81 8 40 [0]	from 15, a' = 0, read 2 tetrads by 10
12	F5 11 42 11	advance store address
13	L0 15 36 11	End test transfer if not end
14	0F 0 00 200	STOP by 10
15	01 8 40 208	End constant

The reading is done via the 81 order. The variant digit 1 indicates initial clearing of the accumulator, and the address of the 81 order, namely 8, specifies that 2 tetrads $(8/4 = 2)$ are to be read from the tape upon execution of the 81 order. The digits read from the tape are shifted into the low order end of A and then are placed in the WM via the 40 order at the RH of 11. Thus, when the above program reaches the stop order (LH of 14) the block at 200 appears as follows.

LOCATION	WORD
200	0000 0000 0000 0000 0000 0000 0000 0000 0000 0001
201	0000 0000 0000 0000 0000 0000 0000 0000 0010 0011
202	0000 0000 0000 0000 0000 0000 0000 0000 0100 0101
203	0000 0000 0000 0000 0000 0000 0000 0000 0110 0111
204	0000 0000 0000 0000 0000 0000 0000 0000 1000 1001
205	0000 0000 0000 0000 0000 0000 0000 0000 1010 1011
206	0000 0000 0000 0000 0000 0000 0000 0000 1100 1101
207	0000 0000 0000 0000 0000 0000 0000 0000 1110 1111

Example 2. Let us now consider a simple code which will read a block
of positive 3 digit decimal integers from the tape, convert these integers into
their binary equivalents, and store the result in a block at 200. The last
decimal integer of the block on the tape will be indicated by punching the
sexadecimal character N as the terminating character on the tape. Suppose the
list of decimal integers to be read is that shown in Figure 15-2.

010
039
146
237
599

Figure 15-2

Three digit decimal integers.

The tape on which these numbers are punched for subsequent reading
by the code is shown in Figure 15-3. Notice that the line feed and carriage
return characters have been included.

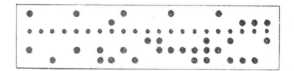

Figure 15-3

Tape with data of Figure 15-2.

An N has also been punched as the terminating character on the tape. If the tape of Figure 15-3 were to be put into the reader of a teleprinter, then the list of numbers shown in Figure 15-2 would be printed (an N would be printed immediately after the last digit so that the last line would appear as 599N).

The decimal to binary conversion is achieved by an iterative procedure. Let the decimal digits be indicated by d_i (i = 1, 2, 3; a three digit number is $d_1 d_2 d_3$), then the iterative scheme is described by

$$S_i = 10 \, S_{i-1} + d_i$$

$$S_0 = 0$$

S_3 = final binary representation of the three digit decimal number.

The flow chart follows:

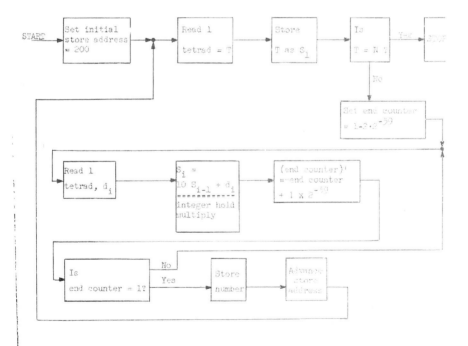

WM	Order Pair	Comments
10	L5 16 42 19	Set initial store address
11	81 4 40 0	from 21; read T store T as S_1
12	L0 23 40 1	T - N temporary store T - N
13	L3 1 32 21	$-\lvert T - N \rvert$ jump if $T \equiv N$
14	L5 24 40 1	Set end counter $= 1-2 \cdot 2^{-39}$ from 18
15	81 4 50 0	read d_i $q' = S_{i-1}$
16	74 22 S5 200	$(aq)' = 10 \times S_{i-1} + d_i$ (integer) by 10
17	40 0 F5 1	store S_i advance end counter
18	32 14 50 0	jump if not end. waste
19	L6 0 40 [0]	by 10, 20; Store S_3
20	F5 19 42 19	advance store address
21	26 11 0F 0	jump to read next integer from 13; STOP when $T \equiv N$
22	00 0 00 10	constant $= 10 \times 2^{-39}$ by 16
23	00 0 00 12	constant $= 12 \times 2^{-39}$ by 12
24	7L 4095 LL 4094	constant $= 1-2 \cdot 2^{-39}$ by 14

The order pair at 10 plants the initial address of the store order which stores the numbers read from the tape into the block at 200. The orders at LH of 10 to RH of 13 test for the termination symbol, N, to determine whether or not all of the data has been read from the tape. The next block of orders up to LH of 18 reads the number from the tape (the first digit of the number is read by the LH of 11) and converts it to a binary number. The order at RH of 19 stores the integer in the list which begins at location 200.

Notice that the multiply order at LH of 16 is a <u>hold</u> multiply order; consequently the tetrad just read at LH of 15 is added as an integer to the integer product to form $10 \times S_{i-1} + d_i$.

The characters having the 5th hole punched, namely the line feed and carriage return characters have no effect on the operation of this code, since the 81 order (and the 80 order) completely ignore any character having the 5th hole punched.

It is possible to read the 5th hole with the 91 order (and the 90 order). The use of this order is indicated in the example below.

<u>Example 3</u>. In this example we consider a code which will read positive integers from the teletype tape and store them in a block at location 200 of the WM. Here the number of decimal digits in the integer will be arbitrary[1], rather than a specified number as in the previous example. The data tape (i.e. the teletype tape on which the decimal integers are punched) is required to have a line feed and carriage return character following each number and the character N following the very last line feed and carriage return to indicate termination of the data. Let us assume the data consists of the following integers

10

5

329

14

1,456

then the data tape will appear as follows:

---

[1] Assuming, of course, that the number remains in the scale of the machine, namely less than 2^{39}.

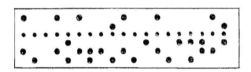

The flow chart and code follow.

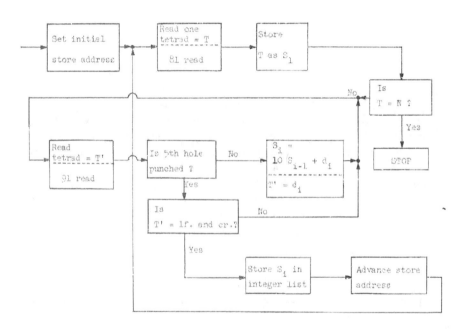

WM	Order Pair	Comments
10	L5 18	
	42 20	from 21; plant store address
11	81 4	Read T
	40 0	
12	LO 23	Test for T = N
	40 1	
13	L3 1	
	36 22	jump if T = N
14	91 4	Read T'; from 19
	32 17	jump if no 5th hole punch
15	LO 24	test for T' = lf. and cr.
	40 1	
16	L3 1	
	36 20	jump if T' = lf. and cr.
17	26 14	jump if T' $\neq$ lf. and cr.
	50 0	from 14
18	74 25	$S_i = 10 S_{i-1} + d_i$
	S5 200	by 10
19	40 0	store S_i
	26 14	jump to read next digit
20	L5 0	from 16
	40 [0]	by 10; store integer
21	F5 20	advance store address
	22 10	jump to read next integer
22	OF 0	from 13; STOP
	00 0	

(Continued on page 108)

WM	Order Pair	Comments
23	00 0	Constant
	00 12	by 12
24	80 0	Constant
	00 2	by 15
25	00 0	Constant
	00 10	by 18

This code is similar to the one in example 2 except that here there is no counter to keep track of the number of digits read, but instead each character is tested to determine whether or not it is a line feed and carriage return (lf. and cr.) character indicating the end of the number. Notice how the test for lf. and cr. is made. First the sign digit is tested at RH of 14; $a_0 = 1$ if the character read from the tape with the 91 order has a 5th hole punch. If this test finds $a_0 = 1$ then a second test is made to determine whether or not the character just read was actually a lf. and cr. character. If this test shows that the character just read was not a lf. and cr. then the jump at LH of 17 is executed, and the next character is read from the tape; this feature makes it possible to "erase" errors on the tape by punching out the fifth hole since any character with a 5th hole punch with the exception of a lf. and cr. character is ignored by this program.

Having discussed some examples of the use of the tape input orders, let us now consider examples of the use of the output orders, namely the 82 and 92 orders.

Example 4. The following is a very simple code for printing the contents of locations 200, 201, ..., 209 as sexadecimal numbers. The numbers are to be printed in a column, each number on a separate line. At the head of the column the word SEXADECIMAL is to be printed. The code follows.

WM	Order Pair	Comments
10	82 131	lf. and cr.
	32 515	delay
11	92 350	letters shift
	92 706	S

WM	Order Pair	Comments
12	92 194	E
	92 451	X
13	92 387	A
	92 67	D
14	92 194	E
	92 835	C
15	92 514	I
	92 643	M
16	92 387	A
	92 962	L
17	92 707	numbers shift
	92 135	lf. and cr. (2)
18	92 515	delay
	15 24	
19	42 20	from 23
	L0 25	end test
20	32 23	jump if end
	L5 [0]	bring number from WM into A
21	82 40	print 10 s-decimal digits
	92 131	lf. and cr.
22	92 515	delay
	F5 20	advance number address
23	26 19	
	OF 0	from 20; STOP
24	32 23	constant
	L5 200	by 4
25	32 23	end constant
	15 210	by 15

The first part of this code comprising the orders at LH of 10 to RH of 16 is used to print the heading. The order pair at 10 punches a lf. and cr. character followed by a delay character. It is always best to precede any printing with a lf. and cr. character to insure that the teleprinter is properly set to begin printing a new line. A delay character should always follow a lf. and cr. character. The delay character provides the teleprinter enough time to properly shift the carriage into position for a new line of printing; omission of the delay will usually result in an uneven margin on the left side of the page. The order at LH of 11 punches a letters shift character. This character causes the carriage of the teleprinter to shift into position for printing letters and special symbols (just as the shift key on a typewriter causes capital letters to be printed). The letter shift character causes the carriage of the teleprinter to be "locked" into the letter printing position so that all subsequent characters will be printed in the letter printing mode until a number shift character appears; the carriage will then be locked into the number printing mode.

One can compute the necessary address for a 92 order to print a given character from the rules given in Appendix 4, p. 264. A complete list of 92 orders for printing teletype characters is given in Appendix 7, p. 273.

At RH of 35 we have the order 92 135 (= 92 [131 + 4]) which will cause two line feed and carriage return characters to be punched. If $4n$ ($n = 1, 2, 3, ..., 14$) is added to the address of any 92 order in the list in Appendix 7, p. 273, then $n + 1$ characters will be punched; thus, 92 135 causes the punching of two line feed and carriage return characters. Similarly the order 92 395 will cause the punching of three A's (after letters shift) or three)'s (after numbers shift); the order 92 98 will cause the punching of nine Q's (after letter shift) or nine 1's (after number shift).

The 82 order at LH of 21 causes the entire contents of A, 10 sexadecimal characters, to be punched ($40 \div 4 = 10$).

Example 5. As a final example in the use of the input-output orders
let us now consider a code for printing a list of twenty positive binary fractions
as decimal fractions. The list begins at location 200 of the WM. The decimal
fractions will be printed to six digits and for simplicity roundoff will be
neglected. The binary to decimal conversion is effected by successively multiplying
the binary fraction by ten, the integer part of the product at each stage being the
desired decimal digit (see Chapter 5, page 25). The flow chart and code follow.

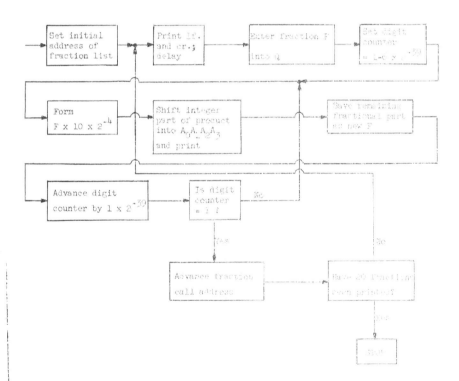

WM	Order Pair	Comments
10	L5 19	plant initial fraction address
	42 12	
11	92 131	lf. and cr., from 18
	92 515	delay
12	50 0	waste
	50 [0]	fraction into Q
13	L5 21	set digit counter
	40 0	from 16
14	75 22	$F \times 10 \times 2^{-4}$
	00 1	position int. part in $A_0 A_1 A_2 A_3$
15	82 4	print $a_0 a_1 a_2 a_3$
	10 40	put fractional part of product into Q.
16	F5 0	step digit counter
	32 13	jump to print more digits
17	F5 12	advance fraction address
	42 12	
18	L0 20	end test
	36 11	jump for next fraction
19	OF 0	STOP
	00 200	by 10
20	J0 0	end test constant
	50 220	by 18
21	7L 4095	$1 - 6 \times 2^{-39}$
	LL 4090	
22	50 0	10×2^{-4} constant
	00 0	

The multiplication at LH of 14 produces the product F x 10 scaled by 2^{-4} since the multiplier is itself scaled by 2^{-4}. Consequently the integer part of the product will be held in $A_1 A_2 A_3 A_4$; it is just this tetrad then that holds the decimal digit which is to be printed. Since the 82 order prints the contents of $A_0 A_1 A_2 A_3$ it is necessary to execute the left shift of one place at RH of 14 in order to put the just generated decimal digit into proper position for printing.

This chapter completes the discussions of the use of the various ILLIAC orders. The complete ILLIAC order code is given in Appendix 4, pp. 251-270.

UNIVERSITY OF ILLINOIS
DIGITAL COMPUTER
CHAPTER 16

SUBROUTINES

Most programs can be divided into a number of parts which are
distinguished by their function in the program. A given program might have
one block of orders which performs the read-in of data, another block to
execute a square root and some other block might compute another special function,
for example the logarithm, and usually a program will have a block of orders
responsible for printing results. One calls such parts of a program "subroutines".
Commonly one portion of the program is designated as "master" or "main part", its
duty being to control the sequencing of the execution of the subroutines.

From the standpoint of simplicity and ease of checking the program it
is a wise practice to attempt to make each subroutine as self-contained as
possible. There will of course necessarily be cross references between subroutines, but one should try to minimize them. There is another important
reason for following this practice. Many times after a program is thought to be
completed, even after it has been used for some time, it will be found desirable
to change a part of the program. It is hard to make substantial changes after a
program has been written (and some of the details forgotten) without spawning
an error, and usually many errors. This spontaneous generation of errors can be
greatly inhibited if the cross references between subroutines are reduced. This
practice will usually result in a slight decrease in the efficiency of a program
from the standpoint of utilization of memory space and time but unless economy
of these items is critical the above practice is a good one to follow.

We distinguish two classes of subroutines called "open" subroutines and
"closed" subroutines. The distinguishing characteristic of a closed subroutine is
that it may be entered via a jump from any location, say p, of the memory and the
subroutine will "remember" the origin of the jump; after the orders of the closed

subroutine have been executed, then a jump to a location relative to p, say p+m, will be executed. On the other hand, an open subroutine is entered from just one position in the memory and after execution of the subroutine exit is made to one fixed position in the memory.

The desirability of the closed subroutine should be fairly evident. A particular function, let us say the square root, may be desired at many different points within a program. It is wasteful of memory space to write out a new set of orders to execute a square root at every point that a square root is needed in the program. Instead the square root subroutine is written as a closed subroutine. It is then possible to obtain $\sqrt{x}$ at any point in the program by simply transferring to the closed subroutine, wherein $\sqrt{x}$ is computed, followed by a transfer back to the main program to resume the course of the computation. One can think of this jump to and from the closed subroutine as equivalent to a single hypothetical order -- extract square root.

Entry and exit to a closed subroutine is indicated schematically in Figure 16-1. On the left of this figure there is indicated a block of orders

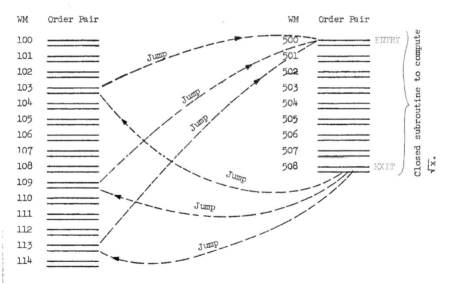

Figure 16-1

Schematic representation of jumps to and from a closed subroutine.

beginning at location 100, representing a portion of the main program; each
horizontal line represents one order. At locations 103, 109 and 113 a computation of $\sqrt{x}$ is needed. On the right of this figure there is indicated a block
of orders at 500 which represents a closed subroutine to compute the $\sqrt{x}$; x is
taken to be the fraction in A at the time of the entry to the subroutine and $\sqrt{x}$
is the number in A at the time of exit from the subroutine. At location 103 the
number whose square root is desired is entered in A and a jump is executed from
the LH side of 103 to location 500 where the square root subroutine begins. A
record is kept of the fact that entry was made from location 103 -- exactly how
this is done will be seen shortly. When the square root has been computed it is
placed in A and a jump from location 508 to the RH side of location 103 is executed.
Again at locations 109 and 113 this process is repeated. If a closed subroutine was
not used but instead an open subroutine to compute $\sqrt{x}$ was used, then this open
subroutine would have to be inserted at the three points in the program where $\sqrt{x}$
is needed.

To establish the link between the main program and the closed subroutine
certain entry rules are necessary. The customary rule with ILLIAC programs is to
enter the subroutine via a jump from the left side of a word. If this word is at
location p+1, then the order immediately preceding the jump (this would be the order
on the right side of location p) must be 50p. Thus to enter the subroutine we have
a sequence of orders that appears as shown in Figure 16-2.

WM	ORDER PAIR
p	-- ---
	50 p
p+1	26 (address of subroutine)
	-- ---

Figure 16-2

Typical entry to closed subroutine.

Notice the consequence of the 50 order. It places the word at p into Q, thus the 50p order itself resides in the right half of Q at the time that the jump is executed. The address p residing in Q is used by the closed subroutine to establish the link for exit. In most cases the custom is to set the link so that the return jump will be made to the order at the right side of p+1.

To illustrate the setting up of the link in the closed subroutine an example is given below. This subroutine sums the digits in a word except w_0 and therefore it resembles very closely the program given in Chapter 12, example 2, where the same computation is done without the program being written as a closed subroutine. It is assumed in this example that entry to the closed subroutine is made by the order sequence shown in Figure 16-2. It is further assumed that the word, x, whose digits are to be summed is in A at the time of entry; the sum of these digits is to be in A at the time of exit from the subroutine. The code follows.

WM	Order Pair	Comments
10	40 0	temp. store x
	K5 0	$a' = q + 2^{-39} \ (p \to p+1)$
11	42 16	plant link
	41 1	clear sum box
12	50 0	$q' = x$
	L5 17	set end counter
13	40 2	from 15
	01 1	move bit into A
14	L4 1	add to sum box
	40 1	restore sum box
15	F5 2	advance end counter
	36 13	jump if not done
16	L5 1	$a' = $ sum of bits
	22 [0]	by 11
17	7L 4095	$1 - 39 \times 2^{-39}$
	LL 4057	= initial value of end counter.

In this code the increment add from Q order, type K, is being used for the first time. This order is exactly like the type F order, which was discussed in Chapter 12, except that the addend is taken from Q rather than the memory. After the K5 order at 10 is executed the right address digits of A contain p+1 and the 42 order at LH of 11 plants this address into the address digits of the 22 order at 16. (Remember that upon entry to this subroutine the Q register will contain p -- See Figure 16-2 -- in the right address digits -- $Q_{30} Q_{31} \cdots Q_{39}$.) The link for the exit has now been established. After the subroutine has been executed the 22 p+1 order at RH of 16 will cause a return to the order following the transfer order which executed the entry into this closed subroutine.

UNIVERSITY OF ILLINOIS
DIGITAL COMPUTER
CHAPTER 17

SADOI - PART 1

In describing the programs in the preceding chapters it has always
been assumed that the orders were already in the memory. In this chapter some
of the steps are discussed which are involved in getting a program
written on a sheet of paper, into the memory of the ILLIAC.

Information which is to be read into the ILLIAC must first be placed
onto teletype tape. In particular the orders which make up the program must
at some time be transcribed from the printed page onto teletype tape. This
tape containing the program must then be read into the ILLIAC and the instructions
inscribed thereon placed in the memory. In order to get this program tape into
the ILLIAC a special "input routine" must first be put into the ILLIAC; the
input routine then reads the program tape and places the orders into the proper
locations in the WM. But of course the input routine itself must get into the
ILLIAC and this is done by a set of orders known as a "bootstrap" which essentially
reads itself and the input routine into the ILLIAC.

The properties of the input routine prescribe the rules for the
transcription of the program onto the teletype tape. It is natural to expect
that the input routine would permit the programmer to put the program onto tape
using a simple and convenient notation. For example it would be inconvenient if
every order pair in the program had to be placed on the tape as a ten character
sexadecimal number; it would be simpler if the address digits of the order
could be written as a decimal integer. The input routine permits the programmer
to do this. In addition to this, the input routine has many other features
designed to permit the programmer to write the orders onto the tape in a simple
and convenient form. One might regard the input routine as a kind of language
translation program which translates the instructions on the tape, written in
the "language" of the programmer into instructions in the "language" of the

ILLIAC, namely the binary words which have already been described. The input routine used with the ILLIAC is known as the Symbolic Address Decimal Order Input -- or more simply SADOI. Let us now consider some of the rules which must be followed by the programmer in writing a program for SADOI.

First, SADOI must be told where the orders on the program tape are to be placed in the ILLIAC memory. This is done with a directive; if a list of order-pairs are to be placed in the memory starting at location m, then the characters 00 mK are punched on the tape just preceding the list of order pairs; m is written as a decimal integer. Thus if the first order pair of the list is to be placed in location thirty nin , then the characters

00 39K

are punched onto the tape preceding the order pairs. The form of this directive is as follows:

(1) the first two characters are zero;
(2) the following characters represent a decimal integer which is the location of the first order-pair in the list following the directive;
(3) the sexadecimal character K follows the address*.

There are other special forms for this directive which will be discussed in a later chapter.

The T and V digits of every order are written as sexadecimal characters on the tape just as we have been writing them in the past; thus a clear add order would be indicated by the characters L5 on the tape.

There are essentially two different forms in which the address may be written: one is the decimal address form and the other is the symbolic address form. In this chapter the former, namely the decimal address, will be considered.

The decimal address, as the name implies, is written as a decimal integer. The decimal address is always followed by a single sexadecimal character K, S, N, J, F or L which signals SADOI that the address digits are terminated and "directs"

---

* The sexadecimal character K is actually printed as a "+" by the teletype equipment. Similarly, the sexadecimal character S is printed as a "-" by the teletype equipment. All other sexadecimal characters are printed properly, i.e. N is printed "N", J is printed "J" and so forth.

SADOI on the interpretation of the address digits. It was already seen above that the termination symbol K is used to direct SADOI on the assignment of memory locations to the subsequent order pairs.

The termination symbol F indicates a _fixed_ address; that is the address digits are interpreted directly as the location in the memory referred to by the function digits. Thus if the word in memory location 175 is to be brought into the accumulator with a clear add order, one would write the order as L5 175F on the teletype tape. Addresses which do not refer to memory locations, for example shift orders, normally have the address terminated by F; thus, a left shift of ten places would be written on the tape as 00 10F.

The termination symbol L indicates a _relative_ address, that is the address is interpreted relative to the address specified by the K directive preceding the list of orders. By this means words within a block of orders may be referred to according to their relative position in the block. For example, if there is a clear add order in the block for which the addend is the forty-third word in the same block one would write L5 43L on the tape for this order. If the first word in this block is at location 100 in the memory then this clear add order would appear in the memory with the address digits equal to 143_D. SADOI achieves this transformation by preserving the "base" address for the block (the directive in this example is 00 100K and the "base" address is 100) and adding it to the address digits of each order terminated by the character L; the base address is also called the relativizer. The relative address feature makes it possible to write a program without explicit reference to the absolute memory location of the orders in the program. After the program is completed the absolute address assignments are made via the 00 mK directives. This is a great convenience which can only be fully appreciated after a little coding experience.

The termination symbol N is used to direct SADOI to relinquish control so that execution of the orders it has just read may begin. The program tape normally ends with an unconditional transfer order to an address, m, where m is the address of the first order in the program, and m is terminated by the letter N. Thus if 26 25N is written at the end of a list of order pairs on the tape it will cause SADOI to relinquish control and a transfer of control to the LH order at location twenty-five will be executed -- this location presumably holding the first order of the program just read by SADOI.

To illustrate the use of the termination symbols K, F, L and N a program is shown below in three stages: (1) as it would be written by the programmer on a sheet of paper; (2) as it appears on the teletype tape; (3) as it appears in the memory of the ILLIAC. This program is the one already discussed in example 3 of Chapter 11.

The program would be written on paper by the programmer as follows:

Address	Order Pair	Comments
	00 10K	
0	41 500F	partial sum = 0
	L5 [201]F	by 3L, from 5L; a' = $x_1, x_2, \ldots, x_{100}$
1	L4 500F	a' = $x_i + z_{i-1} = z_i$
	40 500F	
2	L5 L	Modify address
	L4 6L	
3	42 L	$(10)' = (10) + 2^{-39}$
	L5 7L	
4	L0 6L	End counter
	40 7L	$(17)' = (17) - 2^{-39}$
5	32 L	Transfer when $(17) \geq 0$
	0F F	STOP. Here when $(17) = -1 \times 2^{-39}$
6	00 F	= $1/ \times 2^{-39}$
	00 1F	
7	00 F	= 99×2^{-39} = end counter
	00 99F	by 4L
	26 10N	

Figure 17-1

Sample code showing the use of termination symbols K, L, F and N.

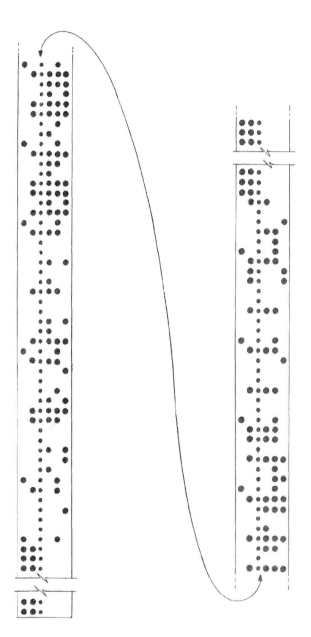

Figure 17-2

Showing the appearance of the code given in
Figure 17-1 when punched onto teletype tape.

W.M. Location (Decimal)	Contents (Binary)
10	0100 0001 0001 1111 0100 1111 0101 0000 1100 1001
11	1111 0100 0001 1111 0100 0100 0000 0001 1111 0100
12	1111 0101 0000 0000 1010 1111 0100 0000 0001 0000
13	0100 0010 0000 0000 1010 1111 0101 0000 0001 0001
14	1111 0000 0000 0001 0000 0100 0000 0000 0001 0001
15	0011 0010 0000 0000 1010 0000 1110 0000 0000 0000
16	0000 0000 0000 0000 0000 0000 0000 0000 0000 0001
17	0000 0000 0000 0000 0000 0000 0000 0000 0110 0011

Figure 17-3

Showing the code of Figure 17-1 in the Williams Memory
after it has been read from the tape of Figure 17-2 by SADOI.

It is to be observed that only the information contained in the column
headed "Order Pair" is typed onto the tape. Leading zeros of the address, relative
or fixed, need not be written explicitly; see the order at LH of 2L, and LH of
6L, Figure 17-1. The remarks made in the comments column vary from programmer to
programmer according to personal taste. The use of the word "by" to describe
modification of the order by some other order is conventional. Also it is common
to use the word "from" to indicate that a transfer from some other part of the
program to the point at hand is made. In general, one should try to make the
remarks in the comments column descriptive. A good guide rule here is to assume
that you had to read and understand the program five years after you had written
it (in other words, after you had forgotten most of it) then put down those
comments which you think would be most helpful for this purpose.

Certain features of the tape should be pointed out. At the very front
of the tape is a portion called the "leader"; 2-hole delay characters are punched
on this part of the tape. The leader should be about eight inches long. If the
leader is too short it will not properly fit into the photoelectric tape reader.
On the leader the coder should write his name and the name of the code. It is

sometimes helpful if the date on which the tape was prepared is also written on the leader. At the end of the tape there is a "tail" which also should be about eight inches long and contains 2-hole delay characters. The lf. and cr., delay (2 hole or 1 hole), and space characters are ignored by SADOI. It is seen in Figure 17-2 that the lf. and cr. is used to separate order pairs; although the two orders of a pair are written on different lines, as in Figure 17-1, it is not the custom to separate them by a lf. and cr. character on the tape. This is only a custom and since the lf. and cr. may appear anywhere without affecting the SADOI "translation" of the code on the tape the programmer may insert lf. and cr. characters on the tape wherever he pleases. It is not customary to follow the lf. and cr. character on a program tape by a delay character, although again this is a matter of taste since the delay character is ignored by SADOI. A delay character is not really necessary in this instance since the length of each line of print is usually so short that there is adequate time for the teleprinter carriage to return to the left margin position for printing the character immediately following the lf. and cr. character. The space character is a convenient one to use for "erasing" tape errors since all five holes are punched out in the space character (hence any character can be changed to a space by simply punching out the remaining holes) and a space character is ignored by SADOI.

In Figure 17-3 it should be observed that the relative addresses have been translated into the proper fixed addresses. Thus the LH order at 2L (or 12 fixed) which is L5 L does indeed have the address digits equal to 10_D when it is in the WM.

The directive 00 10K at the head of the tape and the transfer of control directive 26 10N on the tail of the tape do not actually get placed in the WM as a part of the program. This is natural since they exist only for the purpose of giving certain directions to SADOI and they have no further utility after SADOI has ceased operation and relinquished control to the program.

UNIVERSITY OF ILLINOIS
DIGITAL COMPUTER
CHAPTER 18

SADOI - PART 2

    In this chapter the termination symbol J for fraction input, schemes
for integer input, and the use of symbolic addresses are discussed.

    With the J termination it is possible to write fractions, which might
be constants in the program, in their decimal form, leaving the task of decimal
to binary conversion to SADOI. The fractional digits are written as the digits
of the right address of an order pair. Excepting leading zeros, 12 digits of
the fraction must be written. Examples appear below in Figure 18-1.

Decimal Fraction	Form for writing decimal fraction to be input by SADOI
$\frac{1}{3} = 0.333.$	00 F 00 3333 3333 3333J
$\frac{2}{3} = 0.666.$	00 F 00 6666 6666 6667J
$\frac{1}{12} = 0.08333.$	00 F 00 833 3333 3333J
$\frac{1}{250} = 0.004$	00 F 00 40 0000 0000J

Figure 18-1

Examples of the use of the J termination symbol for
writing positive decimal fractions.

To write negative fractions the sign digit of the order pair is set equal to 1 to make the LH order read 80 F. The sign digit is interpreted to have weight -1 and the fraction -x is written as $\begin{array}{l}\text{80 F}\\ \text{00 x'J}\end{array}$ where x' = 1-x. The same fractions displayed in Figure 18-1 now written as negative decimal fractions are shown in Figure 18-2.

Decimal Fraction	Form for writing decimal fraction to be input by SADOI
$-\frac{1}{3} = -0.333\cdot$	80 F 00 6666 6666 6667J
$-\frac{2}{3} = -0.666\cdot$	80 F 00 3333 3333 3333J
$-\frac{1}{12} = -0.08333\cdot$	80 F 00 9166 6666 6667J
$-\frac{1}{250} = -0.004$	80 F 00 9960 0000 0000J

Figure 18-2

Examples of the use of the J termination symbol for
writing negative decimal fractions.

Notice that the decimal point is always assumed to lie immediately to the left of the first digit of the right address, except when leading zeros are omitted; more generally, the right address x when terminated by J is understood to represent the fraction $x \cdot 10^{-12}$. Leading zeros may be written explicitly if desired; for example,

        00 F
        00 833 3333 3333J
and

        00 F
        00 0833 3333 3333J

are interpreted identically by SADOI.

Two common coding errors with regard to writing fractions are:

  (1) neglecting to write down the proper number of digits in the
      fraction; remember 12 digits must be written with the
      exception of leading zeros, which may be omitted;

  (2) improper entry of negative fractions, writing them in sign
      absolute magnitude form rather than 2's complement form;
      remember, in order to write -x, one sets the sign digit equal to 1 and
      puts 1-x in the right address digits.

Since fractions which terminate in the decimal system generally do
not terminate in the binary system, the fraction x is not exactly represented
when converted by SADOI into the ILLIAC fraction, x^+. In the SADOI conversion
of decimal fractions to binary fractions the maximum error is $\epsilon = 2^{-40}$, i.e.
$-2^{-40} \leq x - x^+ \leq 2^{-40}$.*

Integer constants are easily written for input by SADOI. If the
integer x (positive) is desired, then one writes the order pair

          00 F
          00 xF

where x appears as the address of the RH order. The function digits of the LH
order and RH order and the address digits of the LH order must all be zero. The
address of the RH order can be any integer within machine range ($0 \leq x \leq 2^{39} -1$)
and SADOI will properly make the decimal to binary conversion to obtain the
correct ILLIAC representation of the integer. For example the order pair

          00 F
          00 5497 5581 3887F

will be read by SADOI and converted to the binary word

          0111 1111 1111 1111 1111 1111 1111 1111 1111 1111

which is indeed the correct integer representation of $549,755,813,887 = 2^{39}-1$.

---

* The superscript $^+$ will be used to mean "the number represented by the ILLIAC"
  which ingeneral is not identically equal to the number one is attempting to
  represent because of errors which arise from a variety of sources. The error
  is frequently denoted by ϵ and the relationship between x, the number that
  ILLIAC is attempting to represent, and x^+, the number ILLIAC is actually
  representing, is $x^+ + \epsilon = x$.

Negative integers may be entered using the complement representation, thus, -x is written as

    80 F
    00 2^{39} -x F

In particular, if -x = -10, then 2^{39} - x = 549, 755, 813, 878 and one writes

    80 F
    00 5497 5581 3878F

SADOI will convert this to the binary word

    1111 1111 1111 1111 1111 1111 1111 1111 1111 0110 ,

which is indeed the ILLIAC representation of the integer -10.

This technique is possible because of the way SADOI constructs the binary program words from the code on the tape. This discussion is reserved for the next chapter.

For small negative integers and large positive integers a slightly simpler scheme can be used. First let us notice that certain order pairs have a simple numerical significance:

Order Pair	Fractional Value	Integer Value
80 F	-1	-2^{39}
00 F		
7L 4095F	$1-2^{-39}$	$2^{39}-1$
LL 4095F		
LL 4095F	-1×2^{-39}	-1
LL 4095F		

We immediately see that the large positive integer 2^{39}-p can be obtained from the representation for 2^{39}-1 by subtracting p-1 from it; 2^{39}-1 - (p-1) = 2^{39}-p. Now if p does not exceed 4096 this subtraction is easily executed since only the address digits of the RH order need be considered; if p does exceed 4096 then one has to be careful in handling the borrows from the digits to the left of the RH address digits. In a similar manner one can easily generate the order pair

representations for small negative integers from the above representation
for -1. Some examples of the order pair representations for integers are
given below.

Integer	Order Pair
2^{39}-10	7L 4095F
	LL 4086F
2^{39}-500	7L 4095F
	LL 3596F
-10	LL 4095F
	LL 4086F
-500	LL 4095F
	LL 3596F

One of the most important features of SADOI is that it permits
symbolic address references whereby one can assign a "name" to a word of the
program quite independent of the address of the word in the Illiac memory.
We have seen in preceding examples, that the operand specified by the
address digits of an order is usually a word of the program (this may be an order
pair, a constant, a parameter, etc.). We have also seen that the operand is
referred to by giving its location in the memory, either fixed (if we use the
termination symbol F) or relative (if we use the termination symbol L). However
with the symbolic address convention we can "name" any word of the program which
must be referred to as an operand and then always refer to this word by its
"name" -- i.e. its symbolic address -- writing it as the address portion of
the order. This ability to refer to words in the program independent of their
specific location in the memory, relative or fixed, provides a great convenience
in writing the code which can only be appreciated after a certain amount of
coding experience has been gained. The symbolic address scheme also facilitates
the making of alterations in a code, as we shall see.

A symbolic address is always identified by being enclosed by parentheses;
thus, (1), (A1), (ROOTS), (Z39) are examples of symbolic addresses. The symbolic
address may include up to five characters, letters, figures or symbols;

specifically, any character which is actually printed is considered a part of
the symbolic address. The characters lf. and cr., delay and space are not
regarded as part of the symbolic address and are in fact completely ignored
by SADOI. Below the four symbolic addresses just cited are shown as they might
appear in a section of code:

    L5 (1)
    40 (A1)
    ───────────
    LC (ROOTS)
    36 (Z39)

Here the symbolic addresses appear in the address portion of the order to
indicate the operand referred to by the order. Now the symbolic address (1)
is the "name" for a certain word of the program; let us say that this word
is 00 F 00 10F. When the code is written the word 00 F 00 10F is given
this name, (1), by writing the word as follows.

    (1) 00 F
         00 10F

        SADOI loads the words of the code sequentially into blocks in the
memory as specified by the directives mentioned in the last chapter. When
SADOI reads (1) 00 F 00 10F from the tape it recognizes the (1) as a symbolic
address name for this word and associates (1) with the actual memory location,
say m, into which this word is loaded. Every address reference to (1), as in the
L5 order above, is now interpreted by SADOI to mean a reference to memory location
m (since the word called (1) in the code has been placed in location m) and the
binary address m is inserted for the address digits of the order by SADOI. The
same remarks apply to the other symbolic addresses above, (A1), (ROOTS), and (Z39).
Let us consider a short example:

00	10K

	L5	(1)
	42	(2)

(2)	L0	(3A)
	36	F

(1)	OF	F
	00	100F

(3A)	OF	F
	00	200F

This portion of the code would be printed as follows on the teletype tape:

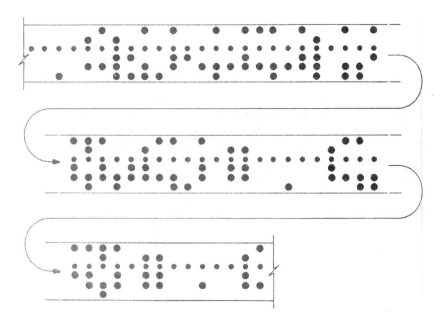

After SADOI reads these orders from the tape they will appear as follows in the memory:

W.M. Location (Sexadecimal)	Order Pair (Sexadecimal)
00K	L500N 4200S
00S	L000J 36000
00N	0F000 00064
00J	0F000 000N8

When the symbolic address appears in the address portion of an order it is called an <u>inside</u> symbolic address. In the first order pair of the above example (1) and (2) appear as inside symbolic addresses. When the symbolic address precedes the order, thus "naming" it, we call it an <u>outside</u> symbolic address. In the second order pair of the above example (2) appears as an outside symbolic address and (3A) appears as an inside symbolic address.

Notice that a letter shift character precedes A (in the symbolic address 3A) since A can only be printed when the teleprinter carriage is in the letters position. SADOI recognizes the letter shift character and accordingly properly distinguishes the characters following it as "letters". Following A a numbers shift character appears. Again, SADOI recognizes the numbers shift character and accordingly distinguishes the characters following it as "numbers". Characters which are the same in either mode, letters or numbers, namely F, J, L and N are likewise regarded as the same in either mode by SADOI. The letter shift character and number shift character are not counted among the five characters which may be used to specify a symbolic address. In general one can say that only those characters count which the teleprinter actually would print.

UNIVERSITY OF ILLINOIS
DIGITAL COMPUTER
CHAPTER 19

SADOI - PART 3

In this chapter additional features of SADOI and some of the logic connected with the operation of SADOI are discussed. The library subroutine write-up of SADOI is contained in Appendix 9, pp. 275-329.

The SADOI program is stored permanently in the auxiliary drum memory of the ILLIAC. When a program tape is to be read into the ILLIAC a series of preliminary routines are first executed which eventually read SADOI from the drum and place it in the WM. Control is then transferred to SADOI and it begins read-in of the program tape. A discussion of the preliminary routines is presented in Appendix 10, pp. 330-337. For the present discussion let us just assume that SADOI can be automatically called forth from the drum, placed in the WM, and control transferred to it.

The program tape must begin with a directive, which is of the form

$$00 \ mK$$

where m signifies a decimal integer. This directive instructs SADOI to store the order pairs which follow in locations m, m+1, m+2, ..., of the WM. This directive also sets a number known as a relativizer which is added to the relative address to form the real address of an order.

The orders are assembled in location 1 of the WM. Let us consider now an intermediate stage in the assembly of a program, where SADOI is ready to read a new order from the program tape. Before read-in of the function digits of an order begins the WM location 1 holds the last two orders read by SADOI; the next-to-the-last order is in the LH order position of location 1 and the last order is in the RH order position of location 1. When the function digits for the new order are read the contents of 1 become shifted 20 places to the left so that now the last order resides in the LH order position at 1, and the function

digits of the new order are in the function digit positions of the RH order
at 1; namely, digital positions 20, 21, ..., 27. The remaining digital
positions of the RH order contain zero at this stage of the read-in --- they
eventually will hold the address of the order now being assembled.

After the function digits have been read, read-in of the address
begins. The address is assembled in WM location 0. The address, as has been
seen, may be either numerical or symbolic. Let us consider the treatment of
the numerical address first. As the digits of the numerical address are read
they are converted to form a binary integer which is stored at location zero.
This decimal to binary integer conversion proceeds until the termination symbol
is read. This computation is executed in such a way that it is possible to write
any decimal integer within machine range on the tape and it will be properly
converted to the binary integer and stored at zero. Different things will now
happen, depending on the termination symbol.

If the termination symbol is K, then SADOI interprets the order as a
directive. So far only one form for the directive has been cited;
actually there are four. They are listed with their meaning below.

Directive   Meaning

00 mK   Load the following order pairs at
                           m, m+1, ... and set the relativizer
                           to m.

00 K   If m is the location of the last
                           instruction pair then set the
                           relativizer to m+1 and load the
                           following order pairs into locations
                           m+1, m+2, ...

01 nK   If m is the value of the relativizer
                           then the following instruction pairs
                           will go into m+n, m+n+1, ... The
                           relativizer is not changed.

Directive	Meaning
02 nK	Set the relativizer to the address m of the preceding instruction and load the following order pairs into locations m+n, m+n+1, ...

The effect of these different directives is illustrated in Figures 19-1 and 19-2.

If the termination symbol is S, then one sexadecimal character which must follow S, and must be 2, 3, 4 ... or L, is read from the tape. This character causes the word, called the S parameter, at the corresponding WM location (2, 3, 4, ... or L) to be added to the integer at location 0. The resultant sum is then added to the word at location 1. Assembly of the new order is now complete. The effect of this termination symbol is illustrated in Figures 19-3 and 19-4.

If the termination symbol is N, then the integer at location 0 is added to the word at location 1. If the integer at zero is less than 999, then the program being assembled is read from the drum, where it is stored during the assembly, into the assigned locations in the WM and control is transferred to the order at the RH of location 1. This order is the last order read, namely the order whose address is terminated by N.

If the integer at location 0 (i.e. the address of the order terminated by N) is 999, then SADOI comes to a stop on the order 24 05J$_S$. A black switch start will cause SADOI to resume reading the program tape. Thus, if a program is on two separate tapes, the first tape is terminated by 24 999N to cause a stop so that the second program tape may be put into the photoelectric reader. Other addresses above 999 which are terminated by N are used in connection with interludes and drum loading; the reader is referred to the SADOI write-up for a discussion of their use.

	ORDER PAIR			ORDER PAIR			ORDER PAIR	
	00	10K		00	10K		00	10K
0	L5	8L	0	L5	8L	0	L5	8L
	40	2L		40	2L		40	2L
1	L5	9L	1	L5	9L	1	L5	9L
	40	3L		40	3L		40	3L
							00	2L
	00	K		01	4K		02	2K
0	[00	F	4	L5	2L	2	L5	L
	00	F]		L4	10L		L4	8L
1	[00	F	5	40	2L	3	40	L
	00	F]		F5	3L		F5	1L
2	L5	L	6	42	3L	4	42	1L
	L4	8L		L0	11L		L0	9L
3	40	L	7	36	2L	5	36	L
	F5	1L		0F	F		0F	F
4	42	1L	8	L5	100F	6	L5	100F
	L0	9L		L4	200F		L4	200F
5	36	L	9	50	F	7	50	F
	0F	F		40	300F		40	300F
6	L5	100F	10	00	1F	8	00	1F
	L4	200F		00	1F		00	1F
7	50	F	11	70	F	9	70	F
	40	300F		40	400F		40	400F
8	00	1F						
	00	1F						
9	J0	F						
	40	400F						

Figure 19-1

Three forms of the same code illustrating the effect of the different directives. Each of these is loaded into the WM by SADOI as shown in Figure 19-2.

138

WM LOCATION	CONTENTS
00K	L5012 4000N
00S	L5013 4000J
00N	00000 00000
00J	00000 00000
00F	L500N L4014
00L	4000N F500J
010	4200J L0015
011	3600N 0F000
012	L5064 L40N8
013	50000 4012N
014	00001 00001
015	J0000 40190

Figure 19-2

Each of the codes shown in Figure 19-1 is loaded into the WM
by SADOI as shown here. All characters are sexadecimal.

WM	ORDER PAIR	
	00 3K	
3	00 F 00 100F	Parameter S3
4	00 F 00 200F	Parameter S4
5	00 10F 00 30F	Parameter S5
6	L5 F 26 64F	Parameter S6
	00 10K	
10	L5 S3 40 2S4	
11	L5 2F 40 S4	
12	L5 1S5 40 6L	
13	L5 2S5 40 3S5	
14	00 F 00 1S6	

Figure 19-3

A portion of a code designed to illustrate the effect of the S termination.
The contents of locations 10, 11, 12, 13, and 14, after this code is read by
SADOI, are shown in Figure 19-4.

WM LOCATION	CONTENTS
00K	L5064 400NK
00S	L5002 400N8
00N	L501L 40010
00J	L502K 40021
00F	L5000 26041

Figure 19-4

The contents of locations 10, 11, 12, 13, and 14, after the portion of code shown in Figure 19-3 has been loaded into the WM by SADOI. All characters are sexadecimal.

Sometimes it is desired to jump to a word in the program identified by a symbolic address, say (A). Rather than figure out the real address, call it 769_D, corresponding to (A) in order to terminate the tape by

26 769N

one can terminate the tape with the pair of orders

26 (A)
26 1N

and achieve the desired effect.

It is important to take notice of the fact that the word in which the order terminated by N is located is never actually assembled as a part of the program. Thus, if the tape ends with the order pair

-- ----
-- ----

OF   F
24 100N

then the order OF is not actually loaded as a part of the program. To get the
order OF into the memory in this instance it is necessary to use a waste half-
order as follows

$$
\begin{array}{ll}
\text{OF} & \text{F} \\
\underline{\text{OO} \quad \text{F}} & \quad\text{waste} \\
\text{24 100N} &
\end{array}
$$

If the termination symbol is J, then the following computation is done:

$$(1)' = (1) + \frac{1}{2} \left[\frac{(0) - 5 \times 10^{11} \times 2^{-39} + 5 \times 10^{11} \times 2^{-78}}{5 \times 10^{11} \times 2^{-39}} \right] + \frac{1}{2}$$

where (1) means the contents of location 1 and (0) means the contents of
location O. This calculation converts the integer, (0), to a fraction and
adds the result to (1). We see now the reasons behind the rules given
earlier for the use of the J termination symbol. Assembly of the new order
is now complete.

It is perhaps worthwhile to digress for a moment to illustrate how the above
calculation does in fact produce the desired result. The number preceding
the J termination is read by SADOI just as any other address and therefore is
held as an integer in location zero when the J termination is read. To convert
this number to a 12 digit fraction it is of course necessary to divide it by
10^{12}. However, it is to be noted that if the number preceding the J was
549 755 813 888 (= 2^{39}) or larger (suppose we wanted to store .999 999 999 999
by writing the order OOF 00 999 999 999 999J) then there will be overflow of
the number into the sign digit. Consequently the integer at location zero is
brought into ILLIAC range by first subtracting 5×10^{11} to form

$$a = (0) - 5 \times 10^{11} \times 2^{-39} \quad .$$

In order to provide for a rounded quotient with a maximum error of 2^{-40} the
number $5 \times 10^{11} \times 2^{-39}$ is placed in Q before division thus making the dividend

$$a + 2^{-39}q = (0) - 5 \times 10^{11} \times 2^{-39} + 5 \times 10^{11} \times 2^{-78} \quad .$$

Division by $5 \times 10^{11} \times 2^{-39}$ is then executed to form

$$q = \frac{(0)}{5 \times 10^{11} \times 2^{-39}} - 1 + 2^{-39} + \delta \, 2^{-39}$$

(where $\delta = 0$ or 1 according as the true quotient does or does not have a 1 in the 2^{-39} bit position.) This quotient is then shifted to the right one place to drop off the division roundoff digit and produce

$$q' = \frac{1}{2} \, q = \frac{(0)}{10^{12} \times 2^{-39}} - \frac{1}{2} + 2^{-40}$$

Next this result is added to 1/2 to form (in the accumulator)

$$a = \frac{(0)}{10^{12} \times 2^{-39}} + 2^{-40}$$

The term on the right provides the desired roundoff error $|\epsilon| \leq 2^{-40}$. Finally, this number is added to the number at location 1 to form

$$a' = (1) + a = (1) + \frac{(0)}{10^{12} \times 2^{-39}} + 2^{-40}$$

permitting the sign digit to be picked up if the fraction was negative.

If the termination symbol is F, then the integer at 0 is added to the word in 1 and the assembly of the new order is complete.

If the termination symbol is L, then the integer at 0 is added to the relativizer (which was set by the directive) and the resultant sum is added to the word in location 1. The assembly of the new order is now complete.

Let us now consider the action taken by SADOI when a symbolic address follows the function digits; this would be an inside symbolic address. First it should be noted that an integer may precede the symbolic address; that is the order may have the form TV n( ) where n is a decimal integer. This form for the address is interpreted to mean that the real address for the order is given

by n + (the address represented by the symbolic address). SADOI reads the
integer n and stores it at location 0, as described earlier for the numerical
address. Notice that during this read-in of n SADOI does not "know" what kind
of an address is present, it may be numerical or symbolic; only when the left
parenthesis, which follows n, is read is the existence of a symbolic address
recognized.

The characters of the symbolic address are read, and encoded into groups
of six binary digits. Five bits are used to specify the tape character and the
sixth bit specifies whether the character was printed in the letter shift mode or
the number shift mode; since the print mode is thus encoded it is not necessary to
specifically encode the number shift and letter shift characters. These six bit
groups which represent the letters of the symbolic address are formed as the
symbolic address characters are read from the tape and they are shifted into a word
from the left hand end. This process proceeds until the right parenthesis is
read and then the word is stored temporarily so that after read-in of the
symbolic address characters this word contains, when read from left to right, the
last 5 coded symbolic address characters in $w_0\ w_1\ \cdots\ w_{29}$. The right-most ten
bits of this word are set equal to zero; later they may hold the real address
corresponding to this symbolic address. Notice that because the actual symbolic
address is composed by this reading and shifting procedure, a cycle which is stopped
only when the right parenthesis is detected, the symbolic address written on the
tape may be composed of an arbitrary number of characters but only the last five,
reading from left to right, will actually be used by SADOI for the symbolic address:
thus,

(13A2Z)
(413A2Z)
(WXYZ16413A2Z)

are interpreted by SADOI as identical symbolic addresses. As was cited earlier
a symbolic address may contain less than five characters.

Having read the inside symbolic address, SADOI begins a search through
a list, known as the symbolic address list in an attempt to find the real
address which corresponds to this symbolic address. This list contains symbolic

address words. Each distinct symbolic address used by the program is represented by a word in this list; the symbolic address represented is located in digital positions w_0 w_1 ... w_{29} according to the encoding scheme described above. The words in this list have two origins. An entry is made in this list each time an outside symbolic address, call it X, is read from the tape. In this case the real address corresponding to X is known; by definition the real address is just the WM location assigned to the order having X as an outside address. The real address is put into the rightmost ten bits of the symbolic address word. The other origin of entries to this list will be seen presently.

In the search of the symbolic address list a symbolic address word holding the "looked-for" symbolic address and the associated real address will be found if the necessary outside symbolic address has already been read from the tape. In this event the real address is extracted from the symbolic address word and is added to the integer at location O; [*] the resultant sum is added to the word at location 1 to complete the assembly of an order having a symbolic address. Now it may be that the outside address has not yet been read from the tape. In this instance the symbolic address of the order being assembled is referring to a word of the program whose location has not yet been assigned; such a reference is known as a forward address reference. (In the previous case where the location had already been assigned at the time of the inside symbolic address reference we had what is known as a backward address reference.) The real address will now not be found in the list. As a consequence of this, the symbolic address word which was formed on read-in of the symbolic address is now added to the symbolic address list; recall that the right most ten bits of this word are zero. This is the other origin of entries to the symbolic address list. It may be that the present symbolic address has already been used as a forward reference in which case the symbolic address will have already been entered in the list; the fact that the right-most ten bits of this word are zero indicates that they do not represent a real address. When an entry from such a previous forward reference is found no new addition to the symbolic address list is made.

---

[*] Remember that location O holds the integer preceding the symbolic address; i.e. (O) = n where the order is of the form TV n ( ).

One can readily see that the forward address reference calls for special attention because the assembly of the order using this forward reference cannot be immediately completed. Provision is made for SADOI to "remember" that the real address of the order is absent so that later after the real address has been obtained it may be substituted in the order. Provision is also made for SADOI to remember the increment that must be made to the address represented by the symbolic address to obtain the real address of the order; this increment is the integer at location 0, earlier designated by n. These provisions are made as follows. If n = 0 then the order being assembled is given an address equal to the memory location of the word in the symbolic address list holding this order's symbolic address. The fact that the address of this order has this special meaning is remembered by SADOI in a special block of 52 words called 2 bit registers. Each binary digit in this block corresponds to an order and if the digit is 1 it means that substitution of the real address in the corresponding order is necessary; if the digit is 0 it means that the corresponding order already contains the real address. As each order is assembled this digit is appropriately set. On the other hand if $n \neq 0$ then the increment to the symbolic address must also be remembered. This is done in another block of words called the additions list. In this case a word, called the additions word, is constructed according to the following prescription: the left most 30 bits hold the right most 30 bits of the word at location zero (i.e. they hold the integer n, provided $n < 2^{30}$); the remaining 10 bits on the right hold the location of the associated symbolic address word in the symbolic address list. This additions word is stored in the additions list. The address portion of the order being assembled is set equal to the location of the corresponding additions word. The 2 bit registers are used as described above to indicate that the real address is still to be substituted.

Whenever an outside symbolic address is read from the tape a search of the symbolic address list is made to determine whether or not it has already been entered in the list. If an entry is found it should have been placed there because of a forward address reference, as described earlier; the real address is now inserted in the right most ten digits of the symbolic address word. It is possible that the programmer has made an error and given two different words of the program the same outside symbolic address. This situation would also cause an entry to be found in the list but it can be distinguished from the above case by examination of the right most ten bits of the symbolic address word: these will be zero if the entry resulted from a forward address reference; they will be non-zero if the entry was due to the earlier use of this symbolic address as an outside address -- this situation causes SADOI to produce an error print (see Appendix 9, pp. 287-289 f∴ a discussion of error stops). In the latter case the "new" real address is substituted into the address digits of the symbolic address word. Thus the real address corresponding to the symbolic address is always the last one assigned if the same symbolic address is used as an outside address more than once.

The operations connected with the reading and assembly of an individual order have now been described. Let us now consider briefly how SADOI assembles these orders into a program.

SADOI must keep track of whether it is working on a left hand order or a right hand order during assembly. In doing this SADOI assumes that the order following a directive or an N termination is a left hand order.

After each right hand order is assembled, the word at location 1 which then holds an order pair is added to a list in the WM that can hold 45 order pairs. When this block becomes filled the order pairs are transferred to the drum memory. Each order pair is stored on the drum in a location that uniquely corresponds to the assigned location of the order pair in the WM (i.e. the location it will occupy in the WM after the assembly is completed); this correspondence is

$$\text{WM location} + 11{,}756 = \text{Drum location} \quad .$$

The assignment of locations in the WM is controlled by a counter which is set by the directive orders.

Whenever the directive or the N termination is detected the word at location 1 is <u>not</u> added to the order pair list, even though it may occur in a RH order. Orders which are directives or are terminated by N are never considered as truly orders of the program, rather they represent instructions to SADOI for the various purposes we have cited. Because of this feature it is important to remember that if such an order does appear in the RH order position, then the preceding order which is in the LH order position also will <u>not</u> get stored as part of the program.

Whenever the K directive or the N termination, with address less than 999 is detected or, as cited above, when the assembly block of 45 words in the WM is filled, the words in the assembly block are transferred to their proper locations in the drum memory. In the event of an order with an N termination and an address less than 999 the program is then read into the assigned locations in the WM and any necessary substitutions of real addresses are made (determined by examination of the two bit registers) and finally control is transferred to the word at the RH order position of location 1 (this being the last order read from the tape).

The available memory space puts a limitation on the size of the symbolic address list and on the size of the additions list. These limits are as follows:

a) The number of words in the symbolic address list (which is equal to the number of different symbolic addresses) must be less than 325;

b) The number of words in the additions list (which is equal to the number of addresses of the form n(-----------) where the symbolic address is a forward address reference) must be less than 315.

The foregoing two chapters and the present one have been presented as an introductory survey to some of the main features of SADOI. Not all features have been discussed; indeed, we have not talked about input of library subroutines from the drum--this will be discussed through examples in a later chapter. For specific details of the SADOI properties the reader should consult the library subroutine write-up.

UNIVERSITY OF ILLINOIS
DIGITAL COMPUTER
CHAPTER 20

PROGRAM ERROR DIAGNOSIS

There is a variety of errors that can be made in setting up a
problem to be run on a computer, and a programmer will frequently make at least
one error, or perhaps more, in a program of reasonable length. Good programming
technique includes knowing how to properly check a program for possible errors
and knowing how to locate the source of any errors detected.

The kinds of errors that occur fall roughly into two general classes.
There are errors due to mistakes in the coding logic -- the programmer thinks
that he has told ILLIAC to do one thing when in fact he has told it to do something quite different. There are errors due to incorrect methods -- ILLIAC does
exactly what the programmer thinks he has told it to do but he has not told it to
do the correct thing. The former type of error is commonly referred to as a
blunder and in comparison with the latter type of error it is relatively easy
to detect. This is so because the blunder will commonly cause the machine to
stop, to loop (execute a block of orders repeatedly without end), or produce
"answers" that are so far from the correct answers that one is immediately aware
that something is wrong. The second type of error on the other hand will usually
produce "answers" which appear to be reasonable, and consequently the errors are
more likely to go undetected. Furthermore, since the latter type of error results
from a conceptual error on the part of the programmer it is still more likely to
be hidden.

When a program has been written, the testing of it for possible errors
is known as code checking. The specific procedures to be used in code checking
a problem of course depend on the problem at hand. One good practice is to check
the individual parts or subroutines of a program by themselves first. Generally
this requires the preparation of a set of "dummy" data to be used as input data
for the subroutine. Furthermore there must be some way of independently checking

the response of the subroutine to this data; e.g. by a hand calculation or from already tabulated values. In doing this it is important that an intelligent choice of input data to the subroutine be made, since it is impossible to test the response of the subroutine to every conceivable set of input data. If the subroutine is supposed to be able to accept a range of values of an input parameter then the response of the subroutine to the limiting values of the parameter should be checked. One should try to pick input data which will give a response by the subroutine that is easy to check by a hand calculation; for example one check is to provide input data which will always give zero's as output data, then it is easy to scan the output data for errors because they will stand out against the background of zeros; another help is to provide sets of input data which yield an output by the subroutine which changes in a simple and consistent way with successive sets of data. After each subroutine is completely checked then they should be assembled together into the final program. Following this a second series of code checks should be made to guarantee that the individual parts of the program have been properly linked together. Although on the surface of it the assembly of the parts into the whole would seem to be a fairly simple task, a little experience will show that great care must be exercised to avoid errors in performing this operation.

If one does not follow the practice outlined above or one similar to it, but tries to check the entire program as a whole without any preliminaries, then errors will usually be difficult to localize and remove. This of course is not true for very short programs.

If one intends to separately test the parts of a program this should be kept in mind while the program is being written so that it is not too difficult to test each part as an independent unit. Some remarks concerning the organization of the program for easy code checking follow. One should minimize the number of cross references between subroutines (for example, subroutine A should not have many orders which refer to specific words in subroutine B as operands). Minimization of cross references will generally result in a somewhat longer program (i.e. more words) but the resultant simplicity is worth the length if memory space is not at a premium.

Another procedure for organizing a program that seems to provide for relatively easy checking is the following. Let the various subroutines be numbered 1, 2, ..., n; i.e. (1) is the outside address of the first word in subroutine number 1, and so forth. Write a master control routine which has the form shown in Figure 20-1.

ORDER PAIR	COMMENTS
(0.1) 24 (1)	to "Read Data Subroutine"
00 1F	
(0.2) 24 (2)	to "Initialization Subroutine"
00 2F	
(0.3) 24 (3)	to "Initial Print Subroutine"
00 3F	
(0.4) 24 (4)	
00 4F	
.	Jumps to subroutines in main
.	part of the program
.	
(0.n) 24 (n)	
00 nF	
OF F	Final stop
OF F	
FF 1F	2 (or more)
26 (---)	special stops.
FF 2F	
26 (---)	

Figure 20-1

Suggested form for master control routine.

When exit is made from each of the subroutines a jump is executed to the
appropriate transfer order in the master control routine. In code checking
the program the black switch stops provide simple blocks between the
subroutines, permitting easy individual checking of each one. The right
half of each transfer word is designed for easily determining which 24 order
causes a stop during a code check, by reading the right address digits of
the order register. After the parts of the program have been checked the
24 orders can easily be changed to 26 orders (notice that a 4 can be changed
to a 6 by simply punching out the 2's hole on the tape). It is usually
convenient to have all stops in the program in the master routine, as
indicated in Figure 20-1.

Another procedure which seems to be quite helpful is to have all
constants used in the program located in a single block of storage. This
is to be preferred over putting constants in unused space scattered throughout the program (unless memory space is at a premium) because one is then
less likely to cause errors when making corrections in a program during the
code checking procedure, or when making changes in the program after it has
been checked; e.g. it is easy to forget that the address digits of some
order are being used as a constant, say to set a base address. Furthermore
from the discussion below it will be seen that this procedure permits one to
easily post-mortem all constants of a program. For similar reasons it is
usually best to put all data or parameters for a program into a separate
storage block.

It should go without saying that the program should be very carefully
prepared in the first place; this includes writing it carefully and reading it
over very carefully, at least twice, before it is even put onto the computer. The
two readings of the program should be separated by a space of time of at least
24 hours to reduce the chance of overlooking the same mistake twice in a row.
Also, the printed copy produced by the teleprinter in making the program tape
should be carefully compared against the handwritten copy. In general the
programmer should take every possible precaution against errors so that he is
as certain as possible that there is no error even the first time the program

is put onto the machine -- unfortunately, there usually will be some errors anyway but hopefully, if all of the precautions have been taken, they will be small in number.

The recommendations expressed in the foregoing paragraphs are not always followed. A number of people feel that one should be moderately careful in preparing the program and adopt the philosophy that any errors that exist in the program can be found and removed during the code check. They claim that the computer will turn up the errors faster than the programmer will by reading the program over and checking it carefully. It is no doubt true that most errors. will be found automatically during the course of a code check, if it has been well designed. Nevertheless, no code check is perfect since one cannot test the output of the program against every conceivable input (if this were possible the program would not have been necessary in the first place). Therefore the probability that an error in the program will get by all code checks without detection is not zero, though it may be small. If the programmer is sloppy, relying on the code checks to turn up his blunders, and his more subtle errors, then the probability of an error getting by all code checks is much greater than for the careful programmer since the careful programmer has fewer errors to begin with. When a code of one hundred instructions is checked and ten errors are found a careful programmer should be very concerned about the possibility of still more errors which were undetected. An experienced programmer should average fewer than one error per one hundred instructions.

When a program is being checked and a failure is found there is a great tendency to blame the computer. After a little experience it will be found that virtually all failures are due to program errors. The programmer should adopt the attitude that every failure is due to the program and then take the necessary steps to find the error in his program. It is of course possible for computer failures to occur. If a program has failed and the programmer has <u>thoroughly</u> checked over his program and still cannot find the error then he may try to run it again on the computer. If it fails again, as before, then it is almost certain that the failure is due to an error in the program and the programmer should look into his program again. On the other hand, if a second running of the program yields a different result than the first running then the programmer can assume that a computer error was the source of the failure; this conclusion is only safe if the same physical program tape is used in both attempts to run the program.

The methods used by programmers for checking the various parts of their program differ in detail. Generally a short routine known as a "driver" must be written. The function of the driver is to supply data to the subroutine being checked and to print information about the operation of the subroutine. These drivers vary in degree of elaborateness. Sometimes a dynamic check of the subroutine is made. In this the driver program interrupts the running of the subroutine under test at various points, known as check points, and prints out specified information about the contents of certain memory locations and certain registers; following this the driver lets the subroutine resume its computations until the next check point is reached. When the master routine is as shown in Figure 20-1 the addresses of certain of the transfer orders are altered so that a jump to the "driver" is made instead. Commonly the altered transfer orders and the driver are on a second tape (an overwrite tape) which is read in after the main program. To facilitate the reading of an overwrite tape the main program tape should end with the following sequence of orders:

$$24 \ 999N$$
$$26 \ (0.1)$$
$$26 \ 1N$$

Here the 24 999N stop permits one to put the overwrite tape into the reader and read it in with SADOT. Alternatively, if no overwrite is desired then a black switch start will cause execution of the program to begin.

A subroutine in the ILLIAC program library, program D1, permits a very flexible dynamic checking procedure. A description of the properties of this subroutine is in Appendix 11, pp. 339-343.

Another checking procedure is commonly used in which the driver simply stores the results obtained from the test data in an unused portion of the memory. After the subroutine has processed the test data, the driver causes a STOP to occur.

The results which have been stored away are then read by one of the post-mortem routines available in the ILLIAC library. They permit a desired portion of the memory, WM or drum, to be printed in different forms; the words may be printed as decimal integers, decimal fractions, order pairs with sexadecimal function digits and decimal address, etc. When a program is being checked the most common occurrence is an unexpected stop, a zero left shift, a : hangup, or the program goes into a loop (i.e. it executes a set of instructions over and over again without termination). To locate the cause of this failure a post-mortem of the program is made. This involves running one or more of the post-mortem routines while the "dead" program (i.e. the program that has just failed) is still in the ILLIAC. A description of the post-mortem routines that are available is provided in Appendix 12, pp. 344-58 and Appendix 13, pp. 359-63.

In using the post-mortem routines a common oversight is to neglect to get all of the desired information printed out; for example the programmer may have the block of words at location 100 to 140 printed as integers only to find out later, after his program has been erased from the ILLIAC, that he also needs the integers in locations 140 to 150. To avoid wasting time, and to insure getting the maximum amount of information out of each code check the programmer should carefully write out in advance the memory locations of all of the words he might want to print out in a post-mortem.

Finally a remark about removing errors from a program. When a program failure occurs, the programmer, usually with the assistance of information gained from a post-mortem, begins a sleuthing job which should ultimately locate an error. Now it may be that the error found does not appear to entirely explain the failure. Before proceeding, however, it is generally worthwhile to remove the error just found and repeat the test. It will frequently be found that this one error just removed does indeed completely explain the failure, and if not it is usually the case that the remaining errors will be found more easily. In other words it is usually best to remove the errors one by one, repeating each code check after removing the suspected error. When errors are located one should be very careful in removing them for it is amazing how easy it is to create more than one new error by the removal of one old error.

UNIVERSITY OF ILLINOIS
DIGITAL COMPUTER
CHAPTER 21

ILLIAC STORAGE UNITS

In this chapter the two memory units of the Illiac, the Williams
memory and the drum storage unit, will be discussed. The use of the Williams
memory (WM) has already been thoroughly discussed on the preceding pages, so
that the following brief description will involve only the physical characteristics
of the WM. The reader is referred to references (2) and (3) (Chapter 1) for a
more detailed discussion of Williams Tube storage devices.[1] The major part of
our attention in this chapter will be directed toward the drum storage unit.

The basic element of a Williams memory unit is the cathode ray tube.
One end of the cathode ray tube holds an electron "gun", an emitter of electrons,
and certain elements for focusing the emitted stream of electrons on any point at
the other end of the tube which has a coating of phosphorescent material. When the
electrons strike the phosphorescent material they give up energy to it and cause
the material to emit light. The Williams memory device does not make use of the
light emitting properties of the phosphor. A small positively charged spot is
created on the phosphor when the electron beam strikes it and this charge will
remain for a short while even after the beam is turned off.[2] A bit of information
can be stored on the phosphor surface by assigning two close-together points on
the surface to one bit and letting a 1 be represented when one of the points is
positive relative to its neighbor and letting a 0 be represented by the inverse
situation, i.e. the neighbor relatively positive. The stored information is "read"
in the following way. A conducting screen is attached to the outside of the tube

[1] The Williams Tube memory belongs to the class of storage devices known as
electrostatic storage devices.

[2] One might think a negative charge should be created instead; however, when the
electrons strike the phosphor they cause electrons to be emitted (secondary
emission) by the phosphor leaving a net positive charge.

at the end having the phosphorescent coating (which is on the inside surface of the tube). To read a bit the electron beam is directed at one of the two points (always the same one) representing the bit and a pulse of current (caused by the redistribution of charge at the surface of the phosphor) is sensed in a wire connected to the conducting screen; the polarity of the pulse depends on whether or not the point at which the beam was directed was the point of the pair that was relatively positive. Reading is destructive; that is, the information that was there may be destroyed by the act of reading, so it is necessary to write the old information anew after reading. Writing information into storage is achieved simply by directing the beam at one of the two points associated with a bit depending on whether a 1 or a 0 is to be written.

The WM of the Illiac is comprised of 40 of these tubes, one tube corresponding to each digital position. The surface of the tube is divided into 1024 point-pairs, one point-pair for each memory location. The point-pairs are arranged in a regular pattern -- a square lattice with 32 point-pairs on a side. With this arrangement it is possible to write or read information by aiming the electron beam in each of the 40 tubes at the spot corresponding to the memory location involved; it is thus possible to read or write digits in a parallel manner.

Now the small charged spots will change with time because of leakage of the charge; therefore the spots must be periodically refreshed. There is a unit in Illiac which keeps the memory continually refreshed; this is done in a systematic way, reading the information in each memory location and writing it back, thus keeping it fresh. This process is known as regeneration. The time taken to regenerate the information in one location is sometimes called a "clock period" or a "basic memory cycle" and it is equal to about 18.5 μsec. Whenever access to the memory for reading or writing is necessary (e.g. for reading order pairs, writing information via a type 4 order, etc.) the current memory cycle must be completed before access to the memory is permitted.

When the same location in the memory is referred to repeatedly the points in the neighborhood of the point representing this location get sprayed with a small amount of electric charge and the information in these neighboring points may be destroyed as a result. The number of times a specific location may be thus referred to before information in a neighboring point is changed is known as the read-around-ratio; this is a statistical quantity and the average value is quite high, about 350. This ratio is so high that before information is lost in a neighboring location because of read-around a complete regeneration of the memory is usually executed and the neighboring points are refreshed. This is not true for all computers. In many computers having the Williams tube memory read-around is a serious problem; in writing codes the coder has to be careful not to refer to the same region in the memory too frequently during the regeneration period for the whole memory. From the standpoint of high read-around-ratio the Illiac is one of the most reliable computers with a Williams tube memory.

It has been mentioned several times previously that the Illiac has an auxiliary memory device, a drum storage unit. Let us now turn our attention to it. The fundamental parts of this unit are a cylinder (length = 15 inches, radius = 4.25 inches) coated with a magnetic material and mounted so that it can be rotated at high speed by a motor; a set of writing heads, devices mounted in a framework around the rotating cylinder, which can induce a small magnetized spot on the surface of the cylinder; a set of reading heads, devices also mounted in a framework around the rotating cylinder, which can sense the magnetized spots on the surface of the drum created by the writing heads. The reading and writing heads correspond to the devices which perform a similar function in a tape recorder. The writing heads of the drum create a magnetized spot on the surface of the drum with the direction of the magnetization having just two possible values corresponding to the writing of a 1 or 0. The reading heads can sense the direction of the magnetization and thus detect whether a 1 or 0 is stored. Unlike the WM, reading the drum does not destroy the information stored there.

The surface of the drum is subdivided into 200 tracks; each track can be regarded as an imaginary circle drawn around the surface of the cylinder as shown below in Figure 21-1. The tracks are numbered 0, 1, 2, ..., 199. Associated with each track is a writing head and a reading head. Each track is divided into 64 sectors. Each sector comprises enough space to record 40 magnetized spots along the track by the associated writing head; thus, each sector represents one Illiac word. A drum location or drum address corresponds to a particular word position on the drum; that is, it corresponds to a particular track and sector. Fourteen binary digits are necessary to represent all possible drum addresses: $2^{14} = 16,384$. The following addressing scheme is adopted: the least significant six digits of the fourteen digit address specify the sector number and the remaining eight digits specify the track number.

It will be noticed that the sectors are not numbered consecutively along the track. Consecutively numbered sectors are separated by four sectors. The order pattern for the numbering of the sectors should be obvious from Figure 21-1. With this arrangement of consecutive drum locations it is said that the locations are interlaced. The reason for the interlacing will soon become clear.

A type 8 order is used to read (playback) information from the drum and write (record) information onto the drum. The drum orders require a complete 40 digit word rather than just a half word as required by all other kinds of orders. The structure of the drum orders is as follows.

Let $\quad w = w_0 \, w_1 \, w_2 \, \cdots \, w_{39}$

be the usual representation for an ILLIAC word. To record the contents of the accumulator onto drum location p the order has the form

$$\underbrace{w_0 \, w_1 \, w_2 \, \cdots \, w_7}_{} = 1000 \ 0110 = 86_S$$

LH function digits

$w_8 \, w_9 \qquad\qquad$ are ignored as usual

$$\underbrace{w_{10} \, w_{11} \, w_{12} \, \cdots \, w_{19}}_{} = 00 \ 0000 \ 1011 = 11_D$$

LH address digits

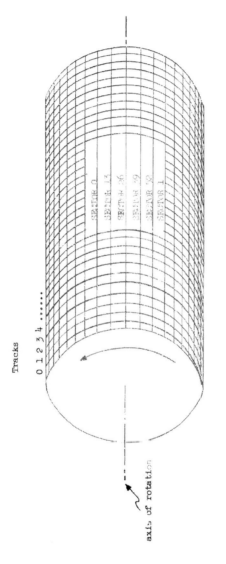

Tracks

0 1 2 3 4 ......

SECTOR 0
SECTOR 13
SECTOR 26
SECTOR 39
SECTOR 52
SECTOR 1

axis of rotation

Figure 21-1

A schematic of the drum showing the orientation of the tracks.

$$w_{20}\ w_{21}\ w_{22}\ \cdots\ w_{25} = 000000 \qquad \text{(normal form)}$$

RH function digits <u>except</u> V_1 and V_2

$$w_{26}\ w_{27}\ w_{28}\ \cdots\ w_{39} = p, \text{ drum location into which information is recorded.}^{*}$$

Thus, the order pair to record the contents of A into location $2,500_D$ of the drum is written in SADOI notation as

    86 11F

    00 2500F

To playback the contents of drum location p into the accumulator the order has the form

$$w_0\ w_1\ w_2\ \cdots\ w_7 = 1000\ 0101 = 85_S$$

LH function digits

$$w_8\ w_9 \qquad \text{are ignored as usual}$$

$$w_{10}\ w_{11}\ w_{12}\ \cdots\ w_{19} = 00\ 0000\ 1011 = 11_D$$

LH address digits

$$w_{20}\ w_{21}\ w_{22}\ \cdots\ w_{25} = 000000 \qquad \text{(normal form)}$$

RH function digits <u>except</u> V_1 and V_2

$$w_{26}\ w_{27}\ w_{28}\ \cdots\ w_{39} = p, \text{ drum location from which playback is to be made.}^{*}$$

Thus, the order pair to playback the contents of location $2,500_D$ on the drum into A is written in SADOI notation as

    85 11F

    00 2500F   .

---

*   If $12,800_D \leqslant p \leqslant 16,383_D$, ILLIAC will stop.

There are several points to be made about the structure of these orders. Notice that the left-hand address digits are equal to 11 (decimal). This must be so for proper operation of these orders (there are certain unusual cases in which the left-hand address digits may be different than 11 but they are of no practical use). Notice that the two least significant function digits of the right half-word, namely V_1 and V_2, are used as the most significant digits of the drum address. Finally, observe that digits $w_{28} w_{29}$, which in all other orders are ignored, are here used as part of the drum address digits.

Execution of the record order causes eleven left shifts of AQ. Thus, unlike storing information in the WM, where the contents of AQ are not altered by the store operation, the storing of information on the drum does cause an alteration of the contents of AQ. Similarly the execution of the playback order involves 11 left shifts of AQ; so, on completion of the playback instruction, the contents of Q will have been shifted 11 places to the left. (In this left shift the digits shifted out of the left end of Q do not go into A, as is also the case with the other 8 orders)

Certain variations of the form of the orders given above are permitted. The most important variation is the following: if $w_{21} = 1$ or $w_{22} = 1$ then the right half-word will be executed as an order immediately following the execution of the drum order. In this case the drum address is interpreted modulo $8192 = 2^{13}$. For example the word, written in SADOI notation,

> 85 11F
> 40 2500F

when executed as an order will first cause a playback of the contents of drum location 2,500. Following this the right half-word will be executed as a normal 40 order, and the contents of A will be stored in the WM location 2500 (mod 1024) = 452. The net effect of these two operations is then to transfer the contents of location 2,500 on the drum into location 452 in the WM. The right half-word will always be thus executed as an order except when the T digit is 0, 1, 8 or 9 (i.e. except when $T_2 = T_4 = 0$). Thus, the following pairs of orders are equivalent

162

to each other and to the above orders wherein the store order is combined with
the drum order in a single word.

85 11F	85 11F
00 2500F	80 2500F
40 452F	40 452F

In making use of this feature one must be careful to take into account the fact
that w_{27} plays a double role: it is the least significant variant digit of the
RH order and also the most significant digit of the drum address.

Other acceptable variations in the form of the drum order include
$V_1 = 7$, J, L. 87 and 8L are record orders, like 86, but 87 first clears
A ($V_1 = 1$) and 8L first sets A = 1/2 ($V_8 = V_1 = 1$). 8J has exactly the same
effect as the 85 order. Some other variations are possible but appear to have
little utility.

When using a drum storage device the timing of memory references
becomes an important consideration. It should be fairly evident from the
preceding physical description of the drum that recording into a given drum
address or playing back from a given drum address can only occur when the
rotating drum is in a certain phase of its rotation, namely when the sector
on the drum surface corresponding to the address in question is under the
recording or reading heads for the track corresponding to this address. If
an order to record is given, the ILLIAC waits until the drum is in position for
recording into the proper address. Now the time required for one revolution
of the drum is 16.9 milliseconds; consequently, if the order to record, say

86 11F

00 pF

is given just after location p has passed under the recording heads, the ILLIAC must wait one revolution time, namely 16.9 ms., until the location p is again in position for recording. On the average, for a location selected at random, the waiting time is just half this, i.e. $\frac{1}{2}$ (16.9) = 8.45 ms. These times are long on the ILLIAC time scale since 16.9 ms. is enough time to execute many standard orders (187 add orders can be executed in 16.9 ms.). It therefore becomes desirable to attempt to minimize the waiting time when executing drum orders. This is achieved by transferring words between the drum and WM in blocks rather than one at a time in a random fashion. Block transfers are efficient because it will be observed that successive sectors and thus successive drum addresses follow each other closely -- thus shortly after sector 0 passes under the recording heads, sector 1 passes under the recording heads and so forth. Consequently, if we do a series of record operations, say record into drum address 1000, record into drum address 1001, record into drum address 1002, etc., we may have to wait 16.9 ms. for location 1000 to come under the recording head but after this the waiting time is short because location 1001 closely follows location 1000 under the recording head, and similarly for 1002, and so forth. Let us now be more specific about these waiting times.

The time required for the digits of one word (one sector interval) to pass a reading or recording head is 0.264 ms. (Notice that 64 x 0.264 ms = 16.9 ms = the time for one revolution of the drum.) Let us consider now a particular drum address $\underline{d}$ and let d correspond to sector $\underline{s}$, track $\underline{t}$. The connections between the ILLIAC and the drum require that an instruction to read from d or write into d must be given one sector interval before sector s is to pass under the reading or writing head for track t -- thus there is an enforced delay of 0.264 ms. Once sector s comes under the reading head it takes .264 ms for all of the digits of this word to pass the head. Immediately after the digits of s have passed under the head the execution of the drum order is complete. Consequently the <u>minimum</u> time taken for the execution of a drum order is two sector intervals or 0.528 ms. If the drum order is given <u>just after</u> the sector preceding s has started to pass under the head then a complete revolution of the drum must take place before s will be in proper position to initiate the execution of the drum order. Thus the maximum time for execution of the drum order is 16.9 + 0.53 = 17.43 ms.

It will be observed in Figure 21-1 that successively numbered sectors are separated by four sector intervals. Suppose we wish to record into sector s, s + 1, and s + 2 of track t. The time taken to record into s will be at least 0.53 ms and at most 17.43 ms. as observed above. Let us assume that recording into s has just been completed. If the order to record into s + 1 is given within the next three sector intervals then this recording can take place without waiting for a full revolution of the drum; if this is done then completion of recording into s + 1 occurs just five sector intervals, or 5 x 0.264 = 1.32 ms, after completion of recording into s. Similarly, after recording into s + 1 one can execute recording into s + 2 without waiting for a whole drum revolution if the order to record into s + 2 is given within three sector intervals after recording into s + 1 has been completed. Notice that the time within which the next record order must be given is three sector intervals rather than four sector intervals; this is because of the enforced delay of one sector interval, mentioned earlier. It is thus possible to record words into successive drum locations at a rate of 1.32 ms. per word (5 x 0.264 = 1.32). The time delays between successive drum locations are the same as just described even when successive drum locations are on different tracks. The foregoing remarks apply to playback as well as recording.

The three sector intervals, 0.792 ms., which may occur before the next record order must be given to achieve the maximum recording rate, are free for executing any ILLIAC orders that may be desired. For example it is common to use this time for bookkeeping operations which must take place between successive drum record operations. The only requirement for achieving the maximum recording rate is that the successive record orders be given within three sector intervals of each other. Because of this requirement it is clear that one must know how to compute the operation time for a sequence of ILLIAC orders.

For the computation of operation times for these purposes it is best to compute the time in units of the basic WM regeneration cycle (18.5 ms) or clock period. The times in these units for the various ILLIAC operations are listed below.

OPERATION	TIME
Readout of each order pair	2
Order types K, S, F, L	4
Order types 2, 4, 5, J	
and 3 when control is transferred	2
Order types 85, 86 and 3	
when control is <u>not</u> transferred	0

Notice especially the first entry in this table. The act of reading out the order pair must be allotted a time equal to 2 clock periods. The times listed are maximum times. The use of these times in computing the operation time for a section of code will be illustrated in examples which follow.

Example 1. Let us assume that a list of 200 numbers x_0, x_1, x_2, ..., x_{199} is stored on the drum in location 3,500 to 3,699 and that this list is to be read from the drum and placed in the WM locations 500 to 699. The code follows.

	WM	Order Pairs	Comments
		00 10K	
	0	15 8L	Initialize drum
		40 2L	read (x_i address = x_0 address)
	1	15 7L	Initialize WM
		42 3L	x_i address.
②	2	85 11F	from 6L
			read x_i from drum
		00 3500F	by L, 4L
⑥	3	50 F	waste
		40 [500]F	store x_i in WM, by 1L, 5L
⑧	4	F5 2L	advance x_i drum
		40 2L	address

(Continued on Page 166)

	WM	Order Pairs	Comments
(8)	5	F5 3L 42 3L	 $i' = i + 1$
(8)	6	LO 9L 36 2L	end test transfer if $i \leq 199$
	7	OF F OO 500F	STOP. $(i = 200)$ R.A. to initialize 3.
	8	85 11F OO 3500F	Constant to initialize drum read.
	9	JO F 40 700F	End Const.

The order at 2L (i.e. 12F) reads an x_i from the drum. The order at 3L
(i.e. 13F) stores the x_i read from the drum into the WM. The addresses of both
of these orders are modified. Notice that in the modification of the drum playback instruction the modified address is restored with a 40 order rather than with
a 42 order. In the present example a 42 order would have worked just as well but
in general a 42 order will not work for this purpose because the address being
modified involves the digits $w_{26} \, w_{27} \, w_{28} \cdots w_{39}$, not just $w_{30} \, w_{31} \cdots w_{39}$, which
are the only ones changed by a 42 order. It is therefore good practice always
to use a 40 order in this instance even though in certain particular cases it may
not be needed.

A computation of the time between successive drum read instructions
has been made. The time for the execution for each order pair is given by the
encircled number to the left of the order pair. This time includes the readout time for the order pair. Thus for the order pair at 3L the time is 6 clock
periods; 2 for readout of the order pair, 2 for execution of the 50 order and 2
for execution of the 40 order. The total time between successive drum read
instructions is seen to be $2 + 6 + 8 + 8 + 8 = 32$. This time must be less than
three sector intervals, or .792 ms.; .792 ms = 42.8 clock periods -- a safe
approximation to three sector periods is then 42 clock periods. Since $32 < 42$
we conclude that readout of the x_i's will be executed in the optimum time.

It is common in transferring lists of numbers between the drum and WM to include a self checking feature known as a check sum computation which will indicate whether or not the transfer of digits has been executed correctly. Examples showing the use of this self checking feature follow.

Example 2. In this example we consider a code which will transfer a list of 200 numbers x_0, x_1, ... x_{199} from the WM locations 500 to 699 into the drum locations 3,500 to 3,699. The check sum (CKS) is computed according to the following iteration procedure:

$$S_{-1} = 0$$
$$S_i = x_i + |S_{i-1}|$$

and the 1's complement of S_{199} is stored at the end of the list, location 3,700.

WM	Order Pairs	Comments
	00 10K	
0	L5 12L	Initialize record
	40 5L	instruction
1	L5 11L	Initialize WM x_i
	42 2L	call address
2 ⑥	41 1F	clear CKS box from 8L
	L5 [500]	$a' = x_i$; by 1L, 7L
3 ⑧	40 F	temp. store x_i
	L6 1F	$x_i + |S_{i-1}|$
4 ⑧	40 1F	store partial CKS = S_i
	L5 F	$a' = x_i$
5 ②	86 11F	record x_i
	00 3500F	by L, 6L

(Continued on page 168)

WM	Order Pairs	Comments
⑨ 6	F5 5L 40 5L	increment x_i drum address
⑧ 7	F5 2L 42 2L	increment x_i WM address
⑧ 8	L0 13L 32 2L	End test transfer if not end
9	50 F F1 1F	waste a' = 1's complement of CKS $= -CKS - 2^{-39}$
10	86 11F 00 3700F	record "CKS" at end of the list.
11	0F F 00 500F	STOP R.A. equals initialization const.
12	86 11F 00 3500F	initialization constant for record instruction
13	N1 1F L5 700F	End constant

The orders at 2, 3 and 4 (relative) are used to compute the check sum. After recording of the list is complete the orders at 9 and 10 (relative) are used to record the digitwise complement of the CKS on the drum.

<u>There is a serious defect in the above code.</u> Notice that the time between successive executions of the record instruction is 48 clock periods, greater than the permitted maximum (42) for optimum execution time. Therefore the execution of the above orders will be significantly slowed down, since a full drum revolution will occur between each recording.

An alternative code is given below which will achieve the same result as the above code but the recording is performed in optimum time.

WM	Order Pairs	Comments
	00 10K	
0	L5 14L	initialize x_i
	42 1L	call address
1	41 F	Clear CKS box
		by L, 3L; from 4L
	L5 [500]F	Form CKS
2	16 F	$x_i + |S_{i-1}| = S_i$
	40 F	Store S_i
3	F5 1L	Advance x_i
	42 1L	call address
4	LC 16L	CKS end test
	32 1L	transfer if CKS not complete
5	L5 15L	here when CKS formed
	40 8L	initialize record order
6	L5 14L	initialize x_i
	42 7L	call address.
(6) 7	50 F	waste
		from 11L
	L5 [500]F	$a' = x_i$; by 6L, 10L
(2) 8	[86 1LF	record x_i
	00 3500F]	by 5L, 9L
(8) 9	F5 8L	advance record
	40 8L	address.
(8) 10	F5 7L	advance x_i
	42 7L	call advance
(8) 11	LO 17L	end test
	32 7L	transfer if recording not done

(Continued on page 170)

WM	Order Pairs	Comments
12	50 F	waste
	F1 F	a' = 1's complement of CKS $= -CKS - 2^{-39}$
13	86 11F	record $-CKS - 2^{-39}$
	00 3700F	
14	0F F	STOP
	00 500F	initialization const.
15	86 11F	initialization const.
	00 3500F	for record order.
16	N1 F	end const. in
	L5 700F	CKS calculation.
17	J0 F	end const. for
	L5 700F	recording.

In the foregoing code it is seen that the check sum calculation is done separately, in advance of the recording. Now there is sufficient time in the recording loop (namely 32 clock periods) to perform the recording in optimum time.

Suppose we now wish to read the list of x_i's back into the WM, then the CKS is used to check that the x_i's played back are the same as those recorded. The playback of the x_i's with checking is executed in the following example.

Example 3. Here we present a code to read the list of x_i's stored on the drum in the preceding example. The x_i's are read into locations 500 to 699 to the WM. A check sum test is made. The code follows.

WM	Order Pair	Comments
	00 10K	
0	15 13L	initialize drum
	40 3L	read order
1	15 2L	initialize x_i store
	42 4L	order
2	41 F	clear new CKS box
	50 500F	initialization const. in R.A.
3 ②	85 11F ⎤	from 8L
		playback x_i
	00 3500F ⎦	by L, 6L
4 ⑥	50 F	waste
	40 [500]F	store x_i, by 1L, 7L
5 ⑧	16 F	form new CKS
	40 F	
6 ⑧	F5 3L	advance x_i
	40 3L	playback address
7 ⑧	F5 4L	advance x_i store
	42 4L	address
8 ⑧	L0 14L	end test
	36 3L	jump if playback not done
9	85 11F	read old $-CKS - 2^{-39}$
	00 3700F	
10	F4 F	$\underbrace{-CKS - 2^{-39}}_{\text{old}} + \underbrace{CKS + 2^{-39}}_{\text{new}}$
	40 F	

(Continued on page 172)

WM	Order Pairs	Comments
11	L3 F	
	32 12L	Jump if old CRK = new CKS
12	FF F	CKS Error STOP
	OF F	Normal STOP
13	85 11F	initialization
	00 55005F	const. for reading.
14	J0 F	end test const.
	40 700F	

In this example it is observed that a new check sum is computed; the orders at 5L do this. When playback of the x_i's is complete then the old CKS is played back, the order at 9L, and it is compared against the new CKS. If the two check sums differ then the error stop FF (this order stops the computer) is encountered. If the two check sums agree then the normal OF stop is encountered.

Agreement of the two check sums does not guarantee that an alteration of the x_i's has not occurred between the recording and playback operations. However the probability is very small that the x_i's would be changed without an alteration of the check sum.

The reason that the digitwise complement of the CKS is stored rather than the CKS itself is to provide a safeguard against the possibility that all the numbers, including the CKS, are cleared to zero. The reason for the absolute magnitude addition is that it makes a single digit error tend to affect the check sum in all digits. With a conventional summation, for example

$$CKS = x_0 + x_1 + \ldots + x_{199} ,$$

a pair of digit errors, in the same digit position of numbers x_i and x_j can compensate each other and cause no alteration in the CKS; for example, if a 1 changes to a 0 in digit position k of x_i and if a 0 changes to a 1 in digit position k of x_j, the CKS is unaltered. However, with the CKS computed as it is in example 2 such "compensating" errors can affect the CKS.

There are subroutines in the ILLIAC program library for transferring information between the WM and drum in optimum time with computation of the check sum. These routines are Y1 and Y5; a description of Y5 is in Appendix 20.

UNIVERSITY OF ILLINOIS
DIGITAL COMPUTER
CHAPTER 22

LIBRARY SUBROUTINES

Many routines, for example routines to compute sin x, $\sqrt{x}$, etc., are
used so frequently that it is worthwhile to write them once and for all and save
them in a central place so that anyone who later needs to use one of them in a
program may simply copy it. At the Digital Computer Laboratory, there is a large
collection of these frequently used subroutines known as the ILLIAC Program
Library. An index to the subroutines currently available in this library is
in Appendix 14, pp. 364-367.

Associated with each routine in the library is a write-up describing
the properties of the routine and how the routine is to be used; an annotated
copy of the code is included with this write-up. A teletype tape copy of the code
is also available in the library. (These items may be secured from the secretary
in the tape preparation room of the Digital Computer Laboratory.) Some of the
routines in the library are actually complete programs. For example, K3, the "Least
Squares" program, is a complete program; the user must only prepare a tape on which
the experimental data is punched and K3 will "read" this data tape and compute and
print the coefficients of the "least squares polynomial". Another example of a
complete program in the library is J2, a program for computing the roots of a
polynomial; here again the user need only prepare a data tape (as specified in
the program write-up) which contains the coefficients of the polynomial and J2 will
"read" this data tape and compute and print the roots of the polynomial. The
library tape copies of closed subroutines are in a form in which they may be directly
copied onto the users' program tape by means of a tape reperforator.

There are certain general rules which apply to the use of the library
subroutines. A standard closed subroutine entry, as described in Chapter 16, is
always to be used unless it is explicitly stated otherwise in the subroutine write-
up. If only one item of data must be supplied to the subroutine (e.g., x for the

square root subroutine to compute $\sqrt{x}$) then it is to be in the accumulator at the time entry is made into the subroutine. If only one item is generated by the subroutine (e.g. $\sqrt{x}$) then it is in the accumulator at the time the exit from the subroutine is made. Variations from these general rules are always explicitly stated in the write-up of the subroutine.

Let us now consider the write-up of a particular library subroutine, namely T4, the Arctan x Subroutine. A copy of the write-up appears on the following page as Figure 22-1; a copy of the code itself is not included. The format for this write-up is typical of most subroutines in the library. The TYPE of routine is specified in the second line, just below the TITLE, and the word "closed" means that this is a closed subroutine. The NUMBER OF WORDS in the subroutine is given on the third line; this subroutine occupies 25 words of the WM. The next line is labeled TEMPORARY STORAGE; it gives the WM locations used by the routine for temporary storage; here it is seen that locations 0, 1, and 2 are used for temporary storage by the program. An error commonly made in using library subroutines is to store a word in a location used as temporary storage by the subroutine and then assume that the word is still there after the subroutine has been used; the word is, of course, no longer there because the subroutine will have overwritten it in using the location for temporary storage. The next line, labeled ACCURACY, describes the precision of the arctan x computed by this subroutine; we see that the maximum error in arctan x is $\pm 2^{-35}$. The next line, labeled DURATION, gives the execution time for this subroutine (i.e., the time between entry and exit); we see that it takes 20 milliseconds to do the arctangent calculation. Following this, a brief description of the method employed by the subroutine is given. It is understood, since there is no statement to the contrary, that the standard closed subroutine entry is to be used. When entry to the subroutine is made, x is in the accumulator, and upon exit from the subroutine, arctan x is in the accumulator.

UNIVERSITY OF ILLINOIS
DIGITAL COMPUTER

LIBRARY ROUTINE T 4 - 140

TITLE	Arctan x Subroutine
TYPE	Closed
NUMBER OF WORDS	25
TEMPORARY STORAGE	0, 1, 2
ACCURACY	Maximum error $\pm\, 2^{-35}$
DURATION	20 milliseconds
DESCRIPTION	Computes arctan x for $-1 \leq x < 1$ by means of a power series involving Tchebyscheff polynomials,

$$\arctan x \;=\; \sum_{i=0}^{27} a_i T_i(x), \text{ where } a_i = 0 \text{ for i even or}$$

where $a_i \;=\; (-1)^{i+3/2}\, (2/i)(\sqrt{2}-1)^i$ for i odd.

(See Hahn, Tables d' Integrales Definis, Table 370,7,8).
Combining coefficients of corresponding powers of x
yields

$$\arctan x \;=\; \sum_{i=0}^{14} C_{2i-1}\, x^{2i-1} .$$

In use, this routine replaces A by arctan A.

Figure 22-1

It is not always necessary to copy a needed library subroutine onto the program tape. Certain of the most commonly used library subroutines are permanently stored on the drum, and it is possible to punch a set of characters on the program tape which will instruct SADOI to read the subroutine from the drum and assemble it into the program.

The first 40 tracks of the drum, that is the first 2,560 drum locations, are used for permanent storage. (This is achieved by disconnecting the writing heads for these tracks--after the desired "permanent" programs have been written into these tracks. The reading heads remain connected, of course.) Certain of the frequently used subroutines[1] are stored on these tracks; also certain of the engineering test programs, and post-mortem routines are stored in this "blocked-off" portion of the drum. If a program erroneously tries to execute a record order having a drum address in this region (0 to 2,559), nothing will be written on the drum; the ILLIAC will not hang up when such a record order is attempted.

SADOI is instructed to assemble into the program one of the library routines on the drum by giving an outside symbolic address to a directive where the symbolic address is the label of the program [e.g., (P16), (Y1), etc.], and the directive specifies where the subroutine is to be loaded; this is called a modified directive. For example, if the library subroutine INFRAPRINT is to be assembled into a program at location 100_D, one would write the following characters on the tape:

(P16)   00 100K

The library subroutine label for INFRAPRINT is P16, hence, one writes the outside address (P16). The directive will cause P16 to be assigned to a block in the WM beginning at location 100_D. Furthermore, the first word in this subroutine will be treated as if it had the outside symbolic address (P16). Thus, entry to P16 can be written as follows in the program:

p	50 p
	26 (P16)
p + 1	-- -- -- --

---

[1] The library subroutines currently on the drum are: P16, Y1, R1, S4, T4, T5, F1, S5, N12, A6, A1, A3, RA1, TA1, SA2, SA3, TA2, A6 (except XA_1).

In fact, any word in P16 can be referred to in the usual way; thus, one can refer to the nth word of P16 by writing the address,

    n(P16)   .

A problem that comes up in assembling a large program composed of a number of subroutines is the assignment of the various subroutines to particular portions of the WM. This assignment is made most efficiently if all of the subroutines and the master routine are assigned to consecutive locations in the memory-- that is, there are no "holes" between parts of the program. If small holes are left between parts of the program, then it may not be possible to get all parts of a long program in the WM when, at the same time, if the holes were closed up, it would be possible to get the entire program into the WM. To achieve this efficient packing, one can carefully count the number of words in each part of the program and assign these word blocks to consecutive regions of the memory by giving the necessary directive address at the start of each part of the program. This assignment process is tedious and subject to error, but fortunately enough, it can be circumvented with SADOI. Consider a program composed of 8 parts: 6 subroutines, a master routine and a block of constants. We will assume that three of the subroutines are library subroutines, namely P16, T4 and R1. The other three subroutines will be labeled simply 1, 2 and 3. If we begin the program at location 100, an efficient packing is achieved by writing the programs on the tape as indicated schematically below.

00100K

| Constants |

(P16) 00K
(T4)   00K
(R1)   00K

00K

| Part 0
Master |

00K

| Part 1 |

00K

| Part 2 |

00K

| Part 3 |

24999N
26(0.1)
24 1N

From the earlier discussion of SADOI it will be recognized that the directive 00K achieves the desired result of packing the parts of the program into successive blocks of the WM. The block of constants and the subroutines are given first on the tape in order to reduce the number of forward address references.

In the above example, one must, of course, be careful not to exceed the capacity of the memory. Only for programs in which the total number of words falls very close to the total capacity of the memory does one need to be careful about an exact word-count. It should be remembered in this connection that SADOI only automatically assembles the program into locations 2-998, inclusive, of the WM. Words assigned to WM locations beyond 998 will be assembled onto the drum according to the usual correspondence rule,

drum address = 11,756 + WM address,

but these words will <u>not</u> be read back from the drum and placed in the WM when the N termination symbol is read.

Library subroutines and, in fact, all standard closed subroutines require the specification of at least one parameter, namely the link address; thus, the standard entry has the parameter p

p	-- ---
	50 p ⟵————Link address
p + 1	26 (address of subroutine)
	-- ---

Many subroutines require more than this one parameter. The parameters which are required fall into two classes, called program parameters and preset parameters. The former is a number which appears in the body of the program and which may be modified <u>while the program is running</u>. An example of the use of such a parameter is provided by the library subroutine R2 which computes $x^{1/\alpha}$ where α is an integer and x is the number in the accumulator at the time of entry to R2. The parameter α is supplied to the subroutine by making the entry in the following way:

p	50 α
	50 p
p + 1	26 (R2)

Thus, at the time of entry α is in the left-hand address digits of Q upon entry to R2. After entry, R2 "reads" the left address digits of Q to mean that the $(\frac{1}{\alpha})^{th}$ root of the number in A is to be computed. Now suppose that the above entry to R2 occurs as part of a loop and that on successive entries to the loop we want different roots: $\frac{1}{\alpha}$, $\frac{1}{\alpha'}$, $\frac{1}{\alpha''}$, etc., then on each pass through the loop the left-hand address at location p is successively modified to read α, α', α'', etc. A parameter which is thus specified <u>within</u> the program (it does not have to be an address; it may be an entire word, or a single bit) and may thus be modified while the program is running is called a program paramter.

The other type of parameter, the preset parameter, does not explicitly appear within the program. It commonly occurs as a parameter for a subroutine which remains constant during the running of the program, but it may be changed from one running of the program to the next. An example of the use of a preset parameter is provided by library routine V1 which computes a table of Legendre polynomials, $P_0(x)$, $P_1(x)$, $P_2(x)$, ... $P_n(x)$, storing them in a block of n + 1 locations of the memory. The location of the first word of the table, i.e., the location of $P_0(x)$, is specified by a preset parameter. In the subroutine, the table addresses are referred to by an S termination symbol; in particular, the first polynomial $P_0(x)$ has address S3 in the program. The real address, m, of $P_0(x)$ is set into location 3 by <u>preceding</u> the V1 subroutine on the tape by

> 00 3K
>
> 00 F   m = address of $P_0(x)$
> 00 mF

By this means it is possible to write the subroutine in a general way so that the polynomial table will be stored at any specified position in the memory. The location of the table is preset by a parameter <u>during the read-in</u> of the program. The parameter is <u>not</u> used during the running of the program to change the location

of the table. A parameter used to thus preset things during the read-in of a
program is called a preset parameter. Further examples of the use of preset parameters
will appear later.

UNIVERSITY OF ILLINOIS
DIGITAL COMPUTER
CHAPTER 23

A COMPLETE PROGRAM AND THE USE OF INFRAPRINT

In this chapter a short program to compute and print a table of square roots of the integers 1 to 99 is presented. This program is used for public demonstrations of the Illiac.

The program is presented on the following page. Two library subroutines are used in this program, namely R1 and P16. R1 is the square root subroutine[1] and P16 is a printing subroutine known as INFRAPRINT; write-ups of these sub-routines are in Appendices 16 and 17. Both of these subroutines are among the subroutines permanently stored on the drum and we see here the modified directive appear at the start of the program for instructing SADOI to read a library subroutine from the drum and assemble it into the program. The P16 sub-routine will be loaded into a block beginning at location 100 and the R1 subroutine will be loaded into a block beginning in the memory location immediately following the last word of P16.

Rules for use of R1 are straightforward. Entry is made in the standard way

p	-- -- -- --
	50 p
p + 1	26 (R1)
	-- -- -- --

from R1

with x in A; upon exit $\sqrt{x}$ is in A and control is transferred to the right hand order at p+1. Rules for the use of P16 are considerably more involved since P16 is a very flexible subroutine permitting a variety of output modes. The entire word at p is used for program parameters to specify the mode of output. In this

---

[1] A discussion of the numerical procedure used by R1 is presented in Chapter 24.

SQUARE ROOT DEMONSTRATION PROGRAM

LOCATION	ORDER		NOTES
	00 10K		
	(P16) 00 100K		
	(R1) 00 K		
	00 K		
0	(1) 41 (N)	from 16	N = 0
	92 131F	from 12	cr. and lf.
1	92 515F		delay
	92 967F		2 sp.
2	50 F		waste
	L5 (N)		
3	(1.1) J2 2F		
	50 (1.1)		
4	26 (P16)		Print N
	92 979F		5 sp.
5	41 F		least sig. part = 0
	50 (N)		$N \cdot 2^{-39}$
6	75 (1.5)		$(.01) \cdot N \cdot 2^{-39}$
	00 39F		$(.01) \cdot N$
7	(1.2) 50 F		waste
	50 (1.2)		
8	26 (R1)		$\sqrt{(.01) N} = \dfrac{\sqrt{N}}{10}$
	50 F		waste
9	J4 111F		
	(1.3) 50 (1.3)		
10	26 (P16)		Print $\sqrt{N}$
	F5 (N)		
11	40 (N)		N' = N + 1
	L0 (1.4)		

(Continued on page 184)

LOCATION	ORDER		NOTES
12	32 (1)		
	92 135F		2 lf. and cr.
13	92 515F		delay
	92 259F		letters
14	92 194F		E
	92 770F		N
15	92 67F		D
	92 707F		Nbr.
16	OF F		STOP
	26 (1)		START OVER
17	(1.4) 80 F		
	00 100F		END CONST.
18	(N) 00 F	by 11	
	00 F		
19	(1.5) 00 F		
	00 0100 0000 0000J		
	26(1) 261N		

square root demonstration program two entries are made to P16; on the first entry
an integer N, $0 \leq N \leq 99$, is printed; on the second entry $\sqrt{N}$ is printed. The
first jump to P16 takes place at the left hand order of location 4 (relative), and
the word at location 3 (relative) is used for program parameter specification. The
left hand order at location 3 (relative) is J2 2F. The first function digit, J, is
used to instruct P16 that the + sign is to be omitted on positive numbers; instead
of + a space character is printed. If this function digit had been 5 instead of
J, then the + sign would have been printed. The second function digit is 2 indicating
that the number in A at the time of entry to P16 is to be printed as an integer without
decimal point. The number of integer digits printed is specified in the address of
this order which is seen to be just 2. Leading zeros are suppressed, the zero being
printed as a space character; thus, the two digit integers

07
08
09
10
11

are printed as

7
8
9
10
11

On the second entry to P16, at location 9 (relative), the $\sqrt{N}$ is printed. When this entry to P16 is made the number in the accumulator is the fraction $\frac{\sqrt{N}}{10}$. Notice that the left hand order at 9 (relative) is J4 111F. The V digit equal to 4 specifies that the number in A is to be printed as a fraction, with decimal point. The address 111 specifies that the decimal point is to be located after the first digit (p = 1) and the fraction is to be printed to 11 digits (n = 11)*. Placement of the decimal point after the first digit in effect multiplies

$\frac{\sqrt{N}}{10}$ by 10 so that $\sqrt{N}$ is indeed correctly printed; had the number in A been $\frac{\sqrt{N}}{10^3}$, then we would have written the address 311 (rather than 111) to place the decimal point after the third digit of the fraction thereby achieving a multiplication by 10^3.

Let us now make some remarks about the number in A at the time of entry to R1 (jump at left side of 8, relative). The number in A is the fraction $\frac{N}{100}$ and upon exit from R1 the number in A is $\sqrt{\frac{N}{100}} = \frac{\sqrt{N}}{10}$. Notice that R1 is not entered with N in the accumulator as an integer, i.e. with $N \cdot 2^{-39}$ in the accumulator. If this had been done then the number in A upon exit from R1 would have been

---

* See the P16 write-up in Appendix 16, pp. 372-378.

$$\sqrt{N \cdot 2^{-39}} = \sqrt{N} \cdot 2^{-\frac{39}{2}} = \sqrt{N} \cdot \frac{2^{-19}}{\sqrt{2}}$$

This result would then have to be multiplied by $\frac{2^{19}}{10} \sqrt{2}$ to get $\frac{\sqrt{N}}{10}$ for printing by P16. This of course is inconvenient. Furthermore, and much more important, is the fact that the error in $\sqrt{N}$ would have been considerably greater if $N \cdot 2^{-39}$ had been taken, as will be seen in Chapter 24.

The first few lines of output from this program are given below.

SQUARE ROOT DEMONSTRATION PROGRAM

NUMBER	SQUARE ROOT
0	.0000000000
1	1.0000000000
2	1.4142135624
3	1.7320508076
4	2.0000000000

The lettered headings were achieved by beginning the program tape with the letter J followed by the desired letters; when the tape is thus headed by a J, a routine is called forth from the drum (not SADOI) which reads and causes a duplication on the output tape of all of the characters following the J until a 1-hole delay character is read. After the 1-hole delay is read, control is relinquished to another routine which reads the next non-fifth-hole character, called the key character, and depending upon this character one of a number of different things may happen; in particular, if the key character is 0 (the first character of the directive 00 nK) then SADOI is called into operation*.

The first directive, 00 10K, is necessary to get SADOI started. The directive address could have any value since it is immediately changed by the next line (P16) 00 100K which causes P16 to be loaded at 100. A program cannot begin with a directive having an outside symbolic address; e.g., this program could not begin (P16) 00 100K.

A copy of the first portion of the program tape is given below to illustrate how the desired lettering is specified on the program tape.

---

* See Appendix 10, pp. 330-338.

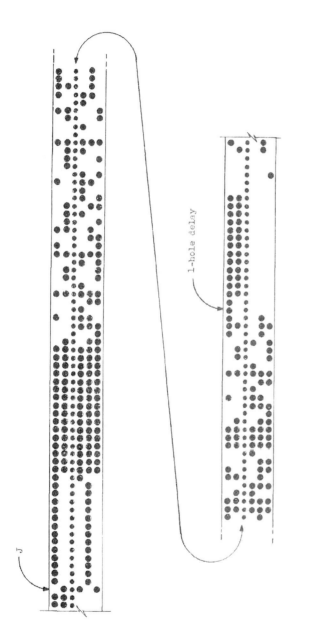

1-hole delay

Figure 23-1

Front end of square root demonstration tape.

UNIVERSITY OF ILLINOIS
DIGITAL COMPUTER
CHAPTER 24

NEWTON'S METHOD FOR THE COMPUTATION OF $\sqrt{a}$

In this chapter we will discuss Newton's method for the computation of $\sqrt{a}$. This method is used in the library subroutine R-1. A copy of the code is in Appendix 17, pp. 379-380.

The procedure for the computation of $x = \sqrt{a}$ is an iterative process described by the relations

$$x_0 = \frac{a}{2} + \frac{1}{2} , \tag{24-1}$$

$$x_{i+1} = x_i + \frac{1}{2} \left(\frac{a}{x_i} - x_i \right) . \tag{24-2}$$

The iteration is stopped when

$$(x_{i+1} - x_i) = \frac{1}{2} \left(\frac{a}{x_i} - x_i \right) \geq 0 \tag{24-3}$$

to within the precision of the machine representation.

This procedure for the computation of $\sqrt{a}$ is characterized by the fact that the error in the ith iterate

$$\epsilon = x_i - \sqrt{a}$$

is always positive and the correction applied to the ith iterate to generate the $i + 1^{st}$ iterate is approximately

$$\epsilon_i \cong -\epsilon + \frac{\epsilon^2}{2\sqrt{a}} \quad (\epsilon \text{ small}).$$

The truth of these remarks is proven below. It is assumed everywhere that we are considering numbers within machine range.

First it will be shown that the initial x_i, namely x_0, is greater than $\sqrt{a}$:

squaring both sides of eq.(24-1) we have

$$x_0^2 = \frac{a^2}{4} + \frac{a}{2} + \frac{1}{4} \ ,$$

now let $x_0^2 = a + \delta$. Then

$$a + \delta = \frac{a^2}{4} + \frac{a}{2} + \frac{1}{4}$$

$$\delta = \frac{a^2}{4} - \frac{a}{2} + \frac{1}{4}$$

$$\delta = \left(\frac{a-1}{2} \right)^2$$

Hence δ is positive (vanishing only when $a = 1$) and $x_0 > \sqrt{a}$. Since $x_0 > \sqrt{a}$ it may now be shown that all of the subsequent iterates are greater than $\sqrt{a}$, i.e. $x_i > \sqrt{a}$ for all i while each iterate is closer to $\sqrt{a}$ than the preceding one; thus, the sequence of iterates x_i, x_{i+1}, x_{i+2}, $\cdots$ approaches $\sqrt{a}$ "from the right". To prove the preceding statement let us note, from eq. (24-2) that the correction term added to each iterate in order to generate the next iterate is $\epsilon_i = \frac{1}{2} \left(\frac{a}{x_i} - x_i \right)$.

We can write this as

$$\epsilon_i = \frac{1}{2} \frac{(a - x_i^2)}{x_i}$$

or

$$\epsilon_i = \frac{1}{2} \frac{(\sqrt{a} - x_i)(\sqrt{a} + x_i)}{x_i}$$

Now $\epsilon = x_i - \sqrt{a}$ is just the error in the ith iterate and substituting this into the above expression for ϵ_i one finds

$$\epsilon_i = -\frac{1}{2} \left(\frac{\sqrt{a}}{x_i} + 1 \right) \cdot \epsilon \qquad\qquad (24\text{-}4)$$

Now if $x_i > \sqrt{a}$ then

$$\frac{1}{2} \left(\frac{\sqrt{a}}{x_i} + 1 \right) < 1$$

and

$$|\epsilon_i| < \epsilon \; ;$$

thus, we see that the correction to the ith iterate is less in magnitude than the error in the ith iterate, consequently the $i+1^{st}$ iterate, x_{i+1}, will also be greater than $\sqrt{a}$, although closer to $\sqrt{a}$ than x_i since ϵ_i is negative. Finally, since we have already shown that the very first iterate, namely x_0, is already greater than $\sqrt{a}$ it follows that the sequence x_0, x_1, x_2 $\cdots$ does indeed approach x_i "from the right". If in eq.(24-4), we replace x_i by $x_i = \epsilon + \sqrt{a}$ then this equation becomes

$$\epsilon_i = -\frac{1}{2} \left(\frac{\sqrt{a}}{\sqrt{a} + \epsilon} + 1 \right) \cdot \epsilon \, ,$$

$$= -\frac{1}{2} \left(2 - \frac{\epsilon}{\sqrt{a}} + \frac{\epsilon^2}{a} \cdots \right) \cdot \epsilon \, ,$$

and for ϵ small we have

$$\epsilon_i \cong -\epsilon + \frac{\epsilon^2}{2\sqrt{a}} \quad .$$

It is to be observed from this result that if the approximant x_i is accurate to p digits, then the approximant x_{i+1} is accurate to about 2p digits.

This process is illustrated graphically in Figure 24-1. Three curves are shown: the straight lines with slopes $\frac{dy}{dx} = -1$ and $\frac{dy}{dx} = -2$, both passing through the point $x = \sqrt{a}$; and the curve $y = \frac{a}{x} - x$, which also crosses the x-axis at $x = \sqrt{a}$. The latter curve falls between the two straight lines, ($\frac{dx}{dx} = -2$, $\frac{dy}{dx} = -1$) for $x > \sqrt{a}$ since

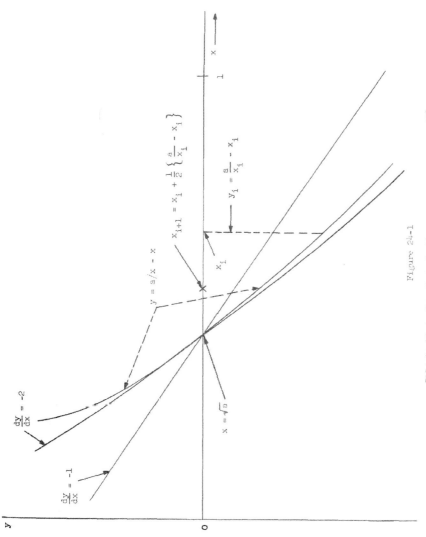

Figure 24-1

Illustration of a stage in the computation of $x = \sqrt{a}$.

$$\frac{dy}{dx} = \frac{d}{dx}\left(\frac{a}{x} - x\right) = -\frac{a}{x^2} - 1$$

that is

$$-2 < \frac{dy}{dx} = -1 - \delta < -1 \; , \quad a < \delta < 1$$

and we have $\delta = 1$ just when $x = \sqrt{a}$. The ith and $i+1^{st}$ iterate are indicated. Since the curve $y = \frac{a}{x} - x$ always lies between the two straight lines for $x > \sqrt{a}$ it is immediately evident that the $i+1^{st}$ iterate will never fall to the left of the point $x = \sqrt{a}$ (because the curve lies above the $\frac{dy}{dx} = -2$ straight line); furthermore the error in the $i+1^{st}$ iterate will be less than half the error in the ith iterate (because the curve lies below the $\frac{dy}{dx} = -1$ straight line).

The iterative formula (24-2) is most easily derived using calculus and Taylor's series. Let us consider the function $f(x) = x^2 - a$. The positive root of this function is $\sqrt{a}$: $f(\sqrt{a}) = 0$. Let x_i be a positive number approximating $\sqrt{a}$. Using the first two terms in a Taylor series we have

$$f(x_i + \Delta) \cong f(x_i) + f'(x_i)\Delta \; ,$$

where $f'(x_i)$ is the derivative of f with respect to x at x_i. We regard Δ as an unknown which is chosen to make $f(x_i + \Delta) = 0$, for then $x_i + \Delta$ will be a new approximation to $\sqrt{a}$. Putting $f(x_i + \Delta) = 0$ and solving for Δ we have

$$\Delta = \frac{-f(x_i)}{f'(x_i)} \; ,$$

so

$$\Delta = \frac{-(x_i^2 - a)}{2x_i} \; ,$$

and if we put $x_{i+1} = x_i + \Delta$, formula (24-2) results.

If all numbers were held to an infinite degree of precision, then the condition (24-3) would never be satisfied; however, since only a finite number of digits are preserved at each stage of the iteration this condition will be satisfied when the two iterates agree to within the precision permitted by the machine representation.

Referring to R1, we see that in the special case of $a = 1 - 2^{-39}$ a difficulty is encountered because in this case $x_0 = a$, and $a \div x_0$ results in a division hangup. Also, when a is negative $|x_0| < |a|$ and $a \div x_0$ yields a division hangup.

UNIVERSITY OF ILLINOIS
DIGITAL COMPUTER
CHAPTER 25

ERRORS IN NUMERICAL COMPUTATIONS - PART 1

In general, numerical computations are accompanied by errors and it is the intention of this chapter and the two succeeding chapters to give some consideration to the kinds of errors which arise and an outline of how they are estimated. The errors discussed here do not include blunders or accidental errors such as saying $1 + 2 = 4$, $2 \times 3 = 7$ or other such mistakes. In principle blunders are avoidable if one is sufficiently careful, but the errors discussed here are a necessary evil of numerical computations and though they may be made small by following proper procedures it is in general not possible to eliminate them entirely no matter how much care is taken. A nice general discussion of errors in computation may be found in Chapter 1 of reference (8) (see Chapter 1 of these notes).

Errors arise in numerical work for essentially two reasons: it is necessary to represent numbers with a finite number of digits; the numerical procedure employed in solving a problem is necessarily limited to a finite number of steps. Errors of a different sort, which we might call "physical" errors, to distinguish them from the fundamentally "numerical" errors above are also present; they include errors from inaccurate data, because the precision of a measurement is necessarily limited; also the mathematical "model" used to represent the physical problem under consideration is in general not completely accurate. Our attention here is directed at the numerical errors.

Let us again consider the representation of numbers in the ILLIAC. Regarding the binary point between digits w_0 and w_1 of an ILLIAC word ($w = w_0\, w_1\, w_2\, \cdots\, w_{39}$) we have said that one can represent fractions x in the interval $-1 \leq x < 1$. Now all numbers in the interval $-1 \leq x < 1$ are represented by the totality of points on the line segment of the x axis shown in Figure 25-1; it is understood that this line segment includes the left end point (-1) but not

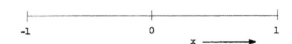

$$-1 \qquad\qquad\qquad 0 \qquad\qquad\qquad 1$$
$$x \longrightarrow$$

Figure 25-1

Points in this interval represent the numbers $-1 \leq x < 1$.

the right end point $(+1)$. The ILLIAC word cannot of course represent <u>all</u> points on this interval but only a discrete set of them and in particular just 2^{40} points are represented; namely, -1 $-1+2^{-39}$, $-1+2 \cdot 2^{-39}$, $\ldots$, $1-2^{-39}$. One could represent the numbers in this interval to a greater precision by assigning two ILLIAC words, w and w', for the representation; w would represent the most significant part of the number and w' would represent the least significant part. With this double precision representation we represent 2^{79} points; namely, -1 $-1+2^{-78}$, $-1+2 \cdot 2^{-78}$, $+ \ldots +$, $1-2^{-78}$. It is of course possible to thus improve the accuracy of the number representation by assigning still more words to the representation but there is a limit to this since there are only a finite number of words in the ILLIAC. The nature of ILLIAC is such that usually numbers are represented "single precision", that is by just one ILLIAC word. Arithmetic operations involving multiple precision numbers are not "natural" for the ILLIAC and require some considerable amount of programming.

The error involved in representing an arbitrary x in the interval $-1 \leq x < 1$ to single precision is given by the neglect of the digits beyond the 2^{-39} th binary digit. Thus, if the exact value of x is

$$x = -w_0 + \sum_{i=1}^{\infty} w_i \, 2^{-i} \qquad\qquad (25\text{-}1)$$

where 2's complement representation is understood, neglect of the digits beyond the 2^{-39} th yields a possible ILLIAC representation

$$x^+ = -w_0 + \sum_{i=1}^{39} w_i 2^{-i} \qquad (25\text{-}2)$$

The error in this representation, namely $\epsilon = x - x^+$ is

$$\epsilon = \sum_{i=40}^{\infty} w_i 2^{-i} \quad . \qquad (25\text{-}3)$$

Clearly the range on ϵ is

$$0 \leq \epsilon \leq 2^{-39} \quad ;$$

The lower limit is achieved when $w_i = 0$ for all i, in which case the ILLIAC representation is exact; the upper limit is achieved when $w_i = 1$ for all i. The representation of x in eq. (25-2) has been achieved by "truncation" (chopping-off) of the exact series representation in eq. (25-1) at the 39th digital position. The error, ϵ, which has resulted is <u>positive</u>, and x^+ is <u>algebraically</u> less than or equal to x, in particular

$$x = x^+ + \epsilon \quad .$$

The error in this representation of x contains one very undesirable property --- it is biased, tending to make <u>all</u> numbers somewhat smaller (algebraically) than they actually are. An unbiased error, that is an error which is distributed uniformly over positive and negative values, is preferred because there is some hope that in a sequence of computations there will be some cancellation of errors with the result that the total error in the computation is reduced.

An unbiased representation of x is achieved if we represent x by the truncated value of $x + 2^{-40}$ or in other words

$$x^+ = -w_0 + \sum_{i=1}^{39} w_i 2^{-i} \qquad \text{if } w_{40} = 0$$

and

$$x^+ = -w_0 + \sum_{i=1}^{39} w_i \, 2^{-i} + 2^{-39} \qquad \text{if } w_{40} = 1$$

Now the error interval is centered on zero, for we have

$$-2^{-40} \leq \epsilon = x - x^+ \leq 2^{-40} \; ;$$

the lower limit is achieved when $w_{40} = 1$ and $w_i = 0$ (all $i > 40$) ; the upper limit is achieved when $w_{40} = 0$ and $w_i = 1$ (all $i > 40$).*

It is sometimes helpful to represent this round-off procedure in a pictorial way. The figure below, Figure 25-1, represents a very small subinterval of the interval $(-1, 1)$ on the x axis. Values of x which may be exactly represented in the ILLIAC are represented by short vertical marks; this subinterval includes just three such points, $x = -1 + n \cdot 2^{-39}$, $x = -1 + (n+1) \cdot 2^{-39}$ and $x = -1 + (n+2) \cdot 2^{-39}$. Any x represented by a point on the interval between these vertical marks, as for example the x represented by the dot between points $-1 + n \cdot 2^{-39}$ and $-1 + (n+1) \cdot 2^{-39}$, cannot be exactly represented. The x represented by this dot, x ($\cdot$) must be represented in the ILLIAC by x^+, a number associated with one of the vertical marks. Since the x ($\cdot$) lies closest to the mark for $x^+ = -1 + (n+1) \cdot 2^{-39}$ it would be natural to use this value of x^+ for representation of x^+; the error ϵ is shown, and is seen to be negative. The long dashed vertical mark divides the interval $(-1 + n \cdot 2^{-39} , -1 + (n+1) \cdot 2^{-39})$ in half, at the point $x = -1 + n \cdot 2^{-39} + 2^{-40}$. If now, numbers in the half-interval to the right of this dashed mark are represented by $x^+ = -1 + (n+1) \cdot 2^{-39}$ (as with x($\cdot$) below) and numbers in the

---

* If one desires to be completely rigorous it should be recognized that

$$\lim_{N \to \infty} \sum_{i=41}^{N} 2^{-i} = 2^{-40},$$ consequently the representations $a_{40} = 1$, $a_i = 0$

(all $i > 40$) and $a_{40} = 0$, $s_i = 1$ (all $i > 40$) are equivalent.

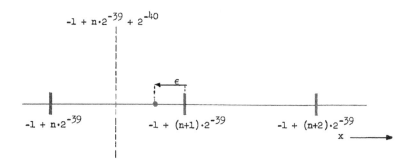

Figure 25-2

A small subinterval of the interval (-1, 1).

left half-interval are represented by $x^+ = -1 + n\cdot 2^{-39}$ and similarly for every other such interval, we have just the rounding procedure described above. This scheme of rounding x to form x^+ is clearly unbiased, since for every x represented by x^+ with ϵ negative (an x in the right half-interval) there corresponds an x' represented by x'^+ with positive ϵ of the same magnitude (the "mirror image" in the left half-interval).

The root-mean-square error of numbers represented by this rounding scheme is given by *

---

* The bar above a quantity indicates the average value of the quantity; thus $\bar{\epsilon}$ is the average value of ϵ.

$$\sqrt{\overline{(\epsilon - \bar{\epsilon})^2}} = \sqrt{\overline{\epsilon^2} - (\bar{\epsilon})^2} = \left[\frac{1}{2^{-39}} \int_{-2^{-40}}^{+2^{-40}} \epsilon^2 \, d\epsilon \; - \; \bar{\epsilon}^2 \right]^{1/2}$$

$$= \left[\frac{1}{2^{-39}} \cdot \frac{\epsilon^3}{3} \Bigg|_{-2^{-40}}^{+2^{-40}} \; - \; 0 \right]^{1/2}$$

$$\sqrt{\overline{\epsilon^2}} = \frac{1}{\sqrt{3}} \cdot 2^{-40} \tag{25-4}$$

In general any problem to be run on the ILLIAC will have associated with it certain parameters, constants and perhaps data. Representation of those numbers in the ILLIAC introduces errors into the calculation known as the initial error. This error will be propagated through the calculation and contribute an error to the final result. The error which is thus propagated through the problem, assuming only the initial error to be present and everything else exact, is called the propagated error. In practice one cannot easily separate out this error but in certain considerations of error analysis it is convenient and useful to distinguish this error from others. For example, numerical procedures which cause a rapid growth of the propagated error are clearly undesirable. Desirable procedures would show a "damping" effect on the propagated error tending to make any contribution of the initial error to the final error negligibly small.

At each stage of the calculation new errors are introduced because the arithmetic is not done exactly and because results of arithmetic operations are not always saved with full precision (for example the product may be rounded off to a single precision number); errors thus introduced during the calculation are called generated errors. The generated errors are propagated through the calculation and thus appear in the final result as a propagated error. Generated error and propagated error are discussed in the following chapter.

UNIVERSITY OF ILLINOIS
DIGITAL COMPUTER
CHAPTER 26

ERRORS IN NUMERICAL COMPUTATIONS - PART 2

During the course of a calculation new errors are generated which propagate through succeeding calculations and contribute to the final error in the result. Let us consider now how these errors are generated and propagated in the elementary arithmetic operations.

Additions and subtractions do not generate errors unless there is overflow. Overflow is a gross error which can be avoided by proper scaling and it will not concern us here. It should of course be noted that these operations propagate errors: thus if ILLIAC numbers x^+ and y^+ have errors ϵ_x and ϵ_y, respectively then the error in $x^+ + y^+$ is just $\epsilon_x + \epsilon_y$,

$$z = x + y = x^+ + y^+ + \epsilon_x + \epsilon_y$$
$$= z^+ + \epsilon_x + \epsilon_y$$
$$= z^+ + \epsilon_z$$

In a practical case one of course does not know ϵ_x and ϵ_y explicitly but knows only certain statistical information about these errors. Many times the statistical information is scanty and it is common to assume that the errors are normally distributed, or uniformly distributed. The latter assumption is somewhat simpler to deal with and generally a reasonable one when information concerning the errors is minimal. In order to get rough estimates on the magnitude of the error one frequently only considers the bounds of the error. In the above case we obviously have

$$|\epsilon_z| \leq \text{Max } |\epsilon_x| + \text{Max } |\epsilon_y| \ .$$

If it is assumed that ϵ_x and ϵ_y are independent and satisfy a normal distribution law;

we have

$$P(\epsilon_x) = \frac{1}{\sqrt{2\pi\sigma_x^2}} \, e^{-\frac{\epsilon_x^2}{2\sigma_x^2}}$$

$$P(\epsilon_y) = \frac{1}{\sqrt{2\pi\sigma_y^2}} \, e^{-\frac{\epsilon_y^2}{2\sigma_y^2}}$$

where σ_x is the standard deviation of ϵ_x and $P(\epsilon_x)$ is the probability density function - - - $P(\epsilon_x) \, d\epsilon_x$ is the probability of an error ϵ_x in the interval $(\epsilon_x, \ \epsilon_x + d\epsilon_x)$ - - - and similarly for y. It can be shown that $\epsilon_z = \epsilon_x + \epsilon_y$ also satisfies a normal distribution:

$$P(\epsilon_z) = \frac{1}{2\pi\sigma_x\sigma_y} \int_{-\infty}^{+\infty} e^{-\frac{\epsilon_x^2}{2\sigma_x^2}} \cdot e^{-\frac{(\epsilon_z-\epsilon_x)^2}{2\sigma_y^2}} \, d\epsilon_x$$

which, after performing the integration, becomes

$$P(\epsilon_z) = \frac{1}{\sqrt{2\pi\sigma_z^2}} \, e^{-\frac{\epsilon_z^2}{2\sigma_z^2}}$$

where

$$\sigma_z^2 = \sigma_x^2 + \sigma_y^2$$

A generalization of this result is the following: the standard deviation of the error in the sum of N numbers, $z = x_1 + x_2 + \dots + x_N$ $(\epsilon_z = \epsilon_1 + \epsilon_2 + \dots + \epsilon_N)$ each ϵ_i being independent and satisfying a Gaussian or normal distribution with standard deviation σ, is

$$\sigma_z = \sqrt{N} \cdot \sigma \ .$$

The standard deviation of the sum thus increases in proportion to the square root of the number of terms in the sum. If N is sufficiently large one can apply the Central Limit Theorem* to obtain a similar result under much more general conditions. This theorem may be stated as follows: given a set $\left\{ \epsilon_i \right\}$ of N mutually independent statistical variables with mean values $\left\{ \bar{\epsilon}_i \right\}$ and standard deviations $\left\{ \sigma_i \right\}$, then

$$E_N = \epsilon_1 + \epsilon_2 + \cdots + \epsilon_N$$

approaches a normal distribution as N tends to infinity with standard deviation, Σ_N, satisfying the equation

$$\Sigma_N^2 = \sigma_1^2 + \sigma_2^2 + \cdots + \sigma_N^2$$

and mean given by

$$\bar{E}_N = \bar{\epsilon}_1 + \bar{\epsilon}_2 + \cdots + \bar{\epsilon}_N \ .$$

It is to be noticed that the distribution of the ϵ_i's does not need to be normal for this result to apply. In fact the only restriction placed on the distribution of the ϵ_i's is that the means $\left\{ \bar{\epsilon}_i \right\}$ and standard deviations $\left\{ \sigma_i \right\}$ exist.

Thus, in a computation of the form $z = x_1 + x_2 + \cdots + x_N$, where the standard deviations and means of the errors in each of the x's is known, one can apply the Central Limit Theorem to get an estimate of the probability distribution of the error in z. The reliability of this estimate will depend of course on the size of N and the extent to which the errors in the x's are mutually independent.

---

* See Feller - "Probability Theory and Its Applications"

Unrounded multiplication in the ILLIAC produces an **exact** product in AQ. If both the most significant part of the product and the least significant part are preserved then no error is generated. Frequently one rounds the double precision product to form a single precision 40 bit number by means of the 7J order. In this instance an error is generated. From the results of Chapter 25 (Eq. 25-4) we see that the root-mean-square deviation of this error is $\frac{1}{\sqrt{3}} \cdot 2^{-40}$, while the maximum of the magnitude of this error is 2^{-40}.

Let us consider now two ILLIAC numbers x^+ and y^+ with respective errors ϵ_x and ϵ_y and find the error in the 40 bit rounded product $z^+ = x^+ \cdot y^+$:

$$x \cdot y = (x^+ + \epsilon_y)(y^+ + \epsilon_y)$$
$$= x^+ y^+ + \epsilon_x y^+ + \epsilon_y x^+ + \epsilon_x \epsilon_y$$

The error term on the right

$$\epsilon_p = \epsilon_x \cdot y^+ + \epsilon_y x^+ + \epsilon_x \epsilon_y \,,$$

is the propagated error since it results entirely from the initial errors in x and y. To obtain the total error, ϵ_z, in the product we must add the generated error, ϵ_g, caused by the rounding of the product to 40 bits, to the propagated error; thus,

$$\epsilon_z = \epsilon_g + \epsilon_p$$
$$= \epsilon_g + \epsilon_z y^+ + \epsilon_y x^+ + \epsilon_x \epsilon_y \,.$$

It will be assumed in the following that the errors are independent of each other and independent of x and y. Let us now consider the bounds on ϵ_z. We know

$$|\epsilon_g| \le 2^{-40}$$
$$|x^+| \quad \text{and} \quad |y^+| \le 1$$

and the bounds on ϵ_x and ϵ_y are not known since they are presumably the results of all preceeding operations involved in the generation of x^+ and y^+. We can neglect the term $\epsilon_x \epsilon_y$ since it will usually be small in comparison with the other three terms, ϵ_g, $\epsilon_x y^+$ and $\epsilon_y x^+$. Consequently the range on ϵ_z is given by

$$- \left\{ 2^{-40} + |\epsilon_x| + |\epsilon_y| \right\} \leq \epsilon_z \leq \left\{ 2^{-40} + |\epsilon_x| + |\epsilon_y| \right\} \ .$$

The root-mean-square error in ϵ_z is given by

$$\sqrt{\overline{(\epsilon_z - \bar{\epsilon}_z)^2}} \ = \ \left[\overline{\left\{ \epsilon_g + \epsilon_x y^+ + \epsilon_y x^+ - [\overline{\epsilon_g + \epsilon_x y^+ + \epsilon_y x^+}] \right\}^2} \right]^{\frac{1}{2}}$$

Making use of the fact that the errors are assumed to be independent, this becomes

$$\sqrt{\overline{(\epsilon_z - \bar{\epsilon}_z)^2}} \ = \ \left\{ \overline{\epsilon_g^2} + (\overline{\epsilon_x^2}) \ \overline{(y^+)^2} + \overline{\epsilon_y^2} \ \overline{(x^+)^2} \right.$$

$$\left. - (\bar{\epsilon}_g)^2 - (\bar{\epsilon}_x)^2 \ \overline{(y^+)^2} - (\bar{\epsilon}_y)^2 \ \overline{(x^+)^2} \right\}^{\frac{1}{2}} \ .$$

Finally, if we assume that x^+ and y^+ are uniformly distributed over the interval $(-1, +1)$, then

$$\overline{x^+} = \overline{y^+} = 0$$

$$\overline{(x^+)^2} = \overline{(y^+)^2} = \frac{1}{3}$$

and recalling (Eq. 25-4) that $\sqrt{\overline{\epsilon_g^2}} = \sqrt{\frac{1}{3}} \cdot 2^{-40}$ and $\bar{\epsilon}_g = 0$ we have finally

$$\sqrt{\overline{(\epsilon_z - \bar{\epsilon}_z)^2}} \ = \ \frac{2^{-40}}{\sqrt{3}} \left\{ 1 + (\frac{\overline{\epsilon_x}}{2^{-40}})^2 + (\frac{\overline{\epsilon_y}}{2^{-40}})^2 \right\}^{\frac{1}{2}}$$

With division, as has been cited earlier, round-off in the ILLIAC is automatic and is achieved by "stuffing" a 1 into the least significant digit of the quotient. Let us now consider the error produced by this mode of rounding and verify that it indeed is unbiased as it has been previously asserted. To do this let us again fix our attention on a small subinterval of the x-axis where the numbers representable by the ILLIAC (in 40 bits) are indicated by short vertical marks; a picture of this subinterval appears below in Figure 26-1. We assume in this figure that n is an even number. Since every rounded quotient in the ILLIAC must have its least significant digit equal to 1 it follows that the possible quotients are restricted to those numbers indicated by the heavy vertical marks in Figure 26-1.

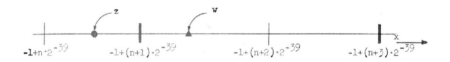

Figure 26-1

A small subinterval of the interval (-1, 1).
Possible quotients are indicated by the heavy
vertical marks.

Let us now consider an exact division $z = \frac{x}{y}$ and let the number z be represented by ● in Figure 26-1. The rounded ILLIAC quotient will be $z^+ = -1 + (n+1) \cdot 2^{-39}$. In fact it is easy to see that any exact quotient in the interval $(-1 + n \cdot 2^{-39}, -1 + (n+1) \cdot 2^{-39})$ will be represented by the rounded ILLIAC quotient $z^+ = -1 + (n+1) \cdot 2^{-39}$. The error for the quotient in this interval, $\Delta x = 2^{-39}$, is negative. Consider now another exact division yielding the quotient $w = \frac{u}{v}$ and let the number w be represented by ▲ in Figure 26-1. The rounded ILLIAC quotient will again be $w^+ = -1 + (n+1) \cdot 2^{-39}$. Noticing the fact that all exact quotients in the interval $(-1 + (n+1) \cdot 2^{-39}, -1 + (n+2) \cdot 2^{-39})$ have their 2^{-39} th digit equal to 1 it follows again that these will be represented by the rounded ILLIAC quotient

$w^+ = -1 + (n+1) \cdot 2^{-39}$. The error for quotients in this interval, $\Delta x = 2^{-39}$, is positive. It follows from these considerations that the error resulting from the division round-off is unbiased; furthermore we see that the range of the error is

$$-2^{-39} \leq \epsilon \leq 2^{-39} \quad,$$

which is just twice the error range resulting from the multiplication roundoff. Assuming a uniform distribution of errors ϵ we compute the root-mean-square error:

$$\sqrt{\overline{(\epsilon - \bar{\epsilon})^2}} = \sqrt{\overline{\epsilon^2} - \bar{\epsilon}^2}$$

$$= \left\{ \frac{1}{2^{-38}} \cdot \int_{-2^{-39}}^{2^{-39}} \epsilon^2 \, d\epsilon \right\}^{\frac{1}{2}}$$

$$= \left\{ \frac{1}{2^{-38}} \cdot \left(\frac{\epsilon^3}{3} \right) \Big|_{-2^{-39}}^{2^{-39}} \right\}^{\frac{1}{2}}$$

$$= \frac{2^{-39}}{\sqrt{3}}$$

Let us now consider two ILLIAC numbers x^+ and y^+ with errors ϵ_x and ϵ_y and find the error in the 40 bit rounded quotient $z^+ = \dfrac{x^+}{y^+}$

$$\frac{x}{y} = \frac{x^+ + \epsilon_x}{y^+ + \epsilon_y}$$

Assuming ϵ_x and ϵ_y small in comparison with x and y this can be written

$$\frac{x}{y} = \frac{x^+ + \epsilon_x}{y^+} \cdot \left(1 - \frac{\epsilon_y}{y^+} + \left(\frac{\epsilon_y}{y^+} \right)^2 - \ldots \right)$$

and neglecting second order terms (all terms involving the square of the error or higher powers) we have approximately

$$\frac{x}{y} = \frac{x^+}{y^+} \left(1 + \frac{\epsilon_x}{x^+} - \frac{\epsilon_y}{y^+} \right) \ .$$

The error term represented by $\frac{x^+}{y^+} \left(\frac{\epsilon_x}{x^+} - \frac{\epsilon_y}{y^+} \right)$ is the propagated error, resulting from the initial errors in x and y. The total error in the quotient is obtained by adding the division roundoff error, i.e. the generated error ϵ_y to obtain finally

$$\epsilon_z = \epsilon_g + \frac{x^+}{y^+} \left(\frac{\epsilon_x}{x^+} - \frac{\epsilon_y}{y^+} \right) \ .$$

Following arguments similar to those used in discussing the multiplication error, one finds for the bounds on ϵ_z

$$- \left\{ 2^{-39} + \left| \frac{\epsilon_x}{x^+} \right| + \left| \frac{\epsilon_y}{y^+} \right| \right\} \leq \epsilon_z \leq \left\{ 2^{-39} + \left| \frac{\epsilon_x}{x^+} \right| + \left| \frac{\epsilon_y}{y^+} \right| \right\} \ ,$$

where we have used the fact that $\left| \frac{x^+}{y^+} \right| < 1$ for ILLIAC division. Here it is seen that the error ϵ_z depends rather critically on the magnitudes of x and y. A root-mean-square error calculation in this case requires special assumptions about the distribution of x^+ and y^+ to be meaningful and is therefore omitted here.

UNIVERSITY OF ILLINOIS
DIGITAL COMPUTER
CHAPTER 27

ERRORS IN NUMERICAL COMPUTATIONS - PART 3

In this chapter we turn attention to the problem of estimating the error in a specific example, namely the computation of e^x $(-1 \leq x < 0)$. It is only fair to point out in the beginning that the example here discussed is a particularly simple one and in general the programmer will not be blessed with such an easy situation: however, it is hoped that this discussion will serve as a guide to the treatment of more difficult problems.

The subroutine which we will consider for the computation of e^x is designed to compute e^x directly from the series expression*:

$$e^x = 1 + x + \frac{x^2}{2!} + \frac{x^3}{3!} + \frac{x^4}{4!} + \cdots$$

The series is truncated at the 15th term to obtain the approximate expression

$$e^x \cong \sum_{i=0}^{15} \frac{x^i}{i!} \quad ; \tag{27-1}$$

it is just this sum which the subroutine must evaluate. The effect of thus truncating the series is easy to estimate. Recognizing that the terms in the series alternate in sign as a consequence of x being negative, it follows that the sum of the neglected terms is less (in magnitude) than the first term neglected i.e.

$$\text{truncation error} < \frac{x^{16}}{16!} \quad .$$

This degree of precision is quite adequate for a single precision computation since $16! \cong 2.1 \times 10^{13}$ and $|x| < 1$ it follows that

---

* This is not the best scheme for computation of e^x from the standpoint of computing time.

$$\text{truncation error} < \frac{1}{2.1} \cdot 10^{-13}$$

which is smaller than the smallest number that can be held in an ILLIAC register; recall that

$$1 \times 2^{-39} \cong 1.8 \times 10^{-12}$$

Thus, by taking the number of terms indicated in eq. (27-1) it has been guaranteed that the truncation error is negligible. The error in e^x, then, will not come from this source but rather it will come from the roundoff errors generated in the course of the computation. To estimate this error let us now consider in detail the subroutine itself.

The series is evaluated using the standard procedure for the evaluation of a polynomial (see page 69) and the coefficients $\frac{1}{i!}$ are stored in a table of constants. A slight trick has been employed in order to accurately handle the coefficient $\frac{1}{1!}$, which consists of storing all coefficients $\frac{1}{i!}$ for i odd as negative numbers (thus we can write exactly -1) and then using negative multiplications by x. It will also be recognized that the first term in the series, 1, is also treated exactly. The code follows.

LOCATION	ORDER PAIR	COMMENTS
0 (EXP)	40 F K5 11L	Store x at 0
1	42 8L L5 10L	Set link
2	40 1F L5 (EXP)	Set sum box $= -\frac{1}{15!}$ Set initial address
3	42 4L 50 1F	of factorials From 7L
4	79 F L4 [0]F	$(-x) \cdot S_{16-i}$ by 3L,6L; $(-x) S_{16-i} + \frac{(-1)^i}{i!}$

(Continued on page 209)

LOCATION	ORDER PAIR	COMMENTS
5	40 1F F5 4L	Store S_{16-i-1} Advance end counter
6	42 4L L0 9L	End test
7	32 3L 50 F	Jump if not end Waste
8	F5 1F 22 [0]F	Exit
9	L9 F L4 26L	End constant
10	80 F 00 999 999 999 999J	$-\frac{1}{15!}$
11	00 F 00 000 000 000 012J	$\frac{1}{14!}$
12	80 F 00 999 999 999 839J	$-\frac{1}{13!}$
13	00 F 00 000 000 002 087J	$\frac{1}{12!}$
14	80 F 00 999 999 974 947J	$-\frac{1}{11!}$
15	00 F 00 000 000 275 573J	$\frac{1}{10!}$
16	80 F 00 999 997 244 268J	$-\frac{1}{9!}$
17	00 F 00 000 024 801 588J	$\frac{1}{8!}$

(Continued on page 210)

LOCATION	ORDER PAIR	COMMENTS
18	80 F 00 999 801 587 301J	$-\frac{1}{7!}$
19	00 F 00 001 388 888 889J	$\frac{1}{6!}$
20	80 F 00 991 666 666 666J	$-\frac{1}{5!}$
21	00 F 00 041 666 666 666J	$\frac{1}{4!}$
22	80 F 00 833 333 333 333J	$-\frac{1}{3!}$
23	40 F 00 F	$\frac{1}{2}$
24	80 F 00 F	-1
25	7L 4095F LL 4095F	$1 - 2^{-39}$

It is seen from this program that the computation proceeds as indicated by
the equation below.

$$e^x = \left(\cdots \left(\left(\left(-\frac{1}{15!} \right) \cdot (-x) + \frac{1}{14!} \right) (-x) - \frac{1}{13!} \right) \cdot (-x) + \cdots -1 \right) (-x) +$$

The constants $\frac{(-1)^i}{i!}$ are each going to be in error by an amount ϵ_i (assuming proper
rounding $|\epsilon_i| \leq 2^{-40}$). Furthermore, each multiplication will cause a roundoff
error, λ_i, consequently the number actually computed is

$$(e^x)^+ = \left(\cdots \left(\left(-\frac{1}{15!} - \epsilon_{15} \right) \cdot (-x) + \lambda_1 + \frac{1}{14!} - \epsilon_{14} \right) \cdot (-x) \cdots + 1 \right)$$

which can be written

$$(e^x)^+ = e^x + x^{15}\epsilon_{15} - x^{14}\epsilon_{14} + \ldots + x\epsilon_1 - \epsilon_0$$

$$+ x^{14}\lambda_1 - x^{13}\lambda_2 + \ldots - x\lambda_{14} + \lambda_{15} \tag{27-2}$$

where the first term on the right, written e^x, is just the truncated series of eq. (27-1). The sum of the remaining terms on the right of eq. (27-2), each of which contains ϵ_i or λ_i as a factor, is the negative of the error, $-E$ (i.e. $e^x = (e^x)^+ + E$. It is to be noted that the errors contributed by the terms involving ϵ_i may be partially fixed by the programmer according to his specific choice of the constants $\frac{(-1)^i}{i!}$. The program has been so written to have $\epsilon_2 = \epsilon_1 = \epsilon_0 = 0$. The error contribution from the terms in ϵ may be further reduced by making slight adjustments in the constants $\frac{(-1)^i}{i!}$ such that when x is close to (-1) there is a tendency for cancellation of these errors.

An upper bound on $|E|$ is obtained by substituting into the expression for E the maximum values of the magnitudes of the various quantities: $|x| = 1$, $|\lambda| = 2^{-40}$, and $|\epsilon_i| = 2^{-40}$ ($i \neq 0, 1, 2$). Carrying out this substitution we obtain

$$|E| < 28 \cdot 2^{-40}$$

It is to be noted that if x is restricted to the range $(-1/2, 0)$ the bound on the error is reduced. In this case an upper bound on the error is

$$|E| < \frac{9}{4} \cdot 2^{-40} .$$

Consequently the user of this subroutine could achieve considerably greater accuracy in the computation of e^x if for values of x in the range $-1 \leq x < -\frac{1}{2}$ he entered the subroutine with $x + \frac{1}{2}$ in the accumulator, rather than x. Upon exit from the subroutine the number $e^{x + \frac{1}{2}}$ would reside in the accumulator; if this is then multiplied by $e^{-\frac{1}{2}}$ (stored as a constant) the desired result is achieved. Alternatively this feature could have been incorporated in the subroutine itself.

UNIVERSITY OF ILLINOIS
DIGITAL COMPUTER
CHAPTER 28

THE RUNGE-KUTTA SUBROUTINE FOR THE SOLUTION OF DIFFERENTIAL EQUATIONS

In this chapter we shall be concerned with the use of library
subroutine F1 which is a routine for numerical solution of a set of
simultaneous first-order differential equations using the Runge-Kutta
method. The write-up for this subroutine is in Appendix 21, pp. 394-404. The
use of the subroutine will be illustrated here in its application to the
solution of Weber's equation:

$$\frac{d^2y}{dx^2} + (n + \frac{1}{2} - \frac{1}{4} x^2) \, y = 0 \tag{28-1}$$

Before proceeding to this example it will perhaps be worthwhile to briefly
review some of the ideas connected with the numerical solution of differential
equations.

The nth-order differential equation describes a relation between
$y, \frac{dy}{dx}, \frac{d^2y}{dx^2}, \ldots, \frac{d^ny}{dx^n}$ and x; thus the general n^{th}-order linear differential

equation has the form

$$\frac{d^ny}{dx^n} + a_{n-1} \, (x) \, \frac{d^{n-1}y}{dx^{n-1}} + \ldots + a_1(x) \, \frac{dy}{dx} + a_0(x) \, y = g \, (x) \; .$$

Ideally one desires to find a function of x

$$y = y \, (x)$$

which when substituted into the differential equation will yield an equation
in x which is satisfied identically. When one cannot find this solution by

analytic means it becomes necessary to use approximate methods, for example
numerical integration. A solution by numerical integration implies that
numerical values for y, $\frac{dy}{dx}$, $\frac{d^2y}{dx^2}$, ... $\frac{d^ny}{dx^n}$ are found at discrete values
of x which when substituted into the differential equation cause it to be
satisfied within the precision of the numerical method.

Let us consider the differential equation

$$\frac{dy}{dx} = f(x) , \tag{28-2}$$

and suppose that the solution $y = y(x)$ is as shown by the curve in Figure 28-1.

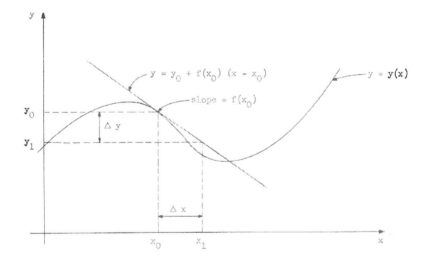

Figure 28-1

Curve showing the solution to $\frac{dy}{dx} = f(x)$.

It follows from the differential equation, eq. (28-2), that the slope of the line drawn tangent to the curve at $y_0 = y(x_0)$ is $f(x_0)$. For a small increment in x, say Δx, the corresponding increment in y, Δy, is given by the approximate expression

$$\Delta y = f(x) \, \Delta x.$$

Thus, if one knows the solution y_0 at $x = x_0$, an estimate of the solution at $x = x_1 = x_0 + \Delta x$ can be obtained:

$$y_1 = y_0 + \Delta y = y_0 + f(x_0)(x_1 - x_0) . \tag{28-3}$$

The estimate of the solution y at $x = x_1$ obtained from this equation is illustrated graphically in Figure 28-1. The error in this estimate is clearly given by the distance between the straight line and the curve $y = y(x)$ at $x = x_1$. Clearly the error will become smaller as Δx becomes smaller and $y = y(x)$ more closely is approximated by a straight line over the interval of interest, Δx. A numerical solution at points x_0, x_1, x_2, ..., x_n can then be obtained by taking steps along the x axis to generate y_0, y_1, y_2, ..., y_n according to the generalization of eq. (28-3):

$$y_i = y_{i-1} + f(x_{i-1})(x_i - x_{i-1}) .$$

To begin this iterative process one must know the value of y for some x say x_0: this is the boundary condition for the process.

In general if one knows the value of a function y for some value of x one can find the value of the function at $x + \Delta x$ from the Taylor expansion of the function:

$$y(x+\Delta x) = y(x) + \frac{dy}{dx} \Delta x + \frac{1}{2!} \frac{d^2 y}{dx^2} (\Delta x)^2 +$$

$$\cdots + \frac{1}{n!} \frac{d^n y}{dx^n} (\Delta x)^n + \cdots$$

The approximation method just described corresponds to truncating the Taylor series at terms involving the first derivative of y. The approximation method is called a first-order method since it agrees with the Taylor expansion to terms of first order in the derivative of the function. Other, more accurate, integration schemes take into account the curvature of y(x) by approximation of the curve over a short interval Δ x by a quadratic in Δ x rather than a straight line as above. Such a scheme can agree with the Taylor expansion to terms of second order in the derivative of y(x); when this agreement obtains it is called a second-order method. This can be extended still further and there are methods which agree with the Taylor expansion to terms of still higher order. In the Runge-Kutta method, employed by Fl, the estimate of y(x $\div$ Δ x) agrees with the Taylor expansion to terms of fourth order.[*]

The above remarks apply if the differential equation, eq. (28-2), assumes the more general form

$$\frac{dy}{dx} = f(x,y) \ ,$$

where now the slope is a function of the dependent variable, y, as well as the independent variable, x. We have discussed only first-order differential equations, let us now turn attention to the problem of solving a differential equation of higher order. It can be shown that the problem of solving a single differential equation of ath order is equivalent to the problem of solving n simultaneous first-order equations. For example consider the third-order differential equation:

$$\frac{d^3y}{dx^3} + a(x) \ \frac{d^2y}{dx^2} + b(x) \ \frac{dy}{dx} + c(x) \ y = g(x) \ , \qquad (28\text{-}4)$$

and define

$$\frac{dy}{dx} = u \ , \qquad (28\text{-}4.1)$$

$$\frac{du}{dx} = v \ . \qquad (28\text{-}4.2)$$

---

[*] The Runge-Kutta method involves terms of higher order in Δx but they do not agree with the Taylor series terms.

Substitution into eq. (28-4) yields

$$\frac{dv}{dx} = -a(x) \, v - b(x) \, u - c(x) \, y + g(x) \quad . \qquad (28\text{-}4.3)$$

Solution of the three simultaneous first-order equations (28-4.1), (28-4.2) and
(28-4.3) is equivalent to the solution of the single equation (28-4); this should
be self-evident since the three functions obtained as solutions to (4.1), (4.2)
and (4.3) are y, $\frac{dy}{dx}$ and $\frac{d^2y}{dx^2}$ of eq. (4). In this way any numerical scheme which
can solve a set of n simultaneous first-order differential equations can be used
to solve a single differential equation of nth order.

It can easily be seen that the simple first-order numerical scheme
already described can be extended to the treatment of simultaneous first-order
differential equations; consider it now in its application to the three equations
above. As boundary conditions to the problem suppose that

$$u = u_0, \; v = v_0, \; y = y_0 \text{ at } x = x_0 \; ,$$

then

$$u(x_0 + \Delta x) = u_0 + v_0 \, \Delta x \; ,$$

$$v(x_0 + \Delta x) = v_0 + \left\{ -a(x_0) \, v_0 - b(x_0) \, u_0 - c(x_0) \, y_0 + g(x_0) \right\} \, \Delta x \; ,$$

$$y(x_0 + \Delta x) = y_0 + u_0 \, \Delta x \; .$$

The process can be repeated to obtain $u(x_0 + 2\Delta x)$, $v(x_0 + 2\Delta x)$, $y(x_0 + 2\Delta x)$
by simply replacing u_0, v_0, y_0 in the above equations by $u(x_0 + \Delta x)$, $v(x_0 + \Delta x)$,
$y(x_0 + \Delta x)$, respectively. The solution to the third-order differential equation
at x_0, $x_0 + \Delta x$, $x_0 + 2 \Delta x$ etc. is thus generated by this simple iterative
process.

Let us now turn attention to the Runge-Kutta method itself. A
characteristic feature of this method is that four estimates $\Delta_1 y$, $\Delta_2 y$, $\Delta_3 y$, and
$\Delta_4 y$ of the increment Δy of the dependent variable are made, corresponding to an
increment Δx of the independent variable. The four estimates of Δy are obtained
using the slope $\frac{dy}{dx}$ evaluated at different points within the interval Δx. The
four estimates $\Delta_1 y$, $\Delta_2 y$, $\Delta_3 y$, $\Delta_4 y$ are combined linearly to obtain the desired Δy:

$$\Delta y = a \, \Delta_1 y + b \, \Delta_2 y + c \, \Delta_3 y + d \, \Delta_4 y$$

The numbers a, b, c and d may be regarded as weighting factors and must satisfy the normalization condition

$$a + b + c + d = 1$$

The approximation thus obtained for Δy agrees with that obtained from a Taylor expansion up to (and including) fourth-order terms.

In the library subroutine Fl the four estimates of Δy are obtained from four estimates of the slope $\frac{dy}{dx} = f(x,y)$ in the interval Δx; specifically these estimates are taken at the left end-point of the interval, twice at the center of the interval and at the right end-point of the interval. The specific form in which the Runge-Kutta method is used by the subroutine is due to S. Gill and for this reason it is sometimes referred to as the Gill-Kutta method. The subroutine is designed to solve n simultaneous first-order differential equations:

$$y_0' = f_0(y_0, y_1, y_2 \cdots y_{n-1}) \ ,$$
$$y_1' = f_1(y_0, y_1, y_2 \cdots y_{n-1}) \ ,$$

$$\cdot$$
$$\cdot$$
$$\cdot$$

$$y_{n-1}' = f_{n-1}(y_0, y_1, y_2 \cdots y_{n-1}) \ ,$$

(y' denotes first derivative of y), where for uniformity of notation the independent variable is identified as one of the y's, say y_0. The values of f_0, f_1 ... f_{n-1} must be supplied to the Runge-Kutta subroutine. The user of the subroutine must write a program which computes the derivatives for given y_0, y_1 ... y_{n-1}; this program is known as the Auxiliary and it must be written in standard closed subroutine form. The Runge-Kutta subroutine jumps to the Auxiliary each time it needs a new estimate for the derivative and the Auxiliary computes the derivatives multiplied by a scale factor, $2^m h$; the scaled derivative is designated by k, thus the numbers computed by the Auxiliary are

$$k_0 = 2^m h \; f_0(y_0, \; y_1, \; y_2 \; \cdots \; y_{n-1})$$
$$k_1 = 2^m h \; f_1(y_0, \; y_1, \; y_2 \; \cdots \; y_{n-1})$$

$$k_{n-1} = 2^m h \; f_{n-1}(y_0, \; y_1, \; y_2 \; \cdots \; y_{n-1}) \; .$$

Since four estimates of the derivative are needed at each Runge-Kutta step, the Runge-Kutta subroutine will make four entries to the Auxiliary to obtain the k_i's at each step.

The scale factor is composed of two parts: h, which is the Runge-Kutta step size (i.e. the increment in the independent variable) for the increments Δy_0, Δy_1 $\cdots$ Δy_{n-1} computed by the Runge-Kutta subroutine; and 2^m where m is chosen to make $2^m h \; f_i$ within machine range but large enough to retain a reasonable amount of accuracy. The need for the factor 2^m to retain accuracy in the computation should be fairly evident. In the first place the derivative itself may become very small and in the computer the effect will be to lose significant digits; loss of accuracy in this instance may be reduced by scaling the derivative up, taking care of course to insure that the numbers stay within machine range. Secondly, the numbers $h \; f_i$, which represent the estimates Δy_i,* will in general be small since the smaller the value one picks for h the smaller will be the truncation error (resulting from the fact that Δy computed from this process deviates from the Taylor expansion in the terms $\frac{1}{i!} y^{(i)} h^i$ for $i \geq 5$). Consequently, to retain significant digits in $h f_i$ it is scaled by 2^m.

It is obvious that at the stage in the computation when Δy_i is to be added to y_i to form the new value of y_i both numbers must be in the same scale. It is quite likely that the increment will be considerably smaller than the function itself, consequently much of the significance in Δy_i can be lost at this point unless special provisions are made; the Runge-Kutta subroutine does make such a provision. Let $\frac{1}{3} q_i$ represent the roundoff error in y_i (in effect this is the least significant part of y_i -- the part which would be beyond the

---

* Not precisely the same Δy's as on page 217.

right end of a 40 bit register) then the number $2^m q_i$ is preserved by the
routine. As roundoff error accumulates to make a net contribution to the
"40-bit-representation" of y_i the contribution is appropriately added to
y_i.

The user of the Runge-Kutta subroutine must provide three blocks
of storage, each of length n, where n is the number of equations being
solved. The first block of storage, the "y-bank", is used to hold the n
variables y_0, y_1, ... y_{n-1}. This bank thus holds the solution to the set
of equations being solved. At the very start of the integration process,
before the first entry to the Runge-Kutta subroutine is made, the initial
values of the variables y_0, y_1 ... y_{n-1} must be loaded into this bank. The
second block of storage, the "k-bank", is used to hold the scaled derivatives
k_0, k_1 ... k_{n-1}. It is the responsibility of the Auxiliary to load this
bank with the scaled derivatives which it computes. The third block of storage,
the "q-bank", is used to hold the numbers $2^m q_i$, just described. This bank should
be cleared to zero at the very start of the integration process, before the
first entry to the Runge-Kutta subroutine is made. If this is not done then
the numbers held in this bank will be treated as roundoff errors to the
functions y_i and consequently will contribute an initial error to the solutions.

Let us now turn attention to the use of the subroutine Fl in its
application to solving eq. (28-1). Let us suppose that in this equation n = 7/4,
the equation becomes

$$\frac{d^2 y}{dx^2} + \left(\frac{9}{4} - \frac{1}{4} x^2 \right) y = 0 \ . \tag{28-5}$$

This equation can be written as the following pair of first-order differential
equations:

$$\frac{dy}{dx} = z \tag{28-6}$$

$$\frac{dz}{dx} = \left(-\frac{9}{4} + \frac{1}{4} x^2 \right) y \ . \tag{28-7}$$

Since the independent variable x appears explicitly in the eq. (28-7) it is necessary to add a third equation to this list, namely

$$\frac{dx}{dx} = 1 \quad .$$

(28-8)

This equation must be added to the list when using F1 to solve equations wherein the independent variable occurs explicitly, because in this instance the value of x at the various points within the interval $h = \Delta x$ must be available for computation of the k_i's by the Auxiliary. If eq. (28-8) is added to the list, then F1 will automatically provide the appropriate value of x in the y-bank.

Let us suppose now that we wish to find the solution in the interval $0 \leq x \leq 2$, and that the boundary conditions are

$$y(0) = 0 \ , \ z(0) = 2 \quad .$$

The variables x, y and z must be scaled so that the scaled values will remain within machine range; the scaled variables will be denoted x*, y* and z*. An appropriate scale factor for x is $\frac{1}{4}$, i.e.

$$x^* = \frac{x}{4} \ ,$$

then $0 \leq x^* \leq \frac{1}{2}$. Notice that a scale factor of $\frac{1}{2}$ would not be sufficient for then at the right end-point of the interval where $x = 2$ the scaled variable would be $x^* = 1$ which is outside machine range. Scale factors for y and z can be obtained from some simple considerations of the differential equation.

Notice that the factor $\frac{9}{4} - \frac{1}{4} x^2$ is everywhere positive in the interval of integration, decreasing monotonically as x ranges from 0 to 2. As a consequence of this

$$\frac{d^2 y}{dx^2} = - \left(\frac{9}{4} - \frac{1}{4} x^2 \right) y$$

has the sign of $-y$ on the interval and is thus always concave toward the x axis. It follows that the straight line

$$y^* = 2x$$

which is tangent to $y = y(x)$ at $x = 0$ satisfies

$$|y(x)| \leq y^+$$

at least until $y(x)$ crosses the axis to assume negative values. y^+ at $x = 2$, i.e. $y^+ = 4$, then will serve as an upper bound on $y(x)$ if it is shown that $y(x)$ does not cross the axis at all in the interval of integration. It should be recognized that the equation we are trying to solve resembles the sin-cos differential equation

$$\frac{d^2y}{dx^2} = -ky \; ,$$

except in our equation k is a variable, $\left(\frac{9}{4} - \frac{x^2}{4}\right)$. The solution to our equation should then appear somewhat like the solution to the sin-cos equation except that the effective period of oscillation in our solution increases with increasing x. It follows then that the solution to

$$\frac{d^2y}{dx^2} = -\frac{9}{4}y \; ,$$

which is the form of our equation when the effective period is least, certainly crosses the axis before the solution to our equation. However, the solution to this equation with boundary conditions stated above is

$$y = \frac{4}{3} \sin \frac{3x}{2} \; .$$

This equation has half period $\frac{2\pi}{3}$ and it is clear that y is positive in the interval $0 \leq x \leq 2$. It follows that the solution to the equation we are trying to solve also does not cross the axis in the interval $0 \leq x \leq 2$. Consequently, according to our previous remarks 4 is a valid upper bound on $y(x)$ in the interval of integration. An upper bound on $\left|\frac{dy}{dx}\right|$ is now readily fixed. The rate of decrease of the slope is certainly everywhere less (in magnitude) than

$$\frac{d}{dx}\left(\frac{dy}{dx}\right) = -\frac{9}{4} \cdot 4$$

where we have put $y = 4$, $x = 0$ on the right side of our differential equation. Hence, the magnitude of the slope is certainly bounded above by

$$| \frac{dy}{dx} | < | (\frac{dy}{dx})_{x=0} - 9 \cdot \Delta x | = | 2 - 18 | = 16$$

Having thus established bounds on y and $z = \frac{dy}{dx}$ suitable scale factors can be picked to give the scaled variables:

$$y* = 2^{-2} y$$
$$z* = 2^{-4} z$$

The three first order differential equations (28-6), (28-7) and (28-8) expressed in terms of the scaled variables become

$$\frac{dy*}{dx*} = 2^4 z* \tag{28-9}$$

$$\frac{dz*}{dx*} = (-\frac{9}{4} + 4 x*^2) y* \tag{28-10}$$

$$\frac{dx*}{dx*} = 1 \tag{28-11}$$

These derivatives must now be scaled by $2^m h$ so that the resulting scaled derivatives k_0, k_1, k_2 will lie within machine range. A suitable scaling factor for this purpose is $2^m h = 2^{-4}$ and the equations for the scaled derivatives are

$$k_0 = 2^m h \frac{dy*}{dx*} = z* \tag{28-12}$$

$$k_1 = 2^m h \frac{dz*}{dx*} = (\frac{-9}{16} + x*^2) y*/4 \tag{28-13}$$

$$k_2 = 2^m h \frac{dx*}{dx*} = \frac{1}{16} \tag{28-14}$$

As mentioned earlier the choice of the factor $2^m h$ is governed by the need to keep the scaled derivatives within machine range and at the same time retain as many significant digits in the scaled derivatives as possible. The choice made here is not necessarily the optimum choice though it is probably close. With a more accurate determination of the bounds of the variables we might have been able to make a somewhat better choice of scale factors (better in the sense that we might not have had to scale down as much, thus preserving more accuracy) however as a practical matter one must decide just how much time and effort it is worthwhile to invest on the determination of a "best" set of scaling parameters. Just as in trying to optimize the number of words in a code one must break off at some point in order to get the code running in a reasonable time, being satisfied that any additional time spent in trying to optimize the code would probably not be worth the effort. It will be noticed that we have everywhere chosen scaling factors which are powers of two. Although it is not necessary to put the scale factors in this form it is usually convenient to do so simply because numbers can be multiplied by powers of two by shifting. The above discussion completes our consideration of the scaling problem.

The question of the choice of the integration step size is not an easily answered one, and a careful discussion of the subject would require an amount of analysis outside of the intended scope of these notes.[*] Consequently we will dispose of this topic by making some qualitative remarks on the type of thinking that must be applied to this problem. It should be fairly apparent that the interval size must be picked in such a way that the solution "does not change much" in the interval. Put in a little more precise way, h must be sufficiently small that the solution $y(x)$ may be satisfactorily represented by just terms up to and including fourth-order terms in the Taylor expansion since the integration scheme takes accurate account of only these terms. In principle an estimate of the truncation error can be obtained by letting this error be represented by just the difference between the fifth-order Taylor expansion term and the term in h^5 of the Runge-Kutta scheme. However, as a practical matter this number is difficult to actually compute.

---

[*] Library routine F 6, which has recently been written, automatically selects the interval size to be as large as possible while maintaining a specified error bound in the solution.

Usually one's judgement on interval size is based heavily on experience. The
rough form of the solution is usually known in advance and consideration of the
interval size that would be needed on a simple function of roughly the same
character usually will lead to an intelligent choice for h. If the programmer
has doubts about the proper choice of interval size he should write the code in
such a way that the interval size is easy to change and then experiment with
different interval sizes to see how much effect is produced on the solution when
the interval size is reduced. It is obvious that the computing time required for
finding the solution to some differential equation on a fixed interval $a \leq x \leq b$
is proportional to the number of integration steps and consequently inversely
proportional to h. Consequently the desire for accuracy through reduction of
the interval size must be tempered somewhat by consideration of the computing
time. Although it might first appear that the accuracy of the solution can be
improved indefinitely by making h arbitrarily small this is not at all true.
The reason is that as the number of integration steps increases the number of
arithmetic operations increases proportionately consequently increasing the
roundoff error. As h is reduced, then, a point will eventually be reached
where the reduced truncation error achieved by the smaller h is counterbalanced
by the increased roundoff error; for still smaller values of h the roundoff
error dominates and causes the total error to increase. For optimum accuracy,
neglecting computing time considerations, the best choice of h is that value
for which the truncation error and roundoff error combine to give a minimum
total error.

In the current example we will take $h = 2^{-8}$. The interval of
integration $\Delta x^* = \frac{1}{2}$ to be divided into $\frac{\Delta x^*}{h} = 2^7$ steps. Since we have
taken $2^m h = 2^{-4}$ it follows that m will be equal to 4.

Let us next assign the S parameters for F1. We will assume that the
function bank, or y bank, begins at location 400, the k bank begins at location
403, the q bank begins at location 406 and the Auxiliary begins at location 500.
The S parameters then are $S3 = 400 \times 2^{-39}$, $S4 = 403 \times 2^{-39}$, $S5 = 406 \times 2^{-39}$,
$S6 = 3 \times 2^{-39}$ (three equations are to be solved), $S7 = 500 \times 2^{-39}$; the
parameters must be loaded into locations 3, 4, ... 7 by SADOI before SADOI reads
an order from the program tape which makes reference to any one of these parameters.

Though our previous considerations were directed at a specific set of boundary conditions it will be instructive to write the code in such a way that the boundary conditions are parameters of the problem which may be varied. (This variation is presumed small, so that the problem does not need to be scaled again.) Consequently, the program is designed to read a parameter tape, using library routine N12 (INFRAPUT)[*], on which the boundary conditions are specified. In particular the form of the data on the tape is as follows:

$y_0/10$ (decimal fraction)

$z_0/10$ (decimal fraction)

N   (end signal for N12)

The solution is to be printed as a table; at each Runge-Kutta step the value of x and y is to be printed. The code follows.

LOCATION	ORDER PAIR	COMMENTS
	00 3K	
		Preset parameters
	00 F	S3: y bank
	00 400F	
	00 F	S4: k bank
	00 403F	
	00 F	S5: q bank
	00 406F	
	00 F	S6: number of equations
	00 3F	
	00 F	S7: location of Auxiliary
	00 500F	
(F1)	00 K	Runge-Kutta Subroutine
(P16)	00 K	INFRAPRINT
(N12)	00K	INFRAPUT

(Continued on page 226)

---

* See APPENDIX 15.

LOCATION	ORDER PAIR	COMMENTS
	00 K	Constants
0	(2) 00 F	
	00 625 000 000 000J	10/16
1	00 F	4/10
	00 400 000 000 000J	
2	80 F	$-1 + 2^7 \cdot 2^{-39}$
	00 128F	
3	00 F	
	00 562 500 000 000J	9/16
		Temporary Storage
	(3) 00 F	
	00 2(3)	
	02 K	Master
0	(1) 50 S3	
	50 (1)	Enter N12 to read $y_0/10$, $z_0/10$
1	26 (N12)	
	19 2F	
2	50 S3	
	74 (2)	$(10/16)\,(y_0/10) + 2^{-42}$
3	00 2F	
	40 S3	$y_0^* = y_0/4$ rounded
4	50 1S3	
	74 (2)	$(z_0/10)(10/16)$

(Continued on page 227)

LOCATION	ORDER PAIR	COMMENTS
5	40 1S3	$z_0^* = z_0/16$ rounded
	41 2S3	$x_0^* = 0$
6	19 3F	
	40 2S4	set $k_2 = \frac{1}{16}$
7	41 S5	clear q_0
	41 1S5	q_1
8	41 2S5	q_2
	F1 2(2)	set integration counter $= 1 - 129 \cdot 2^{-39}$
9	40 (3)	
	22 (1.2)	jump for initial print
10	(1.1) 00 4F	
	50 (1.1)	
11	(1.2) 26 (F1)	enter Runge-Kutta subroutine
	92 131F	prepare to print x
12	92 515F	
	50 2S3	
13	7J 1(2)	$x^* \cdot 4/10 = x/10$
	50 F	waste
14	(1.3) 54 110F	
	50 (1.3)	print x
15	26 (P16)	
	92 963F	space
16	50 S3	
	7J 1(2)	$y^* \cdot 4/10 = y/10$
17	(1.4) 54 110F	
	50 (1.4)	
18	26 (P16)	print y
	F5 (3)	advance integration counter
19	40 (3)	
	32 (1.1)	jump if not end

(Continued on page 228)

LOCATION	ORDER PAIR	COMMENTS
20	24 (1)	BS stop if end
	50 F	waste
	00 500K	AUXILIARY
0	(4) K5 F	
	42 (4.1)	
1	L5 1S3	$k_0 = z*$
	40 S4	
2	50 2S3	$(x*)^2$
	7J 2S3	
3	L0 3(2)	$-9/16 + x*^2$
	40 1(3)	
4	41 F	
	50 1(3)	
5	75 S3	$(- \dfrac{9}{16} + x*^2) \cdot y*$
	F4 F	
6	F4 F	$x \dfrac{1}{4} = k_1$
	10 2F	
7	(4.1) 40 1S4	
	22 [ ]F	exit
	26(1) 241N	

UNIVERSITY OF ILLINOIS
DIGITAL COMPUTER
CHAPTER 29

THE CATHODE RAY TUBE DISPLAY

It is sometimes desirable to plot the results of a computation and for
this purpose a cathode ray tube (CRT) display unit is available. An output command
may be given which will cause a spot, coordinates (x,y), on the face of the tube to
be brightened. The coordinates of the spot to be brightened are specified by the
bit configuration in the accumulator at the time the output command is given.

There are actually three tubes on which the results are plotted in parallel.
Two of these tubes have cameras attached over their faces, making it possible to take
a picture of the set of points brightened -- the sequence of points usually appearing
as a curve in the picture. One of the cameras holds 35 mm film and special ILLIAC
orders may be given to advance the film; thus it is possible to take a series of
35 mm pictures of the sequence of points plotted completely automatically; the other
camera is a Polaroid Land camera and is operated manually. The third tube, operating
in parallel with the other two, is for direct visual observation. This tube is of
a special type, called a Memotron, which has the property that a spot on the tube
face once brightened will remain brightened until the computer operator erases it
manually by throwing a switch on the control panel; thus, with this tube one sees
immediately the picture that is being simultaneously recorded on film since the
tube "permanently" records all brightened spots just as the film does.

To describe the coordinate scheme used with the CRT display consider
Figure 29-1. The origin of the coordinate system is located at the lower left-hand
corner of the tube face. The x and y axes are divided into 256 discrete points
numbered 0, 1, 2 ... 255. A spot on the tube face is specified by the number
pair (x,y) where x and y are allowed just the values given above. The locations
of three points are illustrated in the figure; the point x = 255, y = 255 is located
in the upper right-hand corner; the point x = 128, y = 128 is located at the center;
the point x = 128, y = 64 is located below the center, one-half the distance from
the center of the tube to the x-axis.

230

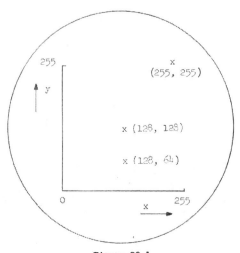

Figure 29-1

Coordinate system for the CRT display unit.

To display a point with coordinates (x,y) the values of x and y are placed in the accumulator according to the following rules:

(1) y is placed in digital positions $A_0 A_1 \ldots A_7$;

(2) x is placed in digital positions $A_8 A_9 \ldots A_{15}$;

(3) digits in the remainder of A have no effect.

Thus, y and x are located in the accumulator as shown below in Figure 29-2.

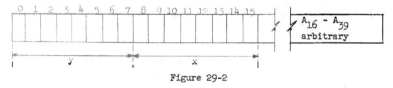

Figure 29-2

Location of digits of x and y in the accumulator to display point (x, y).

Having arranged the digits of x and y in A as shown in Figure 29-2, the execution of the output order 82 16_D will cause the point with coordinates

$$x = a_8 \cdot 2^7 + a_9 \cdot 2^6 + a_{10} \cdot 2^5 + a_{11} \cdot 2^4 + a_{12} \cdot 2^3 + a_{13} \cdot 2^2 + a_{14} \cdot 2 + a_{15}$$

$$y = a_0 \cdot 2^7 + a_1 \cdot 2^6 + a_2 \cdot 2^5 + a_3 \cdot 2^4 + a_4 \cdot 2^3 + a_5 \cdot 2^2 + a_6 \cdot 2 + a_7$$

to be displayed. The execution of the output order will cause 16_D left shifts of the AQ register. The execution time for this output order is about 800 μs.

When making a recording of the points displayed with the 35 mm camera, the following things should be kept in mind. The roll of film in the camera may hold pictures taken by other users; therefore in order to distinguish pictures belonging to a particular user they should be marked in a characteristic way. The film can conveniently be marked with the CRT lettering routine stored on the drum. To use this simply punch the characters to be displayed on a tape, preceding the sequence of characters with the number 9 and terminating the sequence with a one-hole delay. This tape should be read into ILLIAC before the program tape is read. Lettering on the scope will begin in the upper left corner of the scope face and proceed from left to right. A maximum of 18 characters may be placed on one line. A line feed and carriage return character will cause a new line of characters to begin. A maximum of 14 lines may be displayed. If one tries to display more than 18 characters on a line, then a "line feed and carriage return" will automatically be executed. Also, if one attempts to print more than 14 lines, then a film advance will automatically be executed.

If several frames of pictures are taken, it is usually found convenient to mark each frame with some kind of identification symbol. Library subroutine 05 may be used for this purpose. If each frame is not marked, the user should put a mark of some kind after the last picture taken. It is also generally good practice to advance the film one or two frames before the display of points begins; the command 92 769_D will advance the film one frame. Also it is a good idea to advance the film a frame or two after the last picture taken in order to be sure that the next user does not draw a curve on top of the results just obtained by the last user. It is also wise to advance the film to prevent fogging of the picture. The camera has no shutter and as a consequence just the filament light from the CRT will fog the film if the film remains exposed for a long period of time (order of 15 minutes).

The use of the CRT display unit for displaying a curve will now be illustrated in a simple example. Let us suppose that a variable Y which is being computed (for example suppose Y to be the solution to a differential equation) is to be plotted as a function of time, T. The plot is to consist of Y on the vertical axis (ordinate) and T on the horizontal axis (abscissa). We will suppose that bounds on Y have been determined: $-\frac{1}{2} < Y < \frac{1}{2}$. The variable T is held as an integer, i.e. is stored as $T \cdot 2^{-39}$ (the units of T might be those of the integration interval, h, thus T would just be the number of integration steps). Bound on T are such that $0 \leq T < 256$.

Since the variable Y assumes negative as well as positive values with upper and lower bounds symmetrically disposed about zero, we will take the mid-point of the vertical axis to correspond to Y = 0. The proper value of Y for plotting is obtained if we just extract the first 8 bits of Y and add a 1 to the sign digit to shift the origin for the y axis to the center of the tube face. The correct value of T for plotting is obtained if we simply shift this number into digit positions A_8 - A_{15} (least significant digit of integer T in A_{15}).

The code which follows is to be considered as a closed subroutine of a larger program. The purpose of this subroutine is to plot the point (T,Y) on the CRT display unit according to the scheme described above. The subroutine begins at symbolic address (1); on entry to the subroutine it is assumed that Y is in symbolic address (2) and T is in symbolic address 1(2).

LOCATION	ORDER PAIR	COMMENTS
0	(1) K5 F 42 (1.1)	Set link
1	09 1F L4 (2)	Shift Y origin
2	40 F L5 1(2)	Temporarily store Y
3	00 24F 50 F	Put T into position Put Y in Q
4	J0 (1.2) S4 F	Extract Q_0 - Q_7 Put Y in $A_0 \ldots A_7$
5	(1.1) 82 16F 22 F	Plot Y,T Exit
6	(1.2) LL F 00 F	Y extractor
7	(2) Y	
8	$T \cdot 2^{-39}$	

Sometimes it is desired to plot more than one point at a given value
of x; in the preceding example one might desire to plot Y vs. T and $\frac{dY}{dT}$ vs. T
simultaneously. After plotting the point T,Y as just described, then the point
T, $\frac{dY}{dT}$ may be plotted by simply placing $\frac{dY}{dT}$ in the digits of A, A_0 A_1 ... A_7, and
executing the order 82 8. This point will then be plotted with ordinate given
by digits in A_0 A_1 ... A_7 and the abscissa of the preceding point.

UNIVERSITY OF ILLINOIS
DIGITAL COMPUTER
CHAPTER 30

B-LINES AND FLOATING POINT ARITHMETIC

Almost any routine of practical importance contains a number
of loops. A counter is generally associated with each loop which
keeps track of the number of passes through the loop. Usually within
each loop the address of one or more instructions is modified in a regular
fashion; quite commonly, as has been seen in the preceeding chapters, the
addresses are changed by one on each pass. Because these features are so
common in programs a number of computing machines have built into them
special devices called B-lines or index registers which permit counting and
address modification to be performed with considerable efficiency. The
detailed characteristics of the B-lines vary somewhat for different computing
machines but in general they possess the following common features. Each
B-line is a register in the machine comprising n bits, where n is usually
equal to the number of bits in the address portion of an instruction. The
B-line is used to modify the address digits of an instruction; the B-line
which is to do the modification is specified by a set of bits within the
instruction. When the instruction is executed its address is taken to be the
number in the address portion of the instruction modified by the number in the
specified B-line. It is common to perform the modification by adding the
contents of the B-line to the number in the address digits of the instruction.
This modification of the address is not permanent, for the instruction as it
appears in the memory of the computer is <u>not</u> altered, it is only the interpretation of the address by the control unit of the computer at the time the
instruction is to be executed which is modified. To illustrate the preceding
remarks we now consider a computing machine with B-lines.* The form of an

---

* This computer is not necessarily identical to a real computer but its
  properties are similar to those of a real computer with B-lines.

instruction is as shown in Figure 1 below. The instruction is thus composed

FUNCTION (f Bits)	ADDRESS (a Bits)	B-LINE (b Bits)

Figure 30-1

Typical form of an instruction in a computing machine with B-lines.

of three parts, a block of function digits and a block of address digits, as in an ILLIAC instruction, plus a block of B-line digits. Let us consider a specific instruction and its interpretation by the control. We will assume that

(a) the function digits specify a clear add instruction (i.e. L5 in ILLIAC language);

(b) the number in the address digits is 165_D;

(c) the number in the B-line digits is 3_D;

(d) the number in B-line 3 is 40_D;

(e) the number in memory location 205_D is x;

when this instruction is executed the effective address is

$$205_D = 165_D + 40_D$$

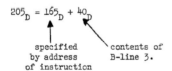

specified
by address
of instruction

contents of
B-line 3.

hence the number from memory location 205, namely x, is brought into the accumulator by this instruction. Our computer will have certain instructions unlike any on the ILLIAC which refer to certain operations on the B-lines.

One instruction we will call "load B-line". This instruction will cause the
number in the address digits of the instruction to be placed in the B-line
specified by the B-line bits of the instruction; thus, the instruction

| Load B-line | 1,000 | 3 |

would cause the number 1,000 to be loaded into B-line 3. Another instruction
will be called "advance B-line". This instruction will cause the contents of
the specified B-line to be incremented by one and then compared with the number
in the address portion of the instruction; if the two numbers are equal the
control skips the instruction immediately following the "advance B-line"
instruction, otherwise the execution of instructions proceeds in the normal
fashion. Any instruction having all B-line digits equal to zero is not to have
its address modified. Let us now write the orders necessary for the evaluation
of the polynomial

$$P_{20}(x) = a_{20}x^{20} + a_{19}x^{19} + \ldots + a_1x + a_0$$

It is assumed that the polynomial coefficients a_{20}, $a_{19} \ldots a_0$ are located in
a block of words in the memory beginning at location 500 and x is in location
600. The code begins at location 100. In this illustration ILLIAC function
digits are used whenever the instruction is a possible ILLIAC instruction.

Instruction Location	Function	Address	B-Line
100	41	0	0
	Load B-line	0	1
101	50	600	0
	7J	0	0
102	L4	500	1
	40	0	0
103	Advance B-line	21	1
	26	101	0
104	OF	0	0

The hold-add instruction at the left-hand side of 102 is B-line modified; the effective address of this order on successive passes through the loop is 500, 501, 502 ... 520, thus calling out the coefficients a_{20}, a_{19}, a_{18}, ... a_0. As long as the contents of B-line 1 are less than 21 the 26 order at RH of location 103 is obeyed. When the contents of B-line 1 are equal to 21 then the 26 order is skipped and the computer will stop on the OF order at 104. One can see from this simple example that the number of orders necessary for "book-keeping" in the loop has been reduced from that necessary in a similar program in the ILLIAC and in addition the bookkeeping is very simply specified---notice that the address in the hold-add instruction at 102 is just the base address of the list of polynomial coefficients and the address of the advance B-line instruction at 103 is just equal to the number of passes through the loop.

A quite different feature also included in many of the present high-speed computing machines is a provision for doing "floating point" arithmetic. The operands in "floating point" arithmetic are called "floating point" numbers which have the form

$$x = a \cdot b^c \quad .$$

The number b is a constant for the machine and is usually either 2 or 10. Let us consider a representation in which b = 2, then the floating point number has the form

$$x = a \cdot 2^c \quad .$$

Each number x in the machine is held in the memory as a number pair (a,c) ; b need not be specified since it is the same for all numbers in the machine. With-in a word one group of bits is used to hold a, called the fractional part of the floating point number (it is a number in the interval $(-1, +1)$, and another group of bits is used to specify c, called the exponent or characteristic of the floating point number.

The aim of the floating point scheme is to increase the range of the numbers which the machine can represent and thereby reduce the scaling problem. Consider a floating point computer with 40 bit words, having bits w_0, w_1 ... w_{32}

assigned for holding the fractional part of the floating point number and bits $w_{33} \cdots w_{39}$ assigned for holding the exponent part of the floating point number. The number range for this representation is then

$$-1 \cdot 2^{63} \leq x < 1 \cdot 2^{63}$$

and, except for x = zero, the range of the magnitude of x is

$$2^{-32} \cdot 2^{-64} \leq |x| < 1 \cdot 2^{63} \, ,$$

the lower bound being achieved when $a = 2^{-32}$ and $c = -64$. In an attempt to preserve significant digits the number a is usually scaled to lie in the range $\frac{1}{2} \leq |a| < 1$; when the floating point number is in this form it is said to be normalized*, or standardized. The number x = 0 is a special case and different computers vary in the detailed manner in which they treat this number. Commonly, whenever the result of an arithmetic operation yields a = 0, then the exponent digits are set to zero (or to -64). Quite commonly also the result of an arithmetic operation is automatically put into normalized form.

The logic of the arithmetic operations is of course different than in fixed point arithmetic, but quite straightforward. We consider addition first, and suppose two numbers

$$x = a_x \cdot 2^{c_x}$$

$$y = a_y \cdot 2^{c_y}$$

are to be summed to form

$$z = a_z 2^{c_z} \, .$$

---

* In general the floating point number is said to be normalized when $\frac{1}{b} \leq |a| < 1$. Thus in a representation $x = a \cdot 10^c$ the normal form is achieved when $\frac{1}{10} \leq |a| < 1$.

To do this sum it is clear that the numbers x and y must be brought into the same scale (that is their exponents must be made equal to each other by appropriately shifting the fractional parts) before the fractional parts may be added to each other. The procedure is to rescale the number with the smaller exponent, thus if $C_x < C_y$ then the first step in the addition process would be to put x into the form

$$x = a'_x \cdot 2^{C'_x} \, ,$$

where

$$a'_x = a_x \cdot 2^{C_x - C_y} \, ,$$

$$C'_x = C_y \, .$$

The fractional part a_x is thus reduced by the factor $2^{C_x-C_y}$ ($C_x-C_y < 0$), this operation being executed in the computer as a right shift of C_y-C_x places. After the two numbers have thus been put into the same scale the fractional parts are added, $a'_x + a_y$, and the exponent associated with the result is just C_y. The alternative procedure of picking the number with the larger exponent and shifting its fractional part left to bring x and y into the same scale is excluded because the most significant digits of the number with the larger exponent would then be "lost" by spilling out of the left end of the shifting register. When the number with the smaller exponent is shifted to the right to bring x and y into the same scale digits also spill out of the shifting register, but these are the least significant digits.

There is the possibility that overflow may occur for it is entirely conceivable that

$$|a'_x + a_y| > 1$$

and it is therefore necessary for the floating-point addition operation to properly detect and treat this situation when it does arise. The scheme is to have a means for detecting and preserving the overflow bit (under any circumstances we must have $|a'_x + a_y| < 2$) and whenever the overflow situation is detected the sum $a'_x + a_y$, including the overflow bit, is shifted to the right once, i.e. it is reduced by $\frac{1}{2}$, and the exponent is increased by 1. The result of an addition may not be in normalized form. In some floating point schemes normalization of the sum is executed automatically, in other schemes the programmer is provided with two types of floating add instructions, one providing for automatic normalization of the sum and the other leaving the sum unnormalized.

Multiplication is not quite so involved. The procedure for multiplication is simply to multiply the fractional parts of the two numbers and sum their exponents

$$x \cdot y = a_x \cdot a_y \cdot 2^{C_x + C_y} = a_z \cdot 2^{C_z} \quad .$$

This may or may not be followed by automatic normalization of the product depending on the scheme used. In this situation overflow of the fractional part is not possible.

Division is slightly more involved than multiplication. Essentially the procedure is to divide the fractional parts and subtract exponents, thus

$$\frac{x}{y} = \frac{a_x}{a_y} \cdot 2^{C_x - C_y} \quad .$$

However, since the division of the fractional parts proceeds as in ordinary fixed point division it is necessary to pre-scale the floating point numbers to insure that the quotient of the fractional parts is itself a fraction. A procedure for handling this is to always first shift the fractional part of the numerator one place to the right, putting x into the form

$$x = \left(\frac{a_x}{2} \right) \cdot 2^{C_x + 1}$$

before executing the division of the fractional parts; it is assumed in this
that both x and y are initially in normal form. This prescaling of x takes
place automatically as an initial step of the floating point division operation.
Normalization after division may be automatic.

While the increased number range permitted by the use of floating
point arithmetic makes it very attractive there are certain problems attending
the use of this scheme of arithmetic which are all too often not fully
appreciated. The primary problem concerns error analysis. It has already been
made apparent that error analysis in fixed point arithmetic is a very difficult
task. In floating point arithmetic these difficulties are greatly exaggerated.
The source of the increased difficulty is that the magnitude of the error is not
absolute as it is in fixed point but relative to the size of the number with which
it is associated. Returning to the floating point scheme described on page 240 where
33 bits were assigned to the fractional part of the number, a number x put into
this form and properly rounded will have an error

$$-2^{-33} \cdot 2^{C_x} < \epsilon < 2^{-33} \cdot 2^{C_x} \ .$$

Thus the bounds on the error of any number are vitally related to the scale
factor of the number itself. In a fixed point calculation a number x' put into
a 33 bit register, and properly rounded, will have its error bounded as follows

$$-2^{-33} < \epsilon < 2^{-33} \ .$$

Of course it is true that x' may have to be scaled by a factor s to bring it
into fixed point range so that the number actually treated in the machine is

$$(x')^* = x' \div s$$

The error in x' is then

$$-2^{-33} \cdot s < \epsilon < 2^{-33} \cdot s \ .$$

This looks very much like the above expression for the error in a floating point computation, but there is one vital difference. In the fixed point computation the scale factor is fixed by the programmer and therefore known to him at all times. In the floating point computation the scale factor is generally assigned automatically when the number is normalized consequently the scaling is taken out of the hands of the programmer and essentially hidden from him and since the bounds on the errors are proportional to the scale factor it follows that the bounds of the errors also become hidden. It is for this reason that the notion that one can bypass the analysis of a problem to determine the sizes of numbers which arise at various stages of a computation by doing everything in floating point is a dangerous one to assume, for it implies that there is very little knowledge of the accuracy of the result---and the result is therefore of very little value.

To further demonstrate the difficulties one can get into in a floating point calculation by neglecting careful consideration of the numbers being dealt with and the errors which are generated, two extreme examples of typical difficulties are now cited. If two numbers of opposite sign and nearly equal magnitude are added to each other there will be strong cancellation in the fractional parts. Let us suppose in fact that the two numbers have the same exponent and that their fractional parts differ (in magnitude) only in the last two bit positions of their fractional part. The resultant sum then has at most two significant digits but after normalization of the sum there is nothing to indicate that only the first two bits of the fractional part of the sum are significant. In the corresponding situation in fixed point arithmetic the non-significant digits are clearly apparent because of the leading zeros which would result. Another difficulty arises in a computation of the following type. Suppose we have a computation to perform which involves the iterative procedure

$$z_i = z_{i-1} + x_i , \qquad i = 0, 1, \ldots N$$
$$z_0 = P .$$

Further let us suppose that the character of the numbers is such that $P >> x_i$ for all i, although

$$\sum_{i=1}^{N} x_i > P \ .$$

If one prepares the floating point program for this computation with no regard to the sizes of the numbers involved, then the sequencing of the sums would probably occur as follows:

$$z_1 = P + x_1$$
$$z_2 = z_1 + x_2 = (P + x_1) + x_2$$
$$z_3 = z_2 + x_3 = (P + x_1 + x_2) + x_3$$

etc.

Consider the first sum. Since $x_1 << P$ the fractional part of x_1 will be shifted far to the right to get it into the same scale as P for the addition; the result is that only a very few significant digits of x_1 are actually used to form the fractional part of $P + x_1$. In an extreme situation the fractional part of x_1 may even be completely lost in the attempt to put the two numbers in the same scale. The same difficulty arises at each successive addition of a new x_i with the consequence that the part of the sum contributed by $x_1 + x_2 + \ldots + x_N$ will be greatly in error; and again in an extreme situation it might even be zero. This difficulty could of course be eliminated easily by simply forming $x_1 + x_2 + \ldots + x_N$ first and then adding P. The point is that to know that this must be done implies that some consideration be given to the sizes of numbers.

The above remarks should make it fairly evident that a careful floating point calculation demands a consideration of the magnitudes of the numbers just as a fixed point calculation does. The question arises as to why floating point should then be used at all, for if one knows enough about the magnitudes of the numbers to properly do a calculation in floating point, then one might just as well write the program in fixed point arithmetic in the first place. This is a controversial point but many hold that floating point arithmetic is a quite useful and practical scheme for a large number of problems.

The ILLIAC does not have the facility for doing floating point arithmetic "wired in". However, it is possible to write a program to make the ILLIAC act as if floating point arithmetic was wired in, just as it is possible by means of a closed subroutine for the computation of $\sqrt{x}$ to make it appear as if there was a single ILLIAC order to execute $\sqrt{x}$. Floating point arithmetic is achieved on the ILLIAC by means of an interpretive subroutine. This interpretive subroutine differs from the subroutines thus far considered in that the program parameters follow the jump order to the subroutine and the "parameters" are actually instructions to execute various floating point arithmetic operations written in a form similar to conventional ILLIAC orders. When the jump to the subroutine is executed the subroutine examines the floating point orders one by one and executes a series of ILLIAC orders designed to produce the desired floating point operation; thus, within the interpretive floating point subroutine there are blocks of orders (regular ILLIAC orders of course) which will operate on the two number pairs

$$(a_x, C_x) \text{ representing } x = a_x 10^{C_x}$$

and

$$(a_y, C_y) \text{ representing } y = a_y 10^{C_y}$$

to form the normalized result

$$(a_z, C_z) \text{ representing } z = a_z 10^{C_z} = x + y;$$

other blocks of orders within the subroutine effect floating point multiplication and so forth. In addition, the floating point interpretive routine permits one to write the floating point instruction as if B-lines were available on the ILLIAC.

The standard library subroutine for executing floating point arithmetic is labeled Al. There are also routines in the library for computation of the frequently used functions in floating point form; routines included in this list are square root (RA1), sine (TA1) exponential (SA2) natural logarithm (SA3), arc tangent (TA2). These routines for computing special functions are always used in connection with A1. There is also in the library a "package" of floating point routines which includes A1 and the above auxiliaries for computing special functions; the "package" is labeled A6. A library write-up of A1, with the code omitted, is given in Appendix 23, pp. 409-415. A library write-up of A6, with the code omitted, is given in Appendix 24, pp. 416-419.

APPENDIX 1

ADDITIONAL LITERATURE REFERENCES

Logical design and circuitry of computers:
    (1A) "Logical Design of Digital Computers", M. Phister, Jr., John
        Wiley and Sons, Inc., New York, 1958.

Programming: These reports by Goldstine and von Neumann are of historical interest.
    (2A) "Planning and Coding of Problems for an Electronic Computing
        Instrument", Herman H. Goldstine and John von Neumann. Re-
        port on the Mathematical and Logical Aspects of an Electronic
        Computing Instrument, Part II, Volume I (1947) and Volume II
        (1948). Institute for Advanced Study, Princeton, New Jersey.

    (3A) "High Speed Data Processing", C. C. Gotlieb and J. N. P. Hume,
        McGraw-Hill, New York, 1958.

    (4A) "Programming the IBM 650 Electronic Data Processing Machine",
        J. V. Andree, Holt, Rinehart and Winston, Inc., New York,
        1958.

    (5A) "Electronic Digital Computers", F. Alt, Academic Press, New York,
        1958.

    (6A) "A Primer of Primer of Programming for Digital Computers", M. H. Wrubel,
        McGraw-Hill, New York, 1959.

    (7A) "Programming for Digital Computers", J. Jeenel, McGraw-Hill,
        New York, 1959.

    (8A) "Mathematical Methods for Digital Computers", A. Ralston and
        H. Wilf, John Wiley and Sons, Inc., New York, 1960.

Periodicals:
    (9A) Communications of the Association for Computing Machinery

(10A) Computing Reviews

(11A) Proceedings of the IRE Professional Group on Electronic
       Computers

(12A) Computer Journal (This is a publication of the British
       Computer Society)

(13A) "Advances in Computers", Volume 1 (1960), edited by F. L. Alt,
       Academic Press, New York.

APPENDIX 2

TABLE OF POWERS OF 2

2^n	n	2^{-n}
1	0	1.0
2	1	0.5
4	2	0.25
8	3	0.125
16	4	0.062 5
32	5	0.031 25
64	6	0.015 625
128	7	0.007 812 5
256	8	0.003 906 25
512	9	0.001 953 125
1 024	10	0.000 976 562 5
2 048	11	0.000 488 281 25
4 096	12	0.000 244 140 625
8 192	13	0.000 122 070 312 5
16 384	14	0.000 061 035 156 25
32 768	15	0.000 030 517 578 125
65 536	16	0.000 015 258 789 062 5
131 072	17	0.000 007 629 394 531 25
262 144	18	0.000 003 814 697 265 625
524 288	19	0.000 001 907 348 632 812 5
1 048 576	20	0.000 000 953 674 316 406 25
2 097 152	21	0.000 000 476 837 158 203 125
4 194 304	22	0.000 000 238 418 579 101 562 5
8 388 608	23	0.000 000 119 209 289 550 781 25
16 777 216	24	0.000 000 059 604 644 775 390 625
33 554 432	25	0.000 000 029 802 322 387 695 312 5
67 108 864	26	0.000 000 014 901 161 193 047 656 25
134 217 728	27	0.000 000 007 450 580 596 923 828 125
268 435 456	28	0.000 000 003 725 290 298 461 914 062 5
536 870 912	29	0.000 000 001 862 645 149 230 957 031 25
1 073 741 824	30	0.000 000 000 931 322 574 615 478 515 625
2 147 483 648	31	0.000 000 000 465 661 287 307 739 257 812 5
4 294 967 296	32	0.000 000 000 232 830 643 653 869 628 906 25
8 589 934 592	33	0.000 000 000 116 415 321 826 934 814 453 125
17 179 869 184	34	0.000 000 000 058 207 660 913 467 407 226 562 5
34 359 738 368	35	0.000 000 000 029 103 830 456 733 703 613 281 25
68 719 476 736	36	0.000 000 000 014 551 915 228 366 851 806 640 625
137 438 953 472	37	0.000 000 000 007 275 957 614 183 425 903 320 312 5
274 877 906 944	38	0.000 000 000 003 637 978 807 091 712 951 660 156 25
549 755 813 888	39	0.000 000 000 001 818 989 403 545 856 475 830 078 125

APPENDIX 3

ADDRESS CONVERSION TABLE

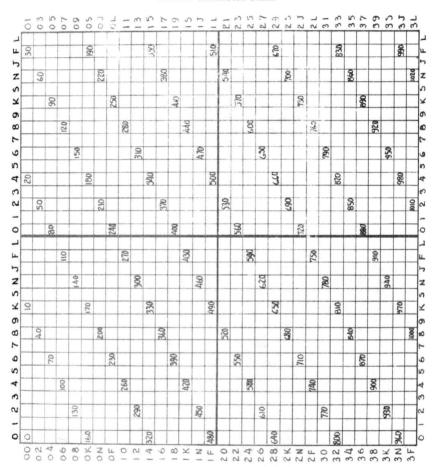

APPENDIX 4

THE COMPLETE ORDER CODE

This appendix has been copied directly from the ILLIAC Programming Manual and the notation used there is slightly different from that used in the present text. The notation of this appendix is defined as follows:

(1) n is used to denote the address digits of an order;

(2) $N(n)$ is used to denote the number in memory location n;

(3) A and Q are used to represent the accumulator and quotient registers, respectively, and they are used to denote the contents of these registers.

OV $\underset{\sim}{n}$ Left Shift (Double)   3 orders
                                 FINAL STOP   1 order

If $n = 0$, the machine will stop. If not, repeat n times the operation which replaces the contents

$$a_0, a_1, a_2, \cdots, a_{38}, a_{39}; \; q_1, q_2, q_3, \cdots, q_{38}, q_{39}$$

of AQ by

$$a_1, a_2, a_3, \cdots, a_{39} \, q_1; \; q_2, q_3, q_4, \cdots, q_{39}, 0$$

leaving q_0 unchanged.

The number n will be interpreted modulo 64.

Variants

0, 2, 4, 6	Order as described above.
1, 3, 5, 7	Clear A and then execute as described.
8, K, N	Illiac will hang up. Avoid these.
9, S, J, L	Clear A, insert 1/2 in A, and then execute order as described above.
F	Final Stop.

Use only 00, 01, 09 for shifts

Use OF with $n = 0$ for final stop

1V n   Right Shift (Halve)   3 Orders

    If n = 0, the machine will stop. If not, repeat n times the
operation which replaces the contents

$$a_0, a_1, a_2, \cdots , a_{38}, a_{39}; \quad q_1, q_2, q_3, \cdots , q_{38}, q_{39}$$

of AQ by

$$a_0, a_0, a_1, \cdots , a_{37}, a_{38}; \quad a_{39}, q_1, q_2, \cdots , q_{37}, q_{38},$$

leaving q_0 unchanged.

    The number n will be interpreted modulo 64.

Variants

0, 2, 4, 6	Order as described above.
1, 3, 5, 7	Clear A and then execute as described.
8, K, N, F	Illiac will hang up. Avoid these.
9, S, J, L	Clear A, insert 1/2 in A, and then execute order as described above.

    Use only 10, 11, 19

Bring the next order pair from memory location n and choose the left or right hand order of this pair, stopping beforehand or not, depending upon V.

Variants

0	Stop. The first order after starting with the START switch will be the right-hand order at memory location n. The stop can be ignored by setting a panel switch.
2	Transfer control to right-hand order at memory location.
4	Same as 0 except take left-hand order.
6	Same as 2 except take left-hand order.
1, 3, 5, 7	Same as 0, 2, 4, 6 except clear A first.
8, K, N, F	Illiac will hang up. Avoid these.
9, S, J, L	Same as 1, 3, 5, 7 except also make A = 1/2 after clearing.

Use 20, 21, 22, 23, 24, 25, 26, 27, 29, 2S, 2J, 2L.

Starting After A Stop. When the Illiac has been stopped by one of the control transfer stop orders, it is usually started again by moving the black switch to START, from which position the switch automatically returns to OBEY.

The Illiac can also be started again by moving the white switch through EXECUTE to FETCH and then back to RUN. If this is done, the control transfer order which stopped the Illiac will be ignored. The normal sequencing

will then follow unless the stop order is a right hand order transferring
control to the right hand side of a word. In this case, the order first
obeyed after starting will be the right hand instead of the left hand order
of the new order pair brought out.

For example consider the following orders:

p	L5 F
	20 p+2
p+1	40 1F
	24 p
p+2	7J 2F
	L4 3F

If we stop with the 20 order, the black switch will start with L4 3F and
the white switch with 24 p. If we stop with the 24 order, the black switch
will start with L5 F and the white switch with 7J 2F.

If $A \geq 0$, bring the next order pair from memory location n and choose the left or right hand order of this pair, stopping beforehand or not, depending upon V. If $A < 0$, go on to the next order.

Variants

0, 2, 4, 6	If $A \geq 0$, do the same operation as for the corresponding 2V order. If $A < 0$, go on to the next order.
1, 3, 5, 7	Identical with corresponding 2V orders.
8, K, N, F	Illiac will hang up. Avoid these.
9, S, J, L	Identical with corresponding 2V orders.

Use only 30, 32, 34, 36.

Starting After A Stop. The discussion given with the 2V orders applies here to the corresponding 3V orders.

4V n   Store   9 Orders

Copy into memory location n all of the contents of A, the contents
corresponding to the address of a left-hand order, or the contents corresponding
to the address of a right-hand order, depending upon V.

Variants

0, 4	Replace N(n) by A.
1, 5	Replace N(n) and A by 0.
2	Replace address digits of <u>right-hand</u> order at memory location n by the corresponding digits of A.
3	Same as 2 except clear A first.
6	Same as 2 except take <u>left-hand</u> order.
7	Same as 6 except clear A first.
8, K, N, F	Illiac will hang up. Avoid these.
9, J	Replace N(n) and A by 1/2.
S	Replace A by 1/2 and address digits of <u>right-hand</u> order at memory location n by 0.
L	Same as S except take <u>left-hand</u> order.

Use only <u>40</u>, <u>41</u>, <u>42</u>, 43, <u>46</u>, 47, <u>49</u>, 4S, 4L.

5V n   Memory to Q   3 Orders

Transfer N(n) to Q

Variants

0, 2, 4, 6,	Transfer N(n) to Q
1, 3, 5, 7	Clear A and transfer N(n) to Q.
8, K, N, F	Illiac will hang up. Avoid these.
9, S, J, L	Put 1/2 in A and transfer N(n) to Q.

Use only 50, 51, 59.

6V n   Divide   3 Orders

     Divide AQ by $N(n)$, placing the rounded quotient in Q (the least significant digit being 1 for the roundoff) and leaving a residue in A. If $|A| > |N(n)|$ the Illiac will stop after dividing. If $|A| = |N(n)|$ and if $A \geq 0$, the Illiac will stop after dividing; if $|A| = |N(n)|$ and if $A < 0$, the Illiac will not stop after dividing.

Variants

6	As described above.
7	Make $A = 0$, then proceed as above.
L, S	Make $A = 1/2$, then proceed as above.
8, K, N, F	Illiac will hang up. Avoid these.
0, 1, 2, 3	These give incorrect results or results
4, 5, 9, J	which are correct only under certain conditions. Avoid them.

    Use only 66, 67, 6L.

7V n   Multiply   12 Orders

Put Q x P(n) + 2^{-39} A into AQ, the least significant 39 digits being in Q with q_0 = 0.

Variants

0	P(n) = - N(n)
1	P(n) = - N(n); A = 0 "Unrounded Negative Multiply"
2	P(n) = - $\|N(n)\|$
3	P(n) = - $\|N(n)\|$; A = 0
4	P(n) = N(n) "Hold Multiply"
5	P(n) = N(n) ; A = 0 "Unrounded Multiply"
6	P(n) = $\|N(n)\|$
7	P(n) = $\|N(n)\|$; A = 0
8, K, N, F	Illiac will hang up. Avoid these.
9	P(n) = -N(n) ; A = 1/2 "Rounded Negative Multiply"
S	P(n) = - $\|N(n)\|$; A = 1/2
J	P(n) = N(n) ; A = 1/2 "Rounded Multiply"
L	P(n) = $\|N(n)\|$; A = 1/2

Use only 70, 71, 72, 73, 74, 75,
76, 77, 79, 7S, 7J, 7L

Transfer words between A and the input tape, output punch, or magnetic drum.

The address n must be a multiple of 4 for the tape and punch orders and must be 11 for drum orders.

Variants

0	Shift AQ four places left as in the 00 order and replace a_{36}, a_{37}, a_{38}, a_{39} by the binary digits corresponding to the sexadecimal character being read. This is done $n/4$ times.
1, 9	Clear A and then do as in 80 order.
2	Punch the digits a_0, a_1, a_2, a_3 as one sexadecimal character and shift AQ four places left as in the 00 order. This is done $n/4$ times.
3	Clear A and do as in 82 order.
5	This is a 40-digit order of the form 85 11 TV p. We distinguish two cases.
	(1) T is not 0, 1, 8, 9. In this case, A and Q are shifted left eleven places as in the 00 order and the word at drum location p is placed in A. Then the T order is executed using address p. Complete freedom is not available in drum addresses because p may interfere with V.

     (2) T is 0, 1, 8, 9. In this case after
     the word at drum location p is placed
     in A the right-hand order is skipped.
     This permits use of any drum address
     for p.

6   This is a 40-digit order of the form 86 11 TV p.
We again have two cases:

     (1) T is not 0, 1, 8, 9. In this case A is
     transferred to drum location p, and A
     and Q are shifted 11 places left as in
     the 00 order. Then the T order is ex-
     ecuted using address p. Complete freedom
     is not available in drum addresses be-
     cause p may interfere with V.

     (2) T is 0, 1, 8, 9. In this case the right-
     hand order is skipped after doing the
     left-hand order as in case (1). This
     permits use of any drum address p.

7   Same as 86 except clear A first.

S   Put 1/2 in A and do as in 82 order.

L   Put 1/2 in A and do as in 86 order.

8, K, N, F   Illiac will hang up. Avoid these.

4, J   These are not useful. Avoid them.

Use 80, 81, 82, 83, 85, 86, 87, 8S, 8L.

When the input order 80 n with n < 4 is executed, it acts like a left shift order, except that digits from Q do not go into A; zeroes go into the low order end of A instead. No tape character is read in this case. The following example illustrates the effect of this order when n = 3:

Initial state of A Q

A a_0 a_1 a_2 a_3 a_4 . . . . a_{36} a_{37} a_{38} a_{39}

Q q_0 q_1 q_2 q_3 q_4 . . . . q_{36} q_{37} q_{38} q_{39}

State of A Q after obeying 80 3

A a_3 a_4 a_5 a_6 a_7 . . . . a_{39} 0 0 0

Q q_0 q_4 q_5 q_6 q_7 . . . . q_{39} 0 0 0

Variants

1   Five hole input. Clear A, shift AQ four places <u>right</u> and replace a_{36}, a_{37}, a_{38}, a_{39} by the binary digits corresponding to the four least significant holes on the tape. Place the contents of the fifth hole in position a_0. The address part of this order must be 4.

2   Letter output. Punch on the tape a character depending upon the address digits n. Three quantities are defined by the 10 binary address digits:

(1) The leftmost 4 digits define the usual 4 digit positions in the output tape.

(2) The rightmost digit defines the 5th hole in the output tape.

(3) The rightmost 6 digits determine the number b of times that the above-defined character is punched and also the number of <u>right shifts</u> executed. The number of characters punched will be found by dividing the number in the rightmost 6 digits by 4 and <u>rounding up</u> to the next integer.

The address n may always be found from the following formula:

$$n = 64a + 4b + c - 2$$

where a is the character punched, a = 0, 1, 2, . . . , J, F, L

b is the number of characters punched, $1 \leq b \leq 16$

c determines the fifth hole, c = 0, 1.

The number of right shifts executed is $4b + c - 2$.

<u>Example</u>. Punch the character 7 thirteen times.

$$n = 64 \times 7 + 4 \times 13 + 0 - 2 = 498$$

It will be found that the last 6 digits contain the number 50 which when divided by 4 and rounded up gives 13. There will be 50 right shifts.

Figure 1 shows the relationship between the tape holes and the address digits of the 92 order. The address shown will print the character 7 thirteen times.

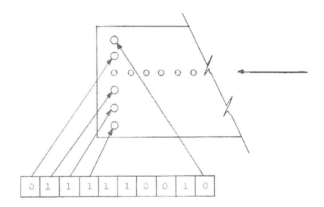

Figure 1

Address Digits of 92 Order

KV n   Increment Add From Q   12 Orders

These orders are identical with the FV orders except that Q is used instead of N(n).

Variants

0	Add $-Q - 2^{-39}$ to A. (See note).
1	Put $-Q - 2^{-39}$ in A.
2	Same as 0 if $Q \geq 0$; same as 4 if $Q < 0$.
3	Same as 1 if $Q \geq 0$; same as 5 if $Q < 0$.
4	Add $Q + 2^{-39}$ to A.
5	Put $Q + 2^{-39}$ in A.
6	Same as 4 if $Q \geq 0$; same as 0 if $Q < 0$.
7	Same as 5 if $Q \geq 0$; same as 1 if $Q < 0$.
8, K, N, F	Illiac will hang up. Avoid these.
9	Put $-Q - 2^{-39} + 1/2$ in A.
S	Same as 9 if $Q \geq 0$; same as J if $Q < 0$.
J	Put $Q + 2^{-39} + 1/2$ in A.
L	Same as J if $Q \geq 0$; same as 9 if $Q < 0$.

Use K0, K1, K2, K3, K4, K5, K6, K7, K9, KS, KJ, KL

NOTE: $-Q - 2^{-39}$ is the digitwise complement of Q.

SV n   Add from Q   12 Orders

Q is added, subtracted, etc.., to A. These orders are identical with the LV orders with Q used instead of N(n).

Variants

0	Subtract Q from A.
1	Put -Q in A.
2	Subtract $|Q|$ from A
3	Put - $|Q|$ in A.
4	Add Q to A.
5	Put Q in A.
6	Add $|Q|$ to A.
7	Put $|Q|$ in A.
8, K, N, F	Illiac will hang up. Avoid these.
9	Put $1/2$ - Q in A.
S	Put $1/2$ - $|Q|$ in A.
J	Put $1/2$ + Q in A.
L	Put $1/2$ + $|Q|$ in A.

Use S0, S1, S2, S3, S4, S5, S6, S7, S9, SS, SJ, SL

JV n   Extract   3 Orders

      If two corresponding digits of N(n) and Q are both 1's, put 1 in that place of Q. Otherwise put 0. This order gives the logical product of N(n) and Q.

Variants

0, 2, 4, 6	As described above.
1, 3, 5, 7	Clear A and do J0 order.
8, K, N, F	Illiac will hang up. Avoid these.
9, S, J, L	Put 1/2 in A and do J0 order.

      Use only J0, J1, J9

FV n   Increment Add   12 Orders
                                  Programmed Stop   1 Order

<u>Variants</u>

0   Add $-N(n) - 2^{-39}$ to A. (See note)

1   Put $-N(n) - 2^{-39}$ in A.

2   Same as 0 if $N(n) \geq 0$; same as 4 if
                     $N(n) < 0$.

3   Same as 1 if $N(n) \geq 0$; same as 5 if
                     $N(n) < 0$.

4   Add $N(n) + 2^{-39}$ to A.

5   Put $N(n) + 2^{-39}$ in A.

6   Same as 4 if $N(n) \geq 0$; same as 0 if
                     $N(n) < 0$.

7   Same as 5 if $N(n) \geq 0$; same as 1 if
                     $N(n) < 0$.

8, K, N   Illiac will hang up. Avoid these.

9   Put $-N(n) - 2^{-39} + 1/2$ in A.

S   Same as 9 if $N(n) \geq 0$; same as J if
                     $N(n) < 0$.

J   Put $N(n) + 2^{-39} + 1/2$ in A.

L   Same as J if $N(n) \geq 0$; same as 9 if
                     $N(n) < 0$.

F   Stop. This stop is used to indicate
                     failure of a programmed check.

       Use F0, <u>F1</u>, F2, F3, <u>F4</u>, <u>F5</u>, F6, F7, F9, FS, FJ, <u>FF</u>, FL.

NOTE: $-N(n) - 2^{-39}$ is the digitwise complement of $N(n)$.

LV n   Add   12 Orders

N(n) is added, subtracted, etc., to A.

Variants

0	Subtract N(n) from A.
1	Put -N(n) in A.
2	Subtract $|N(n)|$ from A.
3	Put - $|N(n)|$ in A.
4	Add N(n) to A.
5	Put N(n) in A.
6	Add $|N(n)|$ to A.
7	Put $|N(n)|$ in A.
8, K, N, F	Illiac will hang up. Avoid these.
9	Put 1/2 - N(n) in A.
S	Put 1/2 - $|N(n)|$ in A.
J	Put 1/2 + N(n) in A.
L	Put 1/2 + $|N(n)|$ in A.

Use L0, L1, L2, L3, L4, L5, L6, L7, L9, LS, LJ, LL.

APPENDIX 5

TIME FOR ORDER EXECUTION

The list below gives approximate execution times for ILLIAC orders which are suitable for estimating the running time of programs. Special timing considerations are necessary for estimating the time for the transfer of information between the drum and the WM (see Chapter 21).

ORDER TYPE	TIME	
0 n, 1 n	16n μsec	
2, 3, 4, 5, J	55 μsec	
3 not executed	18 μsec	
6	800 μsec	
7	700 μsec	
80, 81	4 millisec/char.	
82, 92	17 millisec/char.	(punch)
	1 millisec/char.	(CRT)
K, S, F, L	90 μsec	

APPENDIX 6

THE COMPLETE TAPE CODE

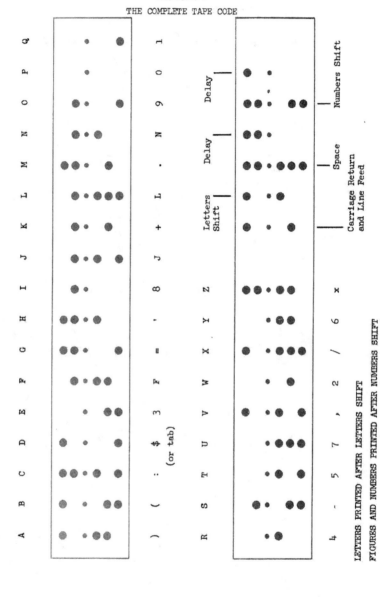

LETTERS PRINTED AFTER LETTERS SHIFT

FIGURES AND NUMBERS PRINTED AFTER NUMBERS SHIFT

APPENDIX 7

92 ORDERS FOR PRINTING TELETYPE CHARACTERS

AND ADVANCING CAMERA FILM

PRINTED CHARACTERS		MACHINE ORDER (DECIMAL ADDRESS)
Space		92 963F
Carriage Return and Line Feed		92 131F
Delay		92 515F
Letters Shift		92 259F
Numbers Shift		92 707F
Film Advance		92 769F
AFTER LETTERS SHIFT	AFTER NUMBERS SHIFT	
A	)	92 387F
B	(	92 195F
C	:	92 835F
D	$ or tab*	92 67F
E	3	92 194F
F	F	92 898F
G	=	92 579F
H	apostrophe	92 771F
I	8	92 514F
J	J	92 834F
K	+	92 642F
L	L	92 962F
M	.	92 643F
N	N	92 770F
O	9	92 578F
P	0	92 2F
Q	1	92 66F
R	4	92 258F
S	-	92 706F
T	5	92 322F
U	7	92 450F
V	;	92 323F
W	2	92 130F
X	/	92 451F
Y	6	92 386F
Z	x	92 899F

Note: These orders change the state of A and Q, see page 264.

*Only one printer has a tabulation mechanism.

APPENDIX 8

96 ORDERS TO SPECIFY OUTPUT MODE

The following 96 orders cause ILLIAC output to be transmitted to the output unit selected.

ORDER	OUTPUT UNIT SELECTED
96 1F	Punch
96 65F	Scope
96 129F	Printer

Once an output unit has been selected, all subsequent output will be transmitted to it until another unit is selected by execution of another 96 order. None of these orders changes the state of A or Q.

SADOI always selects the punch, therefore, unless the programmer gives a 96 order to select another output unit, his output will be on the punch.

APPENDIX 9

ILLIAC LIBRARY DESCRIPTION OF SADOI

LIBRARY ROUTINE X 12 - 235

By   Roger H. Farrell
(Preliminary work also
done by Lily H. Seshu
Raymond P. Polivka,
Gene H. Golub.)

TITLE	Symbolic Address Decimal Order Input (SADOI)
TYPE	Input Assembly Program
NUMBER OF WORDS	615 Words in the locked out section of the drum
WORDS USED	999-1023 in the high speed memory
	11,058-12,799 on drum
TEMPORARY STORAGE	0, 1
DESCRIPTION	

This routine is stored on the drum. It is automatically brought into the Williams memory and is not included on the program tape. It is an input routine designed to read instructions with addresses in decimal or symbolic form. It is compatible with the D.O.I. Any program written for the D.O.I. (library routine X 1) and which refers to the D.O.I. only in standard fashion may be used with SADOI. It may be necessary to recompute sum checks for programs to be input by SADOI.

During input the entire Williams memory is used by SADOI. The instructions in SADOI occupy locations 32-562, 999-1023. The remainder of the Williams memory is used for temporary storage. Instruction pairs of the program being read are initially stored on the drum. The correspondence used is drum address 11756+X ⟷ Williams memory address X. When SADOI is instructed to jump to the program which has been read, words of the program are transferred from the drum to the Williams memory and the jump is executed. A more detailed description is given under interludes.

Initially the reading of a program tape must be started by a hold start or a clear start. In either case Williams memory 2-998 is transferred to drum locations 11,758-12,754. SADOI is then placed in the Williams memory. Input then begins.

Each instruction consists of a pair of _function digits_ and
an _address_. Addresses are written in numerical or symbolic form. _Numerical addresses_
are written and punched in decimal form with non-significant zeros omitted. Thus we
write 1023, 35, 7. Each numerical address is followed by a terminating symbol K, S,
N, J, F, or L. This symbol indicates a method of treating the numerical address and
the instruction. For example, L5 29F and 40 7L. A zero address is indicated by
writing a terminating symbol immediately following the function digits. For example,
00K and 26F.

Symbolic addresses are written and punched as a pair of
parentheses; any combination of symbols or characters may be placed between the
parentheses. Examples of distinct symbolic addresses are ( ), (0), (1), (51372),
(WQXR). Generally speaking, any two combinations of teletype characters which produce
the same sequence of printed characters will represent the same symbolic address.

Numerical and symbolic addresses are most frequently written
to refer to memory locations. When symbolic addresses are used this reference is made
by using the _same_ symbolic address twice. One use is as the address of an instruction.
The other use is as a marker showing which instruction is being referred to. The
instruction 40 (A) says store the contents of the accumulator at (A), using "(A)" as
an address of the instruction. We call this an _inside symbolic address_ or inside
address. Some other instruction pair will use "(A)" as an _outside symbolic address_
or outside address. This instruction pair might be (A) 00F 00F. When this instruction
pair is read by SADOI during input the location at which it is to be stored is
remembered by SADOI as the real address corresponding to "(A)". This real address
is substituted whenever instructions are written with the inside symbolic address (A).

There is no limit to the number of references that may be
made to a particular memory location using symbolic addresses. Further, the word
being referred to may appear anywhere on the program tape. When symbolic addresses
are used SADOI determines the real addresses completely in terms of the relative positions of instructions on the input tape. The programmer will find that he normally
thinks in terms of symbolic addresses while writing a program. Numerical addresses
can be written only after bookkeeping that is made unnecessary by writing symbolic
addresses. Further, the programmer will find that use of symbolic addresses greatly
facilitates making corrections in program tapes. For, instructions often may be
added or deleted without having to change addresses.

TERMINATING SYMBOLS

K is a directive symbol. A directive is an instruction written with a pair of sexadecimal characters, a numerical address and terminated by K. It tells SADOI where to store words of program. In addition it provides an address which is called the relativizer. This address is the origin against which relative addresses are measured (see discussion of L, below). The first instruction on a tape must be a directive. The instruction following a directive will always be a left hand instruction. The directive is never stored as part of the program being read.

There are four types of directives which are written as follows:

00 n K with n a non-zero numerical address. The following instruction pairs on the tape will go into locations n, n + 1, n + 2, ... The relativizer is given the value n.

00 K If m is the location of the last instruction pair, then set the relativizer to m + 1. The instruction pairs following will go into locations m + 1, m + 2, ...

01 nK If m is the value of the relativizer then the instruction pairs following will go into m + n, m + n + 1, ... The relativizer is not changed.

02 nK Set the relativizer to the address m of the preceding instruction. The following instruction pairs will go into m + n, m + n + 1, ... When using this type of directive the preceding instruction will most often be a dummy instruction written solely to provide a value for the 02 K directive. For example, 00 (A) 02 K will result in the real address corresponding to (A) being used as the relativizer. When the preceding instruction (00 (A)) appears on the tape as a left hand instruction, it will not be stored as part of the program being read.

The programmer should be careful to use symbolic addresses with the 02 K directive only in cases where the symbolic address is previously used as an outside address.

F means fixed address. Thus L5 29F 40F when executed instructs ILLIAC to put the number at location 29 into A then, store this number at location 0. The pairs of instructions 00F 00F, 80F 00F, and LL 4095F LL 4095F are particularly useful as they set a memory location to 0, -1, -2^{-39} respectively.

L   means relative address. If n is the value of the relativizer, the instruction
50 3L will have address n + 3.

N   is used with a jump instruction to cause SADOI to jump to a specified location.
Let n be the address of the jump instruction. If n $\leq$ 998 then the words of program
are read back from the drum and put into the Williams memory. Control then transfers
to the word at location n. The jump instruction is stored at location 1. It is not
otherwise stored as part of the program being read.

If the address n $\geq$ 999 then a new address m is computed and substituted into the
jump instruction. m = 93 + (n – 999). The jump (stored at location 1) is then
executed. By this means control may be transferred to any part of the Williams memory
during input. The following jump instructions are useful:

       24 999N: Stop input. This instruction has no other effect.
       26 999N: Use to mark an address (see example 4)
       26 1000N: Special interlude marker (see interludes, below)
       22 1000N: Special drum storage order (see same, below)
       26 1469N: Jump to the first word of temporary storage.

Example 1

00   100 K

L5   L   82 40 F

OF   F   00 F

26 100 N.

In this example instructions are stored at locations 100, 101. Control transfers to
location 100. The first pair of instructions prints itself in sexadecimal.

J   terminations used after right-hand instructions tell SADOI to convert the <u>pair of
instructions</u> into a fraction. It is thus a way of reading a few decimal fractions along
with the instructions of a program. For this purpose <u>instructions</u> are written in a
special form. For example, the fraction .3333 3333 3333 should be written as
00 F 00 3333 3333 3333J and the fraction .1 should be written as 00 F 00 1000 0000 0000J.
The function digits of <u>both instructions</u> are zero and the decimal digits of the fraction
are written as the address of the right instruction. Twelve decimal digits must always
follow the second pair of zeros except that zeros immediately following the decimal point
may be omitted. For example, write .001 as 00 F 00 10 0000 0000J. Any fraction in the
range 0 to .9999 9999 9999 may be written in this way.

We can extend the range by using the function digits of the left instruction. By writing 80 for the function digits we can subtract 1 from the fraction. For example, the number .8888 8888 8889 would be written as 00F 00 8888 8888 8889J while _0.8888 8888 8889 = -1 +.1111 1111 1111 would be written as 80F 00 1111 1111 1111J.

S   This termination is used to refer to S-parameters. Discussion of S-parameters is deferred until later.

USE OF SYMBOLIC ADDRESSES

The use of symbolic addresses can be illustrated by the following example. In this example library subroutine P 10 has been rewritten using symbolic addresses. This routine is used to print headings.

Example 2

(1)	04F	L5 F	
	32 (2)	50 (3)	5th hole character
(2)	26 (4)	50 (1)	non 5th hole character
(4)	00 6F	42 (3)	
(3)	02 1F	92 F	Substitute proper address in the 92 instruction
(5)	91 4F	40 F	Enter loop
	L7 F	32 (1)	5-hold delay? If not, repeat.
	92 707F	26 999F	Exit from loop. See discussion of interludes.
	26 (5)	26 1N	

For this example to be complete it should be preceded by a directive. Each pair of instructions referred to in the program is marked by an outside address. Thus, in the first instruction pair (1) 04F L5F, (1) is used as an outside address. Similarly (2), ... , (5) are used as outside addresses. Certain of the instructions use these symbolic addresses as addresses. For example, 32 (2) 50 (3) which instructs ILLIAC to jump to the right side of (2) if the accumulator is positive. Otherwise, put the contents of (3) into Q register.

It should be noted that forward and backward references can be made. The third word contains the instruction 50 (1). This refers back to an instruction pair already read by SADOI. The reference is called a backward reference. In the same word, the instruction 26 (4) makes a forward reference to an instruction pair not yet read by SADOI.

In example 2, location 0 is used for temporary storage. This means that no matter where the block of instructions is located in the Williams memory, location 0 will be used for storing results temporarily during the computation. Thus, fixed addresses are used. In the first word, for example, the instruction L5F refers to this temporary storage location.

Last, addresses of certain instructions do not refer to memory locations. In shift instructions, for example, the address further supplements the function digits by telling how far to shift. In such cases fixed addresses are almost always written.

WRITING SYMBOLIC ADDRESSES

An outside symbolic address is written before the function digits of __either__ instruction of a pair. In example 2, the first instruction pair could also have been punched as

04 F (1) L5 F

or as   (1) 04 F (1) L5 F

Further, an instruction pair may have several outside addresses. For example, (1) (2) (3) (4) 40 F (5) 81 4 F.

An inside symbolic address is written immediately following the function digits. Only one inside address may be used in an instruction. __It must not be followed by a termination K, S, N, J, F, L.__

Constants may be added to inside addresses. Thus, the instruction L5 21 (N12) will refer to the 21st word past the word marked by (N12) as an outside address. Generally the form "n (   )" will be used to add n to the real address corresponding to (   ).

The full range of available teletype signs may be used in writing symbolic addresses: numbers, letters, punctuation marks, etc. During input the characters placed between parentheses are read and converted to numerical equivalents. From these numerical equivalents a __symbolic address word__ is formed.

As stated earlier, two combinations of teletype characters which produce the same sequence of printed characters will represent the same symbolic address. Delays, spaces, and LF-CR characters do not affect the symbolic address. Figures-shift and letters-shift characters, on the other hand, may affect the symbolic address. After reading the beginning parenthesis of a symbolic address, SADOI assumes each character following is in figures-shift until a letters-shift character is read. Thus, input of a symbolic address is not terminated by "A". The symbolic address (1A) would be punched using the following six characters: "(", "1", "LTR-SH", "A", "FIG-SH" ")". The symbolic address (12) would be punched using four characters.

Thus + and K, - and S are different. Similarly the letter "X" and times "x" are different. The number "O" and letter "O", because they look the same when printed, are given the same numerical equivalent when read. N, J, F, L print the same regardless of the print shift. Each is given the same numerical equivalent in both print shifts when read. The letter "O" or number "O" is different from the absence of a character. Thus, ( ), (O), and (1), (O1) are four distinct symbolic addresses.

The symbolic address recognized by SADOI consists of the last five printed characters. Thus, "(1A2B3C)" is the same as "(A2B3C)" but different from "(2B3C)".

USE OF TEMPORARY STORAGE LOCATIONS 0, 1 BY SADOI

Location 0 is used by SADOI to compute and store numerical addresses during the input of instructions. At the beginning of interludes it is used to compute a sum check.

Location 1 is used by SADOI to form instruction pairs. Once a pair of instructions has formed a word at location 1, the contents of location 1 are stored as part of the program being input. The only cases in which the contents of location 1 are not stored as part of the program being read is when K or N terminated instructions are read.

The right side of location 1 always contains the most recent instruction read. The left side of location 1 always contains the immediately preceding instruction. Consider the following examples:

Example 3

(a)	(b)
00 F 26 100 F	26 100 F 26 1N
26 1N	L5 F 40 F
L5 F 40 F	

In example 3a, the instruction 26 100F appears as a right-hand instruction. The word formed from 00F 26 100F is stored as part of the program being read. When the jump 26 1N is executed, the contents of location 1 is 26064 26001 (sexadecimal). When input resumes, both instructions L5F and 40F must be read before the contents of location 1 are again stored as part of the program. In example 3b, the instruction 26 100F appears as a left-hand instruction. After the right hand instruction 26 1N is read the contents of location 1 appear as before: 26064 26001. This word is not stored as part of the program because of the N termination. As before, the next pair of instructions, L5F and 40F, are read before the contents of location 1 are stored as part of the program being read.

During input when an inside symbolic address is used and a backward reference is made, the real address is substituted immediately into location 1 If an instruction like L5 21 (N12) is written, the numerical part, 21, has been computed and is stored at location 0. When (N12) makes a backward reference, the real address is substituted. Then, N(0) + N(1) is computed and stored at location 1.

When forward references are made during input, sufficient infor mation is retained to allow SADOI to form the correct addresses later. A pseudo addres is temporarily substituted into the word at location 1.

S PARAMETERS

Words stored in locations 2-15 of the Williams memory are called S parameters. These numbers give a way of modifying instructions during input. Following the S termination must be a d = 2, 3, 4, 5, 6, 7, 8, 9, K, S, N, J, F, L. This gives the address (in sexadecimal) of a location which is added to the S-terminated instruction before it is stored in the memory.

The right-hand instruction of an instruction pair stored in locations 2-15 may have an inside symbolic address and still be used as an S parameter. The left hand instruction must not have an inside address if it is to be used as an S parameter.

The directives 00K, 01K and 02K enable the programmer to minimize the number of memory locations needed to store his program. Use of the 02K directive for this purpose is illustrated in example 4. An S parameter is stored at location 5. After the interrupting instructions are read SADOI is set so that the following instructions will be stored immediately after the earlier instructions.

Example 4

```
    L5 F  40 1F
(A) 26 999N              Introduce address (A)
    OO 5K               Store S parameter at 5
    OOF  OO 12F
    OO (A) O2K          Reset SADOI to begin storing at (A)
    L5 1F 82 S5         Instruction using S parameter
```

The instruction (A) 26 999N has no effect other than to introduce the symbolic address (A).

INTERLUDES

Whenever SADOI is told to jump to instructions which have been read, an interlude begins. This is done by writing an N-terminated jump instruction with address less than 999. The jump instruction may appear on tape as if it were a left-hand or a right-hand instruction. Pairs of instructions may be written. For example, the instructions 26 L 26 1N or 26 (A) 26 1N may be used to start interludes. In these cases, the instruction pair is stored at location 1 only.

The system used with the Decimal Order Input (D.O.I.) in which

```
OOF  26L
26 1N
```

is written to begin an interlude may also be used. During input the last two instructions read are stored at location 1. The next to last instruction is always the left-hand instruction of the pair stored at location 1.

There are three types of interludes possible with SADOI.

REGULAR INTERLUDES

Regular interludes happen when SADOI is not explicitly told differently (see below). To get ready for the interlude real addresses are substituted into instructions wherever necessary. After the substitutions are completed drum locations 11,758 to 12,754 inclusive are transferred to Williams memory locations 2-998 inclusive. Control then transfers to the right side of location 1. The interlude begins.

Since at the beginning of a regular interlude substitutions of real addresses are made, the programmer should be careful about putting on tape library routines having interludes. The programmer should put such routines at the beginning of his tape before inside addresses are first used or else convert the interlude to the special interlude discussed below.

Use of a symbolic address as an inside address but not as an outside address is a programming error. SADOI detects all errors of this type before stopping. Information is punched about each error (see below). After all possible substitutions are made and errors indicated, the instructions on the drum are transferred to the William's memory. An FFO31 stop then occurs.

The symbolic addresses used prior to an interlude are remembered This information is stored on the drum during the interlude at addresses higher than 11,000.

A small part of the instructions in SADOI are stored at 999-102: These instructions enable the programmer to jump to SADOI after an interlude for more input. Two types of jumps may be used. When a jump to the left side of location 999 is made the right hand address of the number in Q is used as a new relativizer. If this address has value m then the following instruction pairs will go into m, m + 1, m + 2, .. until a directive is received. When a jump to the right side of location 1014 is made the old relativizer is retained. The right-hand address of A determines where the following instructions will go. If this address has value m the following instruction pairs will go into m, m + 1, m + 2, ...

When a regular interlude is ended by one of these jumps the contents of the Williams memory are put back on the drum. Locations 2-998 are moved to 11,758 - 12,754 respectively. SADOI is then put into the Williams memory, information about the previously used symbolic addresses is restored, and input begins.

SPECIAL INTERLUDES

Special interludes are provided so that a small amount of calculation may be accomplished without requiring substitution of real addresses for symbolic addresses and without transferring all of 1000 words from one memory to another. To write a special interlude precede the first instruction pair to be used by the instruction 26 1000N. The first instruction following an N.termination will always be a left-hand instruction. Follow the last instruction pair by a normal jump instruction terminated by N. Only the instructions lying between the two jump instructions will be brought from the drum for use in the interlude.

<u>Example 5</u>
Input one sexadecimal number
OOK
26 1000N
80 40F 40L
22 1L L5 1L
22 1014F 26L
26 1N
0000000000

The instruction 26 1000N marks the first word to be used in the
special interlude. Let the Williams memory location for this word be n. When 26 1000N
is read n is substituted into the right-hand address of the word in 1022. This address
will have been set to zero previously, and by testing to see whether or not this address
is zero SADOI determines whether a regular or a special interlude is to occur.

Let n_2 be the Williams memory location for the last word of
the interlude which is read from the tape. Then the words brought from the drum will
be placed in locations n_1, $n_1 + 1$, ..., n_2 in the Williams memory. The programmer
should be careful not to store instructions to be used outside this range. This may
happen if directives are used between the 26 1000N instruction and the normal jump
instruction.

Before a special interlude begins, information about symbolic
addresses previously used is stored on the drum. After the interlude this information
is brought back to the Williams memory again.

Special interludes, like regular interludes, are ended by jumps
to 999 or 1014. The meanings of these jumps are the same as for regular interludes.
After the end of the special interlude the S parameters 2-15 are copied onto the corresponding drum locations 11,758 - 11,771. Aside from the S parameters only the words in
locations used for the special interlude are copied onto the corresponding drum locations.

FAST INTERLUDES

Fast interludes may be written when 44 instruction pairs or less
are needed. During input, blocks of instruction pairs are accumulated in the Williams
memory before being transferred to the drum. These transfers to the drum take place
after

(1) 45 instruction pairs are accumulated

(2) a directive is read

(3) an N terminated instruction with address less than 999 is read

(4) an S termination is used <u>and</u> the S parameter has a right inside address for which a real address must be substituted.

The addresses used for the temporary storage are 563 - 607. If the jump 26 1469 + k F is written then according to the rule cited earlier the fixed address 1469 + k is changed to

$$(1469 + k - 999) + 93 = 563 + k.$$

Consequently the instruction 26 1469N will cause SADOI to jump to the left side of location 563.

Fast interludes must be ended by a <u>jump to the left side of 93</u>. Input resumes immediately. If the instructions used in the interlude go to addresses m, m + 1, ..., m + k then the instructions following will go into m + k + 1, m + k + 2, ... until a directive is read.

Example 5 is rewritten for a fast interlude and presented in

Example 6

Input one sexadecimal number

    00 K

80 40F 40 563F

26 93F 00 F

26 1469N

   01 1K

In this example fixed addresses are used throughout. In general the instructions will not go to the same place as that occupied by them when the interlude is executed.

LIBRARY ROUTINES STORED ON DRUM

Certain of the more commonly used ILLIAC library routines have been stored in the locked out section of the drum memory. These routines are, at present,

P16, Y1, N12, R1, S4, S5, T4, T5, F1, A1.

By use of a <u>modified directive</u>, SADOI is instructed to take a specified routine from the drum and insert it in the program being read.

A modified directive like (P12) 00 100K consists of two parts:

(1) An <u>outside</u> address which specifies the library routine.

(2) A directive which specifies the relativizer and first memory location for the program.

Any of the other types of directive may be used. For example, (N12) 00K will cause N12 to be placed following the last instruction read. Similarly, the 01K and 02K type of directives will affect the relativizer and store addresses as described earlier.

When a library routine is obtained using a modified directive, the outside address is inserted into the list of symbolic addresses. The real address which corresponds is the location of the first word of the library routine. Thus, for example, when (N12) 00K is written to obtain N12, the entries to N12 may be written:

50 n

50 q

. . .

26 (N12).

The programmer may use instructions like L5 21(N12) to refer to words interior to a library routine.

When punching teletype tapes the programmer should be careful how he punches P16, Y1, etc. The letters must appear in <u>letters shift</u>. For example, (P16) is punched as

"(", "LTR-SH", "P", "FIG-SH", "1", "6", ")"

using seven teletype characters. Note, also that the use of a hyphen in writing P-16 is incorrect.

Miswriting the designating outside address, or asking for a library routine not stored on the drum will result in an immediate FF 030 stop.

Library routines, stored on the drum, which use interludes (F1 for example) execute their interludes without affecting in any way the symbolic addresses used by the programmer.

SELF CHECKING FEATURES

FF 824   This stop occurs because of a sum check failure in transfers of routines from the locked out section of the drum. Depending on the characters of the input tape last read before the stop, the routine may be

(1) Part of SADOI which was incorrectly placed in the Williams memory

(2) A library routine called for by the input tape which was incorrectly read back from the drum.

FF 030   This stop occurs when the programmer asks for a library routine not stored on the drum. Input stops immediately.

FF 031   This stop indicates that the programmer has misused his symbolic addresses. The nature of these errors is always indicated by output on the punch. The FF stop occurs at the beginning of the 1st <u>regular</u> interlude following an error. At this time all instructions read by SADOI are <u>in the Williams memory</u>.

Three types of coding error are covered by this stop.

<u>S parameters</u>: A word having an inside address is used as an S parameter <u>and</u> the real address corresponding to the inside address has not yet been given to SADOI (by use of an outside address). The punched output appears as S 004 355 H, consisting of "S" which identifies the type of error, two <u>decimal</u> addresses, and the symbolic address involved. The first decimal address specifies the location of the S parameter. The second decimal address specifies the location of the instruction using the S parameter.

If the order was, for example, L5 nS4, then this instruction appear in the Williams memory as L5 nF when the stop occurs.

<u>Outside type error</u>: The same symbolic address is used as an outside address for two instructions having different locations. In this case the punched output appears as

O 367 528 Q. ·

"O" signifies "outside". The first decimal address is the location of the first instruction, the second decimal address is the location of the second instruction. The symboli address involved is printed last.

During input, when the real address corresponding to a symboli address is known, the real address is substituted into instructions immediately. In case of duplicate outside addresses, the most recent real address value is the one saved and used during subsequent input.

<u>Inside type error</u>: When a regular interlude is to begin, real addresses are substituted into instructions. When a zero real address or no real address is available, this type of error is indicated. The punched output appears as:

473 K3.

This first thing punched is the location of the instruction using the inside address. The symbolic address involved is punched second.

FF 032   This stop may occur when a directive appears as a right-hand instruction. The stop indicates that the left-hand instruction which preceded used an inside address which made a **forward** reference. This may mean that input is out of phase one-half word or that an O2K directive cannot be executed. Input stops immediately.

FF 033   This stop occurs when an N terminated order is read and
   (1) it appears as the right-hand order of an order pair, and
   (2) the left-hand order of the order pair has an inside address for which the corresponding real address is not known, and
   (3) the address of the right hand order is ≤ 998.

This error stop may occur at the start of special or regular interludes. The stop is made after the appropriate instructions have been transferred to the Williams memory. There may also be output on the tape punch.

FF 034   This stop occurs when too many instructions of the type AB n (C) are written with n $\neq$ 0. Each time such an instruction is read and the real address corresponding to "(C)" is not known (forward reference), a word is added to the **additions** list. If the real address is known, the additions list is not increased. This list is limited to 314 entries.

FF 035   This stop occurs when too many distinct symbolic addresses are used. The number of symbolic addresses is limited to 324.

SUM CHECKS

Library routine X-7, used for sum checks, is not well suited for use with SADOI. It is written as an interlude ending with a 36 999F jump. Ending an interlude causes SADOI to reload itself into the Williams memory, thus causing additional drum transfers which may be omitted by using a more efficient sum check.

At the beginning of interludes SADOI automatically computes a sum of the words (order pairs or numbers) transferred from the drum memory to the Williams memory. At the end of the transfer this sum is in location zero and may be used by the programmer for checking.

If the words transferred are $x_1, \ldots, x_n$, the sum computed is defined by the relations

$$s_0 = 0$$
$$s_{i+1} = x_{i+1} + |s_i| \qquad i+1 = 1, 2, \ldots, n.$$

A sum check routine suitable for SADOI may be written as follows and placed at the end of a tape.

```
00996K
L3F 36 (A)          Let (A) represent the
FF F 26 (A)         location of the first
000000F000000F      instruction to be obeyed
26L  26 1N          in the program
```

The last word in this routine is the sum check and should be punched by hand in the form of an instruction after the program is tried the first time. This word is obtained then by reading the contents of the accumulator when the FF stop first occurs.

SPECIAL DRUM LOADING TECHNIQUE

A special instruction has been provided which will allow the programmer to load blocks of instructions directly into any desired drum locations. Instructions to be loaded this way must be written without symbolic addresses. A sum check is not computed.

The following sequence must be followed:

(1) A directive, which sets the relativizer.

(2) Follow the directive by OC nF 22 1000N. The order pairs following on the tape are stored on the drum at n, n + 1, n + 2, ...

(3) To stop the direct loading, write a directive or begin an interlude (regular or special).

Library routines stored on the drum and containing less than 45 words may be transferred by this technique. For example,

```
(R1) 00 100K
00 3000F 22 1000N
```

will put R1 on the drum starting at 3000. The relativizer used is 100.

Special care must be taken when this technique is used. All bookkeeping work of SADOI proceeds as if the instructions being read were being normally stored. Consequently, if instructions previously read used inside addresses and if these instructions would be overwritten were the new instructions still normally stored, then the bookkeeping will be incorrect.

DETAILS OF THE FORMATION OF INSTRUCTIONS DURING INPUT

During input, decimal addresses are computed and stored at location 0. The pair of instructions being formed is always stored at location 1. The following sequence is followed:

(I) Instruction type AB n (C)

1. Put $N(1)$ in A.

2. Read two function digits "A" and "B" shifting A left eight places.

3. Shift A left 12 places and store at 1.

4. Read the address n and store at 0.

5. Read the symbolic address (C).

    a. Forward reference (real address not known).

        (1) Substitute a false address into the right-hand instruction at location 1.

        (2) Test for n = 0. If zero, begin reading the next instruction.

        (3) If $n \neq 0$ put a new word into the additions list. Left most 30 bits are used for the number n. Right most 10 bits determine the symbolic address (c) used. Begin reading the next instruction.

    b. Backward reference (real address known).

        (1) Substitute real address into right-hand instruction at 1.

        (2) Form $N(0) + N(1)$ and store at 1.

        (3) Begin reading the next instruction.

(II) Instruction type AB n D   D a K, S, N, S, F, L termination.

1. Repeat steps 1-4 of I above

2. K, N, F; form $N(0) + N(1)$ and store at 1. In case of F, begin reading the next instruction. In case of K, N, finish execution of the termination.

3. L; form $N(0) + N(1)$ + relativizer and store at 1. Begin reading the next instruction.

4. Sk; form $N(0) + N(1) + N(k)$ and store at 1. Begin reading the next instruction.

5. J; form

$$N(1) + \frac{1}{2} \left[\frac{N(0) - 5 \times 10^{11} \times 2^{-39} + 5 \times 10^{11} \times 2^{-79}}{5 \times 10^{11} \times 2^{-39}} - \right] + \frac{1}{2}$$

and store at 1. Begin reading the next instruction.

DATE 7/11/57   RT: 3/5/58; 12/3/58

PROGRAMMED BY R. H. Farrell

APPROVED BY   D. E. Muller

lgr

P R O G R A M N O T E S

INTRODUCTION

The following is by no means a complete analysis of SADOI. Some parts of the program are only named while others are analyzed in detail. The following tries to present the ideas which have made SADOI a usuable input routine. Input is something that happens in time. When one understands the general sequence of steps and a few of the minute details one should then be equipped to understand what actually takes place in ILLIAC.

INPUT STARTS

When instructions being read by SADOI are on tape the input taking place is called tape input. When the instructions are on the drum (reading a library routine) the input taking place is called drum input.

The main part of SADOI fills Williams memory locations 30-604. An input start occurs at any point that the main part of SADOI is written into the Williams memory. Immediately after each input start tape or drum input begins.

Interludes are classed as tape controlled or drum controlled according to the type of input at the start of the interlude. Fast interludes are not followed by input starts (and hence may be used to modify SADOI), while regular and special interludes are. SADOI distinguishes four classes of input start:

(1) a hold or clear start
(2) tape controlled regular interludes
(3) tape controlled special interludes
(4) drum controlled regular or special interludes.

During each input start approximately 200 instructions are used to set up SADOI to begin input. The overall sequence followed during input starts is shown in diagram 1.

TAPE INPUT SEQUENCE

To initiate a clear or hold start one character is read by ILLIAC. SADOI assumes this was the first of a pair of function digits and fakes in a zero for this digit. In this case input starts by reading the second function digit. Consequently, a tape may not be started by a symbolic address.

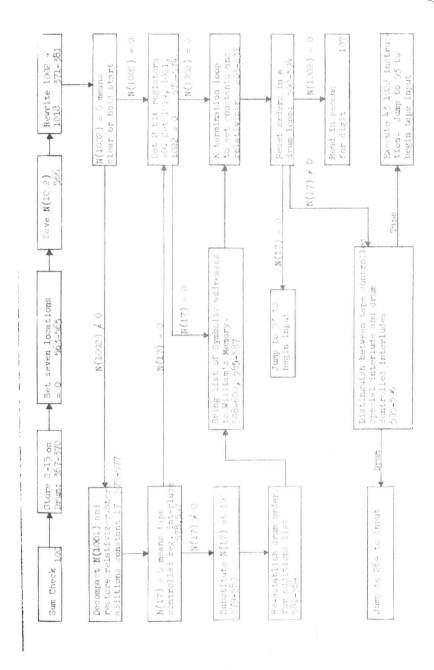

Diagram 1: INPUT START SEQUENCE

Tape input is started (following interludes) by a jump to location 93 after the set up operations. The jump instructions at 93 provide a variable link to the two main input sections of SADOI. A 26 999N instruction, when read by SADOI, also results in a jump to 93.

The input sections are so called because they contain the instructions that read coded information and translate it into numbers. Various other sections are excluded because their functions are to execute the terminations or bookkeeping. Speed of operation while reading tapes was deemed critical. Consequently, some book-keeping uses available time between reading of characters on the tape. In other cases similar bookkeeping operations will be found repeated several times in order to eliminate the need for testing which phase of the input was last completed.

    I. Tape input section: 43-69, 104-147
        A. Read decimal address 43-69
        B. Read symbolic address 115-147
        C. Read second function digit 104-114
    II. Drum input section: 262-327.

The bookkeeping and terminations will be discussed in detail below. The following diagram shows the tape input sequence.

DRUM INPUT SEQUENCE

The maximum compacting by Y4 is to store N words of program in 4/5N locations. Consequently, 36 compacted words placed in the Williams memory will yield at most 45 words of program. For this reason 45 words temporary storage was allowed, locations 563-607. In operation the drum input section brings 36 words from the drum and stores them in locations 572-607. The words are then picked off one at a time and decoded. The resulting instruction pairs are stored in 563-607, starting at 563.

For many library routines stored on the drum 36 words are sufficient to contain the entire routine. When 36 words do not suffice and the current 36 words have been exhausted, the assembled part of the routine is transferred to the drum. Another block of 36 words is put into the Williams memory. The process thus continues until the entire routine has been obtained.

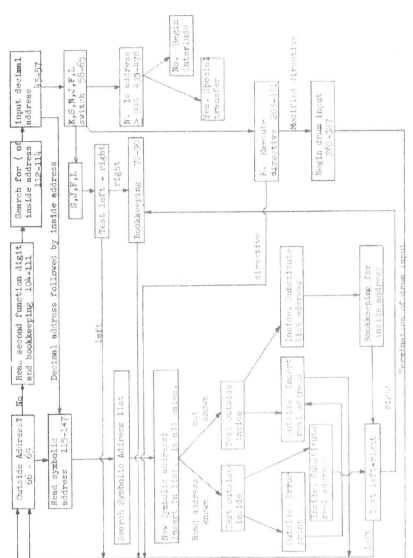

Diagram 2: TAPE INPUT SEQUENCE

If during drum input an interlude is initiated, certain information must be retained in order to restart the drum input after the interlude. Consequently, locations 1019-1021, 1023 are used for temporary storage by the drum input section. They are set equal zero at all times except during drum input. Their use is

1019: A counter for which of the 5 blocks of 8 bits was last taken.

1020: Word currently being decoded.

1021: Drum order set to bring next word from drum.

1023: Sum check on library routines.

In addition 1022 is used when a library routine calls for a special interlude.

Where possible the drum input section was interwoven with other parts of SADOI. This was done to shorten the program but also to keep the drum input compatible with tape input. Thus the K, S, and N termination sections of SADOI are used during both types of input. The bookkeeping section (69-92) is also used during drum input after each instruction pair of a routine is formed. Because of this sharing

(1) S parameters may be automatically preset during drum input

(2) The special transfers (N terminated jumps with address ≥ 999) may be used during drum input

(3) The various types of directives may be used during drum input

(4) S parameters having symbolic addresses will be properly handled.

The following diagram shows the drum input sequence.

READING SYMBOLIC ADDRESSES

The parentheses "(" and ")" have no effect other than to initiate and terminate reading a symbolic address. Each character on the tape following "(" is examined by means of a 32 position switch (132-147) and has one of the following effects:

(1) None. Spaces, delays and LF-CR characters are skipped.

(2) Change from letters to figures shift or from figures to letters shift. Letters and figures shift characters.

(3) Terminate reading of the symbolic address. Closing ")".

(4) Add six bits to the symbolic address word being formed in ILLIAC

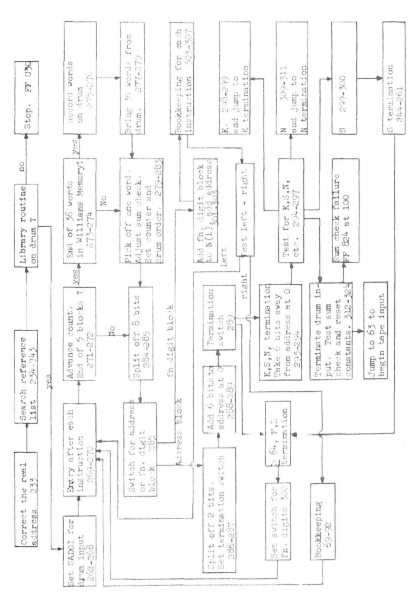

Diagram 3: DRUM INPUT SEQUENCE

in general any character (except parentheses) which will cause
a printed mark causes the addition of six bits to the symbolic address word being formed.
The composition of the block is as follows: let $b_0 b_1 \ldots b_5$ be the digits of the block.
Then

$$b_0 = 0 \qquad \text{figures shift}$$
$$ = 1 \qquad \text{letters shift}$$
$$b_1 = 0 \qquad \text{non-5-hole character}$$
$$ = 1 \qquad \text{5-hole character.}$$

$b_2, \ldots, b_5$ correspond to the 8, 4, 2 and 1 hole positions of the tape respectively and
$b_i = 1$ when the position is punched, $b_i = 0$ when the position is not punched.
Certain exceptions mentioned in the description of SADOI are
made to this rule.

The most recently added block of six bits is always added to the
symbolic address word on the left end by means of a right shift into Q. Part of this
right shift is done by the 90 instruction at 118. The shift of four positions right
occurs before the new digits read from tape are gated into A. Since the 90 instruction
does not clear A, care is taken to make sure $N(A) = 0$ after the right shift. In
particular the constant $N(34) = -1 + 16 \times 2^{-39}$ which is added to $N(A)$ for 5-hole
characters eliminates the minus sign introduced by the 90 instruction.

SYMBOLIC ADDRESS COMPILER

The symbolic address word is formed by successive right shifts
into Q. The first step following the reading is to execute the following instructions:

                    SJ F   00 1F
                    40 946F   43 946F
                    89 1F   L4 946F
                    40945F.

These instructions complete the formation of the symbolic address word and stores it
temporarily at 945, the head of the symbolic address list. The word with sign digit
changed is stored at 946.

Each time a symbolic address is read the list is searched to
determine whether a corresponding symbolic address word is in the list. In long programs
the searching time becomes significant since the total time is an n^2 process. The arrangement used in SADOI results from the following arguments (see words 153-162).

(1) When coding for ILLIAC loop speeds are faster when addresses are increased than when decreased.

(2) If a symbolic address was previously used it was most likely one of the more recently received addresses. Therefore the search through the list should begin at the end of the list containing the most recently received symbolic address words.

(3) The first symbolic address word is therefore stored at 944. Each new word is stored at the next lower address.

(4) By storing each new word temporarily at 945,946 and beginning the search at the low address end, the search will always be automatically terminated, either by finding a word in the list or by finding the new word at the head of the list.

(5) A loop to accomplish the search requires 3-1/2 words with a subloop of 2-1/2 words. Read around ratio for this loop was well above 200. It is consequently duplicated to reduce the read around ratio value.

The right address position of the symbolic address word is used to store the <u>real address</u> corresponding to the symbolic address. When examining a symbolic address word SADUI determines whether the real address has been received by whether the right-hand address is non-zero or not.

When a symbolic address word is already in the list, then, when the search terminates, the right address of $N(A)$ is the right address of the symbolic address word. This address is saved by executing a 42 17F instruction.

An inside symbolic address makes a <u>forward reference</u> when the real address is not known and a <u>backward reference</u> when the real address is known. These cases are treated separately. At some point real addresses must be substituted wherever inside addresses were used. This is done immediately when the real address is known. The compiler thus treats the following cases:

I. Real address known $N(17) \neq 0$

   A. Symbolic address read was an outside address. Then an error has been made. (165-166). Indicate error and proceed as in II B.

   B. Inside symbolic address was read. Substitute real address into right address of $N(1)$. Then form $N(0) + N(1)$ and store at 1. (172-174)

II. Real address not known

    A. New symbolic address. Determine whether word found in the list was N(945). If so put N(945) at the bottom of the list and proceed as in II B or II C.

    B. Outside symbolic address was read. Substitute the real address into the symbolic address word.

    C. Inside symbolic address was read

        1. $N(0) = 0$ so no constant is to be added. Substitute into $N(1)$ the location of the symbolic address word in the Williams memory (a number ≥ 512).

        2. $N(0) \neq 0$. Form a new word composed as follows: The left 30 bits equal the right 30 bits of $N(0)$; the right address is the location of the symbolic address word. Store this word on the drum in the additions list until needed. Substitute into $N(1)$ the location the additions word will have in the Williams memory when it is used (a number < 512).

BACK SUBSTITUTION PROCESS (479-562)

        52 words called 2 bit registers are used by SADOI to keep a record of where real addresses must be substituted later. A digit 1 means a substitution must be made while a digit 0 means no substitution is required. One register thus serves 40 instructions or 20 instruction pairs that have been read. Let an instruction pair have location n (the address it will ultimately have in the Williams memory) and let

$$n = 20q + r \qquad \text{with} \qquad 0 \leq r < 20.$$

Then $947 + q$ is the location of the 2 bit register. After each directive this constant is computed by the X-termination section (see 217-226) and stored at 26. If $a_0 a_1 \ldots a_{39}$ is the 2 bit register then a_{2r} is the digit position for left instructions, a_{2r+1} for right instructions.

        Throughout input a counter word is stored at location 25. This word has one non zero digit a_i where $i = 2r$ or $2r + 1$ according as the instruction being read is a left or right instruction. The counter word is used to add or delete non zero digits from the 2 bit registers as each new instruction is read.

        During the back substitution for real addresses the 2 bit registers are successively tested to determine whether they are equal zero. When a non-zero 2 bit register is found the corresponding 20 words are brought from the drum. The required substitutions are made and the 20 words replaced on the drum.

The parts of SADOI required during the back substitution are the temporary storage locations 16-29, the numerical constants 30-42, and instructions 357-562. The list of additions words stored on the drum are transferred to the Williams memory overwriting locations 43-356 (the upper limit is variable). The list of symbolic addresses is then transferred to the drum overwriting the additions list (which is not to be saved). The back substitution then begins.

When a substitution is required the address n of the instruction involved is examined:

(1) $n < 512$ means an addition is required.

(2) $n > 512$ means no addition is required.

The following diagram shows in detail the operation of instructions 479-562.

USE OF THE WILLIAMS AND DRUM MEMORIES AND SUM CHECKS

SADOI is permanently stored at locations 1027-1641 on the drum. It is set so that the first word of the reference list is stored at 1850. To change this address it is necessary to change the drum instruction at 1252 and adjust the sum check at 1612.

When a clear or hold start is used the drum bootstraps load locations 1614-1640 into the Williams memory locations 999-1025. Control transfers to 1020 of the Williams memory. The words at 1019-1025 are used during hold or clear starts to restore Williams memory locations 2-32 after the drum bootstraps have finished their work. They are not reloaded into the Williams memory during other input starts.

The sum check at 1641 is used by the drum bootstrap routines but not otherwise. The sum check at 1612 is used each time the main part of SADOI is put into the Williams memory. Let $N(n) = X_n$ be the number stored at location n while the main part of SADOI is being brought to the William's memory. The drum loop computes the following sum

$$Y_{31} = X_{31}$$

$$Y_{n+1} = X_{n+1} + |Y_n|$$

The values Y_n are stored at 31. Let $X_{603} = - |Y_{602}| + X_{604}$. X_{603} is the sum check constant stored on the drum at 1612. X_{604} is the last word brought from the drum. Therefore $Y_{604} = X_{604} + |Y_{603}| = X_{604} + |X_{603} + |Y_{602}|| = X_{604} + |X_{604}|$. Since X_{604} is a negative number, $Y_{604} = 0$.

302

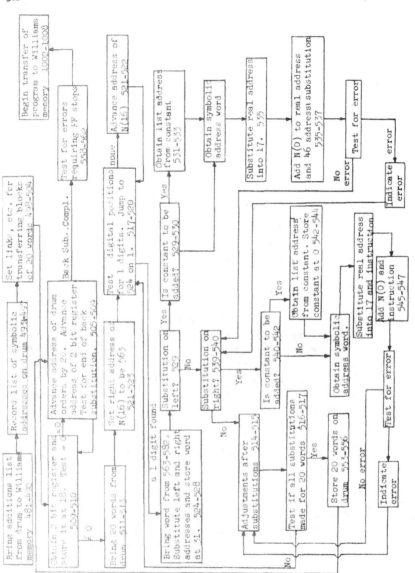

Diagram 4: BACK SUBSTITUTION

During input instruction pairs are stored on the drum. Locations 11,756-12,799 are allocated for this purpose. The correspondence used is location $X \longleftrightarrow$ drum address $11,756 + X$. The bookkeeping of SADOI is so set that any location $0 \le X \le 1039$ may be used. However, only words having locations $2 \le X \le 998$ will be brought from the drum during interludes. The extra words which are available on the drum can be obtained only by special coding.

Storage locations with addresses $11,000 < u \le 11,755$ are used to store the various lists computed by SADOI.

During input the only other material stored on the drum are the additions constants. Small blocks (13 words) are held temporarily in the Williams memory at 608-620. When a full block is accumulated the words are transferred to the drum reversing their order during the transfer. The first block of 13 are stored at 11,742-11,754.

During interludes the manner in which the various lists are moved depends on the type of interlude.

I. Regular tape controlled interludes

The additions list and 2 bit registers are not saved. The list of symbolic addresses is stored on the drum. The order of the list is reversed during the transfer so that the low address end of the list is stored at 11,754.

II. During all other types of interludes (excluding fast interludes)

The three lists are stored on the drum. The additions list, already there, is not moved. The Williams memory from the low end of the symbolic address list to 998 is stored on the drum "below" the additions list, the order being reversed during the transfer. The combined length of 2 bit registers, symbolic address list and additions list cannot exceed 700 words.

The use of the Williams memory is:

0. Sum check and decimal addresses computed during input.

1. Instruction pairs being formed

2-15. S parameters

16-31. Temporary storage for SADOI

16. General purpose temporary storage

17. During input of symbolic addresses, $N(17) = 32 \times 2^{-39}$ for letters shift, $= 0$ for figures shift. Used only for right address substitution otherwise.

18. Used during reading of symbolic addresses and back substitution.

19. General purpose storage

20. = 0 if no outside addresses for current instruction pair. Otherwise contains the location of the most recently received outside address for the instruction pair.

21. ≠ 0 when reading outside addresses
    = 0 when reading inside addresses

22. A word with at most 2 non zero digits. These digits are the positions in the 2 bit register corresponding to current instruction pair.

23. Bits to be added to the two bit register

24. Temporary storage for the current 2 bit register

25. Counter word

26. Address for current 2 bit register in list

27-28. Set aside for use by the error print sections

29. Counter word delayed one right shift

30. The constant zero

31. $N(31) = -1/2$ when reading right instructions
    $= 1/2$ when reading left instructions

32-562. Instructions of SADOI

563-604. Instructions of SADOI used only during input starts

563-607. Temporary storage for blocks of 45 instruction pairs

43-357. William's memory storage for additions list during back substitution

608-620. Temporary storage while 13 additions words are accumulated

621-944. List of symbolic addresses

945-946. Temporary storage for symbolic address word during search of the list

947-998. The 2 bit registers

999-1025. The part of SADOI put into the Williams memory by the drum bootstrap routines

1001. Relativizer

1019-1025. Used only during input starts after clear or hold starts to restore 2-32 of the Williams memory. Otherwise

1019. = 0 except during drum input. Used for counter

1020. = 0 except during drum input. Store word being decoded

1021. = 0 except during drum input. Store drum order

1022. Used to indicate errors have been made. Also used to indicate special interludes

1023. Use to store accumulated sum during computation of sum check when reading back a library routine.

1002-1018. Is spoken of as the control block. These locations are rewritten at each input start.

84. Right address = location for the current instruction pair

86. Right address = location in 563-607 where next instruction pair will be stored temporarily

180. Right address = one less than the location in 608-620 where next additions word will be stored

190. Right address = one less than the location the next additions word will have in the Williams memory.

999. Right address = location of last word in symbolic address list.

BOOKKEEPING

Each new instruction (except K and N terminated) is treated by SADOI as overwriting instructions already stored. The memory location may be zero as after clear starts. This case is also included. The 2 bit registers must therefore be modified continually during input in order to keep track of where substitutions of real addresses must be made.

Since a word is added to the instructions being accumulated on the drum only after complete instruction pairs are received modification of two positions in a 2 bit register is made simultaneously after the complete instruction pair is received

After the instruction pair is received the previous two digits of the register are irrelevant. These positions are therefore set to zero. New 1 digits are then added for each instruction of the pair that will require a substitution later.

Accumulation of information for the bookkeeping is accomplished by use of five storage locations 22-26.

26. The location of the current 2 bit register

24. Temporary storage of the 2 bit register (to avoid many address substitutions)

25. The counter word. This word is as described earlier. During input of the function digits it is shifted right one shift. A copy of the unshifted word is stored at 29.

22. Before the right shift of $N(25)$, the sum $N(22) + N(25)$ is formed and stored at 22. After two instructions are read $N(24) - \left[N(24) \cdot N(22)\right]$ sets two positions of the 2 bit register $= 0$, where "." means logical and.

23. For each instruction which requires a substitution later, $N(23) + N(29)$ is formed and stored. The total correction of the 2 bit register after an instruction pair has the form $N(24) - \left[N(24) \cdot N(22)\right] + N(23)$. See 69-73

When the right instruction of a pair is terminated by K or N $N(1)$ is not stored as part of the program being read. Modification of the 2 bit register does not take place. However, $N(22)$ and $N(23)$ are computed. Since $N(23) \neq 0$ means the use of a forward reference in the instruction pair the test $N(23) \neq 0$ results in the FF032 and FF033 stops.

During input starts, after K, and after instruction pairs are read, $N(22)$ and $N(23)$ are set to zero. N terminations with addresses ≥ 999 get special treatment. It was decided that before executing a special jump SADOI should be reset so that the next instruction would be a left instruction and in general that the N terminated instruction was not read. Words 439-444 therefore

(1) back up the counter word to its previous position,

(2) destroy information about inside and outside addresses having been used:
$N(20) = 0 \quad N(22) = 0 \quad N(23) = 0$,

(3) set for left-hand instruction: $N(31) = 1/2$.

The 2 bit register held at 24 is replaced in the list when K, S, N terminations are read or when $N(25) = 0$.

S TERMINATIONS

Use of S parameters is made almost unnecessary by the details of SADOI. They were included, however, to make SADOI compatible with the D.O.I. In certain cases it is convenient not only to use S parameters but to have a facility allowing use of inside addresses. Some provision is made for this in SADOI.

First, any number which may be used as an S parameter is stored simultaneously in the Williams memory and on the drum. These are the words having locations 2, 3, ..., L. If the number is not used as an S parameter then it may have inside addresses on both sides which make forward references. Backward references never cause difficulty because the real address is substituted immediately. If it is used as a S parameter only the right instruction may use an inside address making a forward reference.

When an S termination is written SADOI checks the 2 bit register at 947 to determine whether a substitution is needed. The current 2 bit register at 25 is replaced in the list just to make sure the register at 947 is actually there. In case a substitution is needed, then the 2 copies of the S parameter must be changed. The instruction pairs (563-607) being held temporarily in the Williams memory are put on the drum to make sure the second copy of the S parameter is actually on the drum. SADOI then determines whether the required real address has been received. If so corrections are made. Otherwise, an error is indicated by the tape punch.

After special interludes which end with 999 or 1014 jumps to SADOI locations 2-15 are transferred to the corresponding drum locations regardless of the locations specified for the special interlude.

LOCATION	ORDER	NOTES	X 12
027	40 1012	Words of bootstrap stored on drum at	
	26 1012	1027-1039. These set up a loop at	
028	F5 607	Williams memory locations 604-609	
	40 1015	to read main body of SADOI into the	
029	40 1016	Williams memory. Remainder of boot-	
	26 1012	strap is in Williams memory 1013-	
030	40 604	1016. Start at 1013.	
	26 607		
031	00 0		
	F5 607		
032	40 605		
	26 607		
033	40 607		
	L5 608		
034	40 606		
	26 607		
035	L4 604		
	46 608		
036	40 609		
	26 607		
037	40 31		
	22 604		
038	40 608		
	26 607		
039	40 31		
	L6 31		
040	00 0	First words of main part	
31	00 0	of SADOI.	
041	00 0	Stored at 31, 32.	
32	00 2		

WILLIAMS MEMORY LOCATIONS ONLY ARE INDICATED.   DRUM
LOCATIONS ARE 1009 GREATER THAN WILLIAMS MEMORY LOCATIONS

LOCATION	ORDER				NOTES	X 12
30	00	0	00	0		
1	00	0	00	0	Numerical Constants	
2	00	0	00	2		
3	00	0	00	10		
4	80	0	00	16		
5	00	0	00	20		
6	00	0	00	32		
7	00	0	00	40		
8	00	0	00	999		
9	741701		282048			
40	7L4095		LL3072			
1	7L4095		LL2048			
2	00	0	00	132		
3	40	16	41	0	_____Read in Decimal Address _____	
4	49	21	L5	16	Set up	
5	LO	33	36	56		
6	L4	33	40	0		
7	91	4	32	48	Read Loop	
8	26	53	LO	33		
9	36	56	10	3		
50	F4	0	00	2		
1	F4	0	00	1		
2	40	0	26	47		
3	FO	32	40	16	Check 5-hole characters for	
4	L7	16	36	47	start of inside address	
5	22	115	FF	53		
6	F4	56	42	57	Set switch	
7	L5	0	26	0		
8	L5	70	22	74	K	
9	L5	251	22	74	S	

LOCATION	ORDER				NOTES	X 12
60	L5 158		22	74	N	
1	50	39	22	97	J	
2	L4	1	26	64	F	
3	L41001		L4	1	L and final operations of	
4	40	1	L1	31	J and S.	
5	40	31	32	69	Left-right switch. Jump after right inst.	
6	91	4	36	104	Search for (of	
7	FO	32	40	16	outside address.	
8	L7	16	36	66		
9	26 116		50	24		

Bookkeeping

70	JO	22	−1	203	Modify current 2-bit reg. after	
1	L4	24	L4	23	inst. pair	
2	40	24	L3	25	Test counter word for zero	
3	36	74	22	81		
4	F5	74	42	77	Replace 2-bit register in list	
5	L5	26	42	76	when counter = 0 or for K, S, N	
6	L5	24	40	0		
7	50	30	26	0		
8	89	1	40	25	When counter word = 0, get next	
9	F5	26	42	80	2-bit register and reset counter word.	
80	42	26	L5	0		
1	40	24	41	22		
2	41	23	L5	84	Store S parameters in Williams Memory.	
3	LO	91	36	85		
4	L5	1	40	0		
5	F5	84	40	84		
6	L5	1	40	563	Store inst. pair temporarily at	
7	41	20	F5	86	563 − 607	
8	40	86	LO	92		
9	32	90	50	89		

LOCATION		ORDER		NOTES	X 12
90	26 357		26 66		
1	L5 1		40 16		
2	75 1		40 608		
3	26 66		22 63	26 999N	
4	22 101		26 95	26 1000N	
5	L5 1		10 20	Set drum input	
6	L4 103		40 362		
7	26 93		LO 39	J termination	
8	66 39		10 1		
9	—J 0		22 63		
100	L3 31		32 361	Sum check test	
1	FF2084		L5 84	Set special interlude address	
2	421022		26 93		
3	86 11				
4	10 4		L5 25	Read second function digit;	
5	40 29		L4 22	Save old counter word and	
6	40 22		L5 1	advance counter word one	
7	00 4		80 4	shift.	
8	50 30		00 12		
9	40 1		L5 25		
110	10 1		32 111		
1	L4 25		40 25		
2	91 4		36 43	Search for (of	
3	FO 32		40 16	inside address.	
4	L7 16		36 112	---------Input Symbolic Address---------	
5	41 0		41 21		
6	L1 42		40 18	Set for fig. shift	
7	41 17		51 17		
8	10 2		90 4	Core of input loop	
9	L4 42		42 120		

LOCATION	ORDER				NOTES				X 12
120	L4	18	26	0	Jump to switch				
1	LO	17	26	118	Entry for N, J, F, L				
2	L4	34	26	118	Entry for "normal" 5-hole char.				
3	L5	36	40	17	Change of letters-figures shift;				
4	LO	42	40	18	entry when character is skipped.				
5	01	4	22	118					
6	40	16	L3	17	) or A				
7	36	148	L5	16					
8	26	122	40	16	zero or P				
9	L3	17	36	131					
130	L5	16	26	118					
1	F5	37	26	118					
2	32	128	26	125	0	delay	P	delay	
3	36	118	26	122	1	S	Q	D	
4	36	118	26	125	2	CR-LF	W	CR-LF	
5	36	118	26	122	3	(	E	B	
6	36	118	26	123	4	Ltr.Sh.	R	Ltr.Sh.	
7	36	118	26	122	5	,	T	V	
8	36	118	26	126	6	)	Y	A	
9	36	118	26	122	7	/	U	X	
140	36	118	26	125	8	delay	I	delay	
1	36	118	26	122	9	=	O	G	
2	36	118	26	122	+	.	K	M	
3	36	118	23	123	−	Nr.sh.	S	Nr.Sh.	
4	36	121	26	122	N	'	N	H	
5	36	121	26	122	J	:	J	C	
6	36	121	26	122	F	x	F	Z	
7	36	121	26	125	L	space	L	space	
8	−J	0	30	1	--------Symbolic Address List Comp------				
9	40	946	43	946					

LOCATION	ORDER		NOTES	X 12
150	89 1	36 151		
1	L4 946	40 945		
2	L5 999	22 153		
3	F5 160	42 154	Search list of symbolic addresses.	
4	L1 946	L4 0	Note double loop because of high	
5	36 159	L4 40	read around ratio.	
6	36 159	42 17		
7	L5 154	42 160		
8	26 163	00 435		
9	F5 154	42 160		
160	L1 946	L4 0		
1	36 153	L4 40		
2	36 153	42 17		
3	L3 17	36 167	Test real add. = 0	
4	L3 21	32 172	Test inside-outside	
5	L5 160	42 20	Outside. Word in list has	
6	42 171	26 323	non-zero address.	
7	L5 160	L0 198	Test for new sym. Add.	
8	36 192	L3 21	Test inside-outside.	
9	36 175	L5 160	1st time outside. Substitute	
170	42 171	42 20	real address.	
1	L5 84	42 0		
2	26 66	L5 17	Inside when real address is	
3	L4 0	L4 1	known.	
4	40 1	26 138		
5	L3 0	32 185	Inside when real address is	
6	F5 180	42 180	not known. Jump to 185 when	
7	50 30	L5 100	no constant to be added.	
8	42 17	L5 0	Otherwise add new word to	
9	00 10	L4 17	additions list.	

LOCATION	ORDER		NOTES	X 12
180	50 30	40 607		
1	L5 180	L0 199		
2	32 447	26 184		
3	L5 261	42 180		
4	F5 190	42 190		
5	26 186	L5 160	For inside, subst. list address	
6	42 1	L5 . 29	and add bit to those to be added	
7	L4 23	40 23	to 2 bit register.	
8	49 21	L1 31	Bookkeeping after inside add.	
9	40 31	32 69		
190	26 66	00 42		
1	+6 66	00 357		
2	L5 999	F0 30	New symbolic address. Decrease	
3	42 999	42 160	list address by one and add new	
4	42 195	89 1	word to the list.	
5	L4 946	40 0		
6	L1 999	L4 200	Test if list capacity is exceeded.	
7	32 204	22 168		
8	L1 946	L4 945		
9	50 30	40 620		
200	491002	-5 620		
1	L5 151	42 999		
2	26 66	00 93		
3	L3 23	32 204	-----------K Termination------------	
4	26 480	L5 1	Test for error	
5	10 16	40 1	Determine function digit and set switch	
6	01 4	L4 221		
7	42 208	50 207		
8	26 357	26 0		
9	L5 0	22 214	00 X	

LOCATION	ORDER		NOTES	X 12

01 K

02 K

LOCATION	ORDER	
210	L51001	22 212
1	L5 1	10 4
2	421001	L4 0
3	42 84	42 0
4	22 217	401001
5	L3 0	32 216
6	23 212	L5 84
7	26 212	50 0
8	09 1	40 25
9	67 35	40 18
220	FO 30	42 224
1	11 1	-5 209
2	L4 254	42 26
3	42 225	L3 18
4	32 225	19 0
5	40 25	L5 0
6	40 24	L5 367
7	L4 0	40 362
8	49 31	49 21
9	41 22	41 23
230	L3 20	36 93
1	L5 20	42 232
2	L51001	42 0
3	L5 242	40 235
4	411023	41 20
5	85 11	
6	36 238	LO 32
7	36 479	L4 32
8	LO 945	32 239
9	221 240	L4 41

Compute address and position of bit in counter word.

Set drum order

Test whether outside address calling for library routine. Set correct real address. Search reference word list on drum. End search on -1.

LOCATION	ORDER		NOTES	X 12
240	36 262	F5 235		
1	40 235	26 235		
2	85 11	001850		
3	81 5	42 247	-----------S Termination------------	
4	10 1	42 248	Read extra character and set addresses.	
5	42 260	L4 367		
6	40 259	49 16		
7	50 16	11 0		
8	J0 947	L5 0	Determine is inside address used.	
9	42 251	40 16		
250	22 250	-3 243	Is correction to be made?	
1	36 260	L5 0		
2	42 17	42 16		
3	L3 17	36 341	Can correction be made?	
4	L5 947	-0 947	Change 2 bit register	
5	40 947	L5 26		
6	42 257	50 256	Record words on drum.	
7	26 357	L5 0	Replace 2 bit register and correct	
8	40 24	L5 16	copies of S parameter.	
9	86 11			
260	L5 16	40 0		
1	L4 0	22 93	------------Modified Y2------------	
2	L0 41	L4 242		
3	401021	491019	Store drum order and modify counter	
4	L51022	40 19	Save info. on spec. interludes and errors.	
5	411022	L5 296	Modify important jump addresses.	
6	42 90	L5 325		
7	40 93	L5 92	Set end constant.	
8	42 379	26 269		
9	41 0	50 0		

LOCATION	ORDER		NOTES	**I 12**
270	F5 270	42 285	Set add.-fn. dig. switch.	
1	L51019	00 1	Advance count. End of 5 blocks?	
2	401019	32 283		
3	F5 279	40 279	End of 36 words from drum?	
4	L0 327	32 279		
5	L5 294	42 279	Record words on drum.	
6	42 375	50 276		
7	26 357	L51021	Bring next group of 36	
8	40 374	50 278	words from the drum.	
9	26 373	L5 608	Pick off one word. Adjust	
280	401020	L61023	sum check, drum order, counter.	
1	401023	F51021		
2	401021	19 4		
3	401019	L51020		
4	50 32	10 8	Split off 8 bits.	
5	401020	22 0	Add.-fn. dig. switch.	
6	LN 0	01 2	Set termination switch.	
7	F4 287	42 289		
8	L5 0	00 6	Add 6 bits to address at 0.	
9	40 0	26 0		
290	26 271	00 607	$\geq$ 64	
1	L41001	40 0	L	
2	40 16	22 300	F	
3	L5 0	10 6	K, S, N.	
4	40 0	-3 572	Test for interlude	
5	32 309	L4 286	Test for termination of drum input.	
6	32 312	-5 269	Test for K, S.	
7	L4 286	32 299		
8	I5 16	40 0	K termination.	
9	26 58	01 7	S termination.	

LOCATION	ORDER		NOTES	X 12
300	22 244	F5 300	Set switch for fn. digits.	
..	22 270	L5 1	Read fn. digit block.	
2	00 20	L4 0	Add to word and bookkeeping.	
3	40 1	L5 25		
4	L4 22	40 22		
5	..) 25	20 1		
6	36 307	L4 25		
7	40 25	L1 31		
8	40 31	32 69		
9	26 269	L5 1	N termination.	
310	L0 16	40 1		
1	L5 16	40 0		
2	26 60	49 21	Test sumcheck. Reset constants,	
3	L5 327	42 279	addresses. Terminate drum input.	
4	L5 19	401022		
5	L51021	40 317		
6	F5 317	401021		
7	85 11			
8	F41023	401023		
9	L31023	32 320		
320	26 101	L5 324		
1	42 90	L5 326		
2	40 93	411019		
3	411020	411021		
4	49 31	26 66		
5	26 269	22 291	Constants	
6	26 66	22 63		
7	+6 373	L5 608		
:	41 27	L5 84	--------Print Outside Type Error--------	
9	L0 17	42 27		

LOCATION	ORDER		NOTES	X 12
330	L3 27	36 66		
1	92 131	92 2		
2	92 963	L5 20		
3	42 382	L5 17		
4	42 27	50 334		
5	26 407	L5 84		
6	42 27	50 336		
7	26 407	F5 337		
8	26 382	89 1		
9	L41022	36 171		
340	401022	26 171		
1	92 131	92 259	----------Print S type error----------	
2	92 706	92 707		
3	92 963	41 27		
4	L5 253	42 382		
5	50 32	L5 248		
6	42 27	50 346		
7	26 407	L5 84		
8	42 27	50 348		
9	26 407	F5 349		
350	26 382	L31019		
1	36 354	89 1		
2	L4 19	36 356		
3	40 19	26 356		
4	89 1	L41022		
5	36 356	401022		
6	L5 0	22 93		
7	+5 0	42 366	-------------------	
8	L5 368	42 361	Store words on the drum.	
9	L5 86	42 369	Closed subroutine. Set	

LOCATION		ORDER		NOTES	X 12
360	L5 361		LO 369	initially to store 2 - 15	
1	32 365		L5 2	on the drum.	
2	86 11		023566		
3	F5 362		40 362		
4	F5 363		40 363		
5	22 360		L5 368		
6	42 86		23 563	Link.	
7	86 11		023564		
8	00 0		00 563		
9	32 365		L5 16		
370	86 11		023563		
1	30 374		22 0	Link. Bring words	
2	00 0		42 375	from the drum. Closed	
3	+5 507		42 371	subroutine. Set initially	
4	85 11		001617	to rewrite 1002 - 1018.	
5	32 375		401002		
6	F5 374		40 374		
7	F5 375		40 375		
8	LO 379		26 371		
9	-2 375		401019		
380	85 11		023564		
1	85 11		023563		
2	42 388		L5 0	Entry. Print symbolic address.	
3	10 10		40 27	Closed subroutine. Address of word	
4	41 28		19 3	to be printed is substituted in	
5	40 21		26 390	382.	
6	L5 21		36 389		
7	L5 28		32 388		
8	92 707		22 0	Link.	
9	04 1		40 21		

LOCATION	ORDER				NOTES	X 12
390	50	28	L5	27		
1	10	6	40	27		
2	−5	0	00	2		
3	40	946	10	2		
4	43	946	−3	0		
5	36	386	−J	0		
6	36	400	89	1		
7	L4	28	40	28		
8	32	399	92	259		
9	26	400	92	707		
400	51	946	01	4		
1	−4	0	36	403		
2	50	405	22	403		
3	50	389	00	3		
4	00	3	42	405		
5	02	1	92	0		
6	26	386	00	549		
7	+5	0	42	416	Entry. Convert binary	
8	50	32	L5	27	address to decimal and print.	
9	00	20	50	417	Closed subroutine. Address	
410	−0	0	36	410	to be printed is stored at 27.	
1	−4	0	50	418		
2	−0	0	36	412		
3	−4	0	46	27		
4	00	12	L4	27		
5	00	8	82	12		
6	92	963	22	0	Link.	
7	00	99	L0	0		
8	00	9	LL	0		
9	41	27	L5	532	Print inside type error.	

LOCATION	ORDER		NOTES	Y 12
420	42 434	L5 531		
1	LO 551	36 423		
2	L5 533	26 424		
3	L5 535	10 20		
4	42 382	22 427		
5	41 27	L5 406		
6	42 434	L5 544		
7	42 382	92 131		
8	L5 381	LO 367		
9	LO 368	L4 16		
430	42 27	50 430		
1	26 407	F5 431		
2	26 382	89 1		
3	L41022	32 434		
4	401022	26 0		
5	L5 1	L4 0	---------N Termination---------	
6	40 1	L5 0	Construct jump instruction.	
7	LO 38	32 438		
8	26 445	L4 202	Jumps with address ≥ 999.	
9	42 1	41 22		
440	41 23	L1 31		
1	36 442	23 442		
2	L5 29	L4 29		
3	40 25	49 31		
4	41 20	22 1		
5	41 0	50 445	Record words on drum.	
6	26 357	F5 456	Set link and record remainder	
7	42 457	L5 180	of additions list on drum.	
8	42 452	L5 370		
9	L4 458	FO 452		

LOCATION	ORDER		NOTES	X 12
450	40 453	40 370	Note that the order is reversed	
1	L5 452	50 30	during the transfer.	
2	22 456	L5 0		
3	86 11			
4	F5 453	40 453		
5	L5 452	F0 30		
6	42 452	L0 458		
7	32 452	26 183		
8	22 456	L5 603		
9	L51022	42 17	Test for special interlude.	
460	L3 17	32 476		
1	L5 17	421008	Set addresses in control block	
2	421003	L4 367	(999 - 1018) for special interlude.	
3	401009	L0 478		
4	401002	L5 84		
5	421017	421018		
6	L31019	36 468	Test for tape-drum input.	
7	L5 19	401022		
8	L3 23	36 470	Test for error in jump at	
9	L 480	40 1	location 1.	
470	L5 190	50 32	Compact address at 190 with	
1	10 10	-5 0	relativizer and store at 1001.	
2	L41001	401001		
3	L5 523	42 452	Store 2 bit registers and symbolic	
4	L5 999	42 458	address list on drum.	
5	L51005	42 457		
6	22 448	L31019	Test for drum or regular interlude.	
7	36 481	26 467		
8	01 0		————————Back Substitution and————————	
9	FF 48	FF 49	Regular interludes for tape input	

LOCATION	ORDER		NOTES	X 12
480	FF 50	FF 51		
1	L5 190	42 488	Transfer additions list from drum to	
2	LO 191	32 483	Williams memory. This loop is set	
3	FF 52	L5 381	initially to bring symbolic address	
4	FO 488	L4 497	list, etc., from the drum during	
5	40 487	L5 488	input starts.	
6	50 30	22 491		
7	85 11	023563		
8	32 488	40 0		
9	F5 487	40 487		
490	L5 488	FO 30		
1	42 488	LO 497		
2	36 487	26 588	See word 593. Changed during input starts.	
3	42 458	L5 513	Store list of symbolic addresses	
4	42 452	F5 491	on drum.	
5	42 457	L5 478		
6	L4 381	26 449		
7	32 488	40 43		
8	L5 367	40 381		
9	L5 380	40 374		
500	L5 368	L4 35	Set links, etc., for transferring	
1	42 369	42 379	blocks of 20 words to and	
2	L5 373	46 361	from the drum.	
3	46 369	L5 556		
4	42 371	22 509		
5	L5 381	L4 35	Advance addresses.	
6	40 381	LO 478		
7	40 374	F5 509	Entry after transfer to drum.	
8	40 509	LO 557		
9	36 558	Fl 947	Test 2 bit register for 0.	

LOCATION	ORDER				NOTES	X 12
510	40	18	F3	18		
1	36 505		L5	368	In case 2 bit reg. $\neq$ 0,	
2	42 361		42	375	bring 20 words from the	
3	26 374		00	944	drum.	
4	40	16	L5	18	Adjustment after subst.	
5	80	2	F4	32	real addresses.	
6	40	18	F3	18	Test for completion of subst.	
7	36 553		L5	18	Test for inside addresses requiring	
8	36 524		80	1	substitution of real addresses. Both	
9	36 524		80	1	instructions of a pair tested each	
					time through loop.	
520	F4	32	40	18		
1	F5	16	40	16		
2	22 517		L5	368	Entry after bringing 20 words.	
3	22 521		00	998		
4	L5	16	42	525	Set up for address substitution.	
5	42 549		L5	0		
6	46 531		42	542		
7	46 535		42	544		
8	40	31	F1	18	Substitution for left instruction.	
9	36 539		L5	531	Test is constant to be added?	
530	L0 551		32	534		
1	L5	0	42	533	Set up if constant to be added.	
2	40	0	50	539		
3	43	0	L5	0		
4	22 535		41	0		
5	L5	0	42	17	Substitution of address in left	
6	00	10	L4	0	instruction.	
7	00	10	46	31		
8	L3	17	36	419	Test for error.	
9	F1	18	80	1	Substitution for right instruction.	

LOCATION	ORDER			NOTES	X 12
540	36 549	41	0	Test is constant to be added to	
1	L5 542	LO 552		right instruction?	
2	32 544	L5	0	Set up if constant is to be added.	
3	42 544	10 10			
4	40 0	L5	0		
5	42 17	43 31		Substitute address.	
6	L5 17	L4 31			
7	L4 0	40 31			
8	L3 17	36 425		Test for error.	
9	L5 31	40	0		
550	F5 16	26 514			
1	L5 512	42 533		Constants	
2	32 544	L5 512			
3	L5 381	40 362		Record modified words on drum.	
4	L4 35	40 381			
5	L5 16	42 369			
o	22 361	00 522			
7	36 558	F1 999		Test for error in jump instruction	
8	L51022	36 560		at location 1. Begin interlude.	
9	L5 479	40 1			
560	L3 23	361002			
1	L5 480	40 1			
2	261002			--------Input Starts--------	
3	23 107	41 0			
4	41 30	41 17		Entry at right of 563 from 366.	
5	41 20	41 1			
6	L51002	42 0		Save information on type of start.	
7	40 16	50 567		Rewrite 1002 - 1018.	
8	26 373	L3 16		Hold or clear start when N(16)=0	
9	32 570	26 575			

LOCATION	ORDER		NOTES	X 12
570	42 574	41 947	Set 2 bit registers = 0	
1	F5 570	40 570		
2	L0 601	32 570		
3	411019	411021	Set locations for special interludes,	
4	411022	22 588	errors and drum input.	
5	501001	01 10	In case of interludes decompact 1001.	
6	40 17	11 10	Re-establish relativizer.	
7	-5 0	401001		
8	L3 17	32 597	N(17)= 0 means regular interlude.	
9	F5 579	42 594	For special and drum input interludes	
580	L5 17	42 190	replace constant at 190. Re-establish	
1	42 488	L5 487	drum orders for additions list and	
2	L4 497	F0 488	bring back symbolic address list and 2 bit	
3	40 487	L4 478	registers.	
4	40 370	L5 523	Transfer lists to Williams memory.	
5	42 488	L5 999		
6	42 497	L5 487		
7	26 484			
8	41 1	L5 600	Enter K termination loop to set up	
9	42 231	L5 16	constants for SADOI	
590	36 210	26 214		
1	L5 202	42 231		
2	L5 112	42 497	Reset some orders and start input.	
3	L5 602	40 492		
4	50 30	26 563		
5	L51021	32 596	Distinguish between special and	
6	26 264	431022	drum input interludes.	
7	26 93	F5 597	Regular interludes	
8	26 570	L5 202		
9	42 594	L5 513		

LOCATION		ORDER	NOTES	X 12
600	26 585	00 591		
1	N2 574	41 999	Constants	
2	36 487	L5 999		
3	00 0	00 0	sum check constant.	
4	80 0	26 100	Overwrite bootstrap to start SADOI	
1614	49 1002		999 type interludes	
999	55 945			
1615	42 1002			
1000	22 1008			
1616	00 0		Relativizer	
1001	00 0			
1617	85 11			
1002	02 3566		Bring assembled	
1618	32 1003			
1003	40 2		program to	
1619	L6 0			
1004	40 0		Williams memory.	
1620	F5 1002			
1005	40 1002			
1621	F5 1003			
1006	40 1003			
1622	L0 1018			
1007	36 1002			
1623	22 1			
1008	L5 16		Put contents of	
1624	86 11			
1009	02 3580		Williams memory	
1625	F5 1009			
1010	40 1009		on drum.	
1626	F5 1008			
1011	40 1008			

OCATION	ORDER	NOTES	X 12
1627	LO 1017		
1012	32 1008		
1628	F5 1015	Bootstrap start	
1013	40 607		
1629	26 1015	Waste	
1014	26 1000	1014 interludes	
1630	85 11		
1015	00 1027	for main part of	
1631	40 608		
1016	26 607	SADOI	
1632	K2 1		
1017	L5 999	constants.	
1633	S2 1003		
1018	40 999		
1634	05 11	2 - 31	
1019	03 512	Restore	
1635	85 11		
1020	03 482	after SADOI	
1636	32 1021		
1021	40 2	is first	
1637	F5 1021		
1022	40 1021	called for. Used	
1638	F5 1020		
1023	40 1020	as storage locations	
1639	LO 1019		
1024	36 1020	by SADOI.	
1640	41 1002		
1025	22 1008		
1641	85 1759	Sum check	
	13 2340		

APPENDIX 10

A DESCRIPTION OF ROUTINES EXECUTED SUBSEQUENT TO THE CLEAR START

AND PRELIMINARY TO THE ROUTINE SELECTED BY THE KEY CHARACTER

        In this appendix the details of the logical operations subsequent
to the "clear start" * are presented. These include the operation of the
drum bootstrap and four routines identified as routines 1, 2, 3, and 4.
This appendix is essentially a copy of File No. 228 of the DCL except for
certain minor changes which have been made to bring it up to date.

        A schematic diagram of the sequence of logical operations subsequent
to the hold start is presented in Figure 1**. The material in this appendix
covers the operations from the clear start up to the sixteen position switch,
with just a partial description of the operations executed by routine 4. In
broad outline the function of these routines is to bring a routine from the
drum, preserving as much as is possible of the Williams Memory (WM) on the
drum, which will read a single character from the tape, known as the key
character, interpret the key character and execute certain operations corresponding to the one of sixteen possible logical paths it specifies. The bulk
of the operations are devoted to the preservation on the drum of that portion
of the WM which must be used to hold the routine which will do the reading
and interpretation of the key character.

        Pages 332,333 contain a complete list of the instructions in the drum
bootstrap, and routines 1, 2, 3, and 4. The drum location of each instruction
pair is indicated in the first column. The WM location of the instruction pair
at the time of its execution is indicated in the second column. All of the
characters are sexadecimal including the numbers appearing in the "remarks"
column.

        The operations of routines 1, 2, 3, and 4 are reasonably straight-
forward and may be relatively easily followed from the instruction list alone.
The operation of the drum bootstrap, however, is too complex to be followed
easily from the instruction list. Its operation is hopefully clarified by
Figure 2 wherein the successive states of all registers and WM locations
significantly involved in the operation of the drum bootstrap are recorded.
Time is regarded as increasing from the top of the figure to the bottom. Each
register and WM location is to be considered as holding the entry last recorded

* The discussion also applies to a "hold start".
** Figures and Tables are at the end of this appendix.

in the column corresponding to it; its state changing only when a new entry
is made in the corresponding column. The first entry into the control counter
and order register is made by the hold start. No drum location is altered
by the drum bootstrap, and it of course is assumed that the state of the drum
memory is as indicated in the instruction list. Exit is made from the drum
bootstrap into routine 1 via the order 26 3L8.

Since it is sometimes helpful to have a convenient reference to the
transfer of information from the WM to the drum and vice versa, Table 1 has
been constructed. Table 1 indicates the transfer of information between the
WM and the drum during each routine. Except for the information transfer
denoted by * for the drum bootstrap the transfer is always one-to-one; thus,
in routine 2 the contents of WM location 2 are placed in drum location 31F2,
the contents of WM location 3 are placed in drum location 31F3 etc., and
finally the contents of WM location 1L are placed in location 31LL of the drum.

In routine 3 the key character, k, is read from the tape. This key
character corresponds to a key word held in location 14+k on the drum. The key
word contains all the necessary information for the setting of addresses in
routine 4. The detailed structure of the key word illustrating the significance
of the various bit positions is shown in Figure 3. In Table 2 the sixteen key
words, corresponding to the sixteen key characters are listed. The name of the
program which the key character eventually calls into operation is also listed.
The routine which is called from the drum into the WM, and subsequently executed,
is called routine 5.

The routines described in this appendix evolved from the work of many
people, particularly J. Fishel, D. Gillies, D. Muller, and J. Robertson. The
present form of these routines was prepared by D. Gillies.

Drum Address	Williams Mem. Address	Order Pair	Remarks
			Routine 1:
3L6	3L6	F5 3L7	Reads in recording routine which records
		42 3L7	WM (2) → (1L) on the drum; also loads WM
3L7	3L7	85 008	(1) → (13) from drum (1) → (13).
		40 (3L9)	
3L8	3L8	00 008	
		56 3L6	Negative 1st time when drum location zero is read. On second pass negative when drum location one is read.
3L9	3L9	00 001	
		32 001	Negative on 1st pass, positive on second pass. Transfer to loc. 1 when recording completed.
			Routine 2:
3LK	3LK	K6 3L6	Record W.M. (2) → (1L)
		L5 (002)	on drum (31F2) → (31LL)
3LS	3LS	86 008	
		03 1F2	
3LN	3LN	F5 3LS	Advance recording address
		40 3LS	
3LJ	3LJ	F5 3LK	Advance call address
		42 3LK	
3LF	3LF	L0 3LL	end test
		32 3LK	end transfer
3LL	3LL	26 3L6	here when recording of W.M. (2) → (1L)
		L5 020	completed.
400	0	85 008	
		40 3L8	
401	1	42 000	Drum Bootstrap
		26 000	
0	0	85 NOS	
		40 401	
1	1	26 3L8	Routine 3: Prepare switches in Routine 4
		81 004	Read key character from tape
2	2	L4 00K	Form key character + 014
		42 003	and plant call address for key word
3	3	85 008	Read key word from the drum
		00 (014)	

Drum Address	Williams Mem. Address	Order Pair	Remarks
4	4	42 009	Plant initial Illiac store address minus 1 of Routine 5.
		10 015	Form and plant drum read instruction
5	5	L4 003	with read address equal to
		40 00F	drum location minus 1 of Routine 5.
6	6	01 007	Form and plant address for transfer
		L4 009	into Routine 5.
7	7	42 012	
		01 00K	Form and plant end constant
8	8	L4 00F	for drum read loop. Constant also serves as
		40 010	read instruction for fiducial check sum.
9	9	23 00K	Enter drum read loop.
			Routine 4: Read block from Drum into W. M. as specified by key character.
		40 (000)	Store drum word in W.M. Mod by 4, S
K	K	L6 014	Accumulate drum sum check
		40 014	at 014.
S	S	F5 009	Advance W.M. storage address
		42 009	
N	N	F5 00F	Advance Drum read address
		40 00F	
J	J	L0 010	Test for end of drum read loop
		36 010	Transfer if end of drum read loop.
F	F	00 000	Read word from drum. Word plant
		00 000	by 5. Mod. by N
L	L	22 009	
		00 022	
10	10	00 000	end constant for reading program from drum and drum read to obtain fiducial sum check
		00 000	number. Set by 8.
11	11	L4 014	
		40 014	Form drum sum check test number
12	12	F3 014	address set by 7
		56 (000)	transfer to program selected by key character
13	13	FF 824	here if drum sum check fails
		23 012	

334

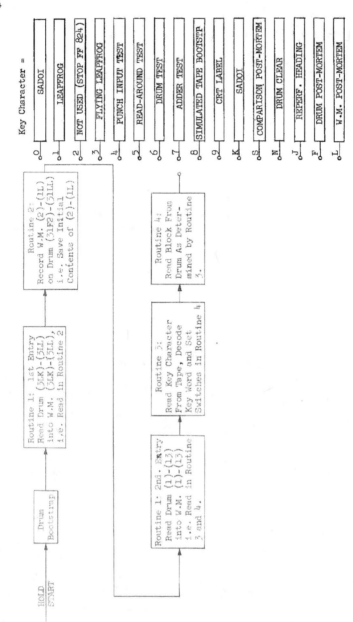

Figure 1

Schematic of Operations Subsequent to Hold Start

CONTROL COUNTER	ORDER REGISTER	ACCUMULATOR	0	1	3L6	3L7	3L8	3L9
0	85 00S							
	40 000	85 NOS						
	40 401	40 401	85 NOS					
			40 401					
1	85 NOS							
	40 401	42 000						
		26 000		42 000				
				26 000				
2	42 000							
	26 000		85 NOS					
0			40 400					
1	85 NOS							
	40 400	85 00S						
		40 3L8	85 00S					
			40 3L8					
2	42 000							
	26 000		85 00S					
0			40 3L6					
1	85 00S							
	40 3L8	00 008						
		36 3L6					00 008	
							36 3L6	
2	42 000							
	26 000		85 00S					
0			40 3L6					
1	85 00S							
	40 3L6	F5 3L7						
		42 3L7			F5 3L7			
					42 3L7			
2	42 000							
	26 000		85 00S					
0			40 3L7					
1	85 00S							
	40 3L7	85 00S						
		40 3L9				85 00S		
						40 3L9		
2	42 000							
	26 000		85 00S					
0			40 3L9					
1	85 00S							
	40 3L9	00 001						
		32 001						00 001
								32 001
2	42 000							
	26 000		85 00S					
0			40 001					
1	85 00S							
	40 001	26 3L8						
		61 004		26 3L8				
				61 004				
2	26 3L8							
	61 004							

FIGURE 2

DETAILED SEQUENCE OF THE OPERATIONS INVOLVED IN THE DRUM BOOTSTRAP

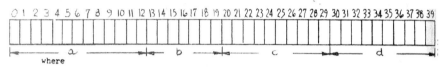

where

$a + k + 15_\varepsilon$ = drum location of Routine 5

k = key character

$d + 1$ = Williams Memory location of Routine 5

$d + b$ = entry address of Routine 5

$c - 1$ = number of words in Routine 5

Figure 3

Structure of Key Word

Routine	Words Transferred	
	W.M.	Drum
	0, 1 [*] ⬅—	0, 1, 400, 401 [*]
Drum Bootstrap	3L6 - 3L9 ⬅—	3L6 - 3L9
Routine 1: 1st entry	3LK - 3LL ⬅—	3LK - 3LL
Routine 2	2 - 1L —➤	31F2 - 31LL
Routine 1: 2nd entry	1 - 13 ⬅—	1 - 13
Routine 3	no transfer	no transfer
Routine 4: k = 0	3F7 - 1 ⬅—	64F - 668
" " k = 1	3N8 - 3LL ⬅—	S7 - FS
" " k = 2	Not used	
" " k = 3	3F7 - 1 ⬅—	S7 - FS
" " k = 4	3KL - 3LF ⬅—	133 - 17L
" " k = 5	109 - 173 ⬅—	19F - 211
" " k = 6	K1 - 189 ⬅—	23J - 325
" " k = 7	101 - 129 ⬅—	213 - 239
" " k = 8	3LK - 1 ⬅—	3FJ - 3L4
" " k = 9	20 - 76 ⬅—	380 - 3J6
" " k = K	3F7 - 1 ⬅—	64F - 668
" " k = S	18 - 1L ⬅—	37K - 37F
" " k = N	3L6 - 7 ⬅—	184 - 195
" " k = J	3LK - 0 ⬅—	3J8 - 3JF
" " k = F	1L - J6 —➤	66L - 726
" " k = L	3L6 - 3L9 —➤	708 - 72G

Table 1

Transfer of Words Between Williams Memory and
Drum Memory Subsequent to a Hold Start

[*] Transfer not one-to-one

KEY CHARACTER	KEY WORD	PROGRAM NAME
0	31N96073F6	SADOI
1	050820JSNK	Leapfrog
2	LJ98100800	Not used and causes stop FF 824
3	04L810JSNK	Flying leapfrog
4	08J01147KF	Punch input test
5	0N2011J4LL	Read-around test
6	111303K8K0	Drum test
7	0LS840K900	Adder test
8	1F802027L9	Simulated tape bootstrap
9	1S1561601L	CRT label
K	31796073F6	SADOI
S	1KJ010181K	Comparison Post-Mortem
N	0S19004LL5	Drum clear
J	1JS07023L9	Reperforate
F	326012F41F	Drum Post-Mortem
L	38203017L5	WM Post-Mortem

Table 2

Index to key words

APPENDIX 11

ILLIAC LIBRARY DESCRIPTION OF D1:

THE CHECK POINT CODE

LIBRARY ROUTINE D 1 - 95

TITLE   Check Point Code II

TYPE   Special

NUMBER OF WORDS $57 + 3\ell + s + j$ (see text)

DESCRIPTION:

      This code is designed to print out intermediate information
about the operation of some other code. Its purpose is to help the programmer locate mistakes in a code which is not working properly, or else to
verify that a code suspected of working properly is actually doing so. The
principle of operation of the check point code is to place "blocking orders"
at particular points of your program (these points to be specified by you on
a specification tape to be discussed later). Each blocking order results in
a transfer of control to Code 95. When control is transferred, Code 95 prints
out the location (fixed) of the order at which the block has been placed,
and then prints out other information which you think will help you in
locating the mistake in your program. The nature of the other information
to be printed out at the checkpoint is also specified on the specification
tape. This other information is printed out before the blocked order is
finally obeyed. The blocking order itself is placed in the left hand side of
the blocked placed in the memory.

      For each checkpoint, the programmer can specify how many times
no printing is to occur (e.g., do not print the first 14 times) and how often
to print thereafter (e.g., print 18 times and then print no more). In this
particular case, the following things would happen: When Code 95 is read
in, it places a blocking order at the checkpoint. The first 14 times the
blocking order is reached, control is transferred to Code 95. Code 95 prints
nothings, executes the blocked order, and transfers control back to your
program. The 15th time the blocking order is reached, control is transferred
to Code 95. Code 95 prints two line feed characters, the location of the
blocking order, and prints such other information as you have asked it to
print (on the specification tape). It then executes the blocked order, and
transfers control back to your program. The 16th time the blocking order is
reached, printing occurs, and so on. The 32nd time (32 = 14 + 18) the blocking

order is encountered, printing occurs, the blocked order is obeyed, and the blocked order is restored to its rightful place in the memory the 33rd time. The 34th time the previously blocked order is encountered, it is simply obeyed just as if it had never been blocked, and the same occurs forever thereafter, until your program terminates with an OFF order, or fails someplace else.

Certain precautions must be obeyed in deciding on the location of blocking orders:

(1) The blocked order must not be overwritten by your program during the time it is blocked (however, it may be overwritten after code 95 has relinquished control).

(2) The blocked order must not be used as a number by your program during the time it is blocked (however, it may be used as a number after Code 95 has relinquished control).

(3) It is not necessary to avoid locating your checkpoint at a place which contains a control transfer order. The printing occurs before any transfer of control (to another part of your program) is obeyed.

(4) It is not necessary to make special provision for identifying each checkpoint (assuming that you have decided to insert several blocking orders), since Code 95 always prints the location of the checkpoint before any other information.

(5) Blocking orders can be overwritten by Code 95, i.e., it is possible to print information at some particular checkpoint the 47th time it is reached, the 58th time it is reached, but at no other times. The specification tape necessary for this will be discussed later.

NATURE OF INFORMATION WHICH CAN BE PRINTED AT EACH CHECKPOINT

At each checkpoint, we may take a number from any place in the memory, or from R_1, or from R_2, and print it in a number of ways:

(1) As an order pair

(2) As a right hand address

(3) As a left hand address

(4) As a ten character sexadecimal word

(5) As a signed integer

(6) As a signed 12 figure decimal fraction, not rounded

(7) As a signed 5 figure fraction, not rounded

The number of items to be printed at each checkpoint is arbitrary and so is the number of different checkpoints. Both are limited only by the memory space available for the operation of Code 95.

Code 95 will print two line feed and carriage return characters before each checkpoint print, but it will not print such characters during each checkpoint print unless the programmer so specifies. If the amount of printing you want to do at a given checkpoint exceeds the capacity of a line on the teletype machines (about 60 characters), you can and should specify additional carriage returns and line feeds by means of the specification tape.

If the number to be printed consists of a sign digit only (i.e., the sexadecimal word is 8000000000) the following things will be printed:

Order pair: 80 0 00 0
R. H. address: 0
L. H. address: 0
Sexadecimal: 8000000000
Signed integer: -0
Signed 12 figure fraction: = -000000000000
Signed 5 figure fraction: = -00000

Zero is always preced by a + sign.

Two spaces are left between any two printed items.

Non-significant zeros are omitted in the printing of integers or addresses. Zero is printed as a single zero. The integer 1235×2^{-39} is printed as + 1235, not as +000000001235.

THE SPECIFICATION TAPE

For each checkpoint, we must specify the location of the checkpoint, the nature of the information to be printed at the checkpoint, how often the printing is to be suppressed at first, and how often printing should occur thereafter until the order is unblocked. This is done as follows:

(1) Let "c" be the location of the checkpoint. Put cL on the specification tape.

(2) Let "f" be the number of times printing is to be suppressed (f = 14 in the example on page 1 of this write-up). Put fF on the specification tape. f must lie between 0 and 511. If f = 0, i.e., if you wish to print the very first time your program reaches the blocking order at c, you do not need to specify f at all.

(3) Let "k" be the number of times printing is to occur before the order is unblocked (k = 18 in the example on page 1 of this write-up). Put kK on the specification tape. If k = 1 (i.e., if you wish to print once and once only at this check point), you need not specify k at all.

(4) Let a, b, c,..., be the addresses of words you wish to have printed at this checkpoint. Let "G" be any one of the following seven sexadecimal characters: G = 0, 2, 5, 6, S, N, F. The character G specifies the way in which the number is to be printed:

(i)   As an order pair: G = 0

(ii)   As a right hand address: G = 2

(iii)   As a left hand address: G = 6

(iv)   As a ten-character sexadecimal word: G = S

(v)   As a signed integer: G = N

(vi)   As a signed twelve figure fraction: G = F

(vii)   As a signed five figure decimal fraction: G = 5

Put on the specification tape: aSG_a, bSG_b, ..., where G_a specifies the way $N(a)$ is to be printed, G_b specifies how $N(b)$ is to be printed, and so on.

If you wish to print the number in R_1, specify the location of word 0 of Code 95, (this is 900 if you use the ILLIAC copy).

If you wish to print the number in R_2, specify the location of word 1 of Code 95, (this is 901 if you use the ILLIAC copy).

If you wish to print a line feed and carriage return character, specify the symbol "J" on the specification tape.

(5) After all the checkpoints and the printing at each checkpoint have been specified, we conclude the specification tape with nNB where "n" is the location of the first order in your program which you wish to have obeyed, and "B" is a sexadecimal character which specifies the nature of the control transfer (in practice, B will be one of 0, 2, 4, 6, in most cases). The control transfer is accomplished by means of a 2Bn order.

(6) If we wish to print, say, the order pair at location 12 during the 10th and 20th times control passes the check point at c, this may be done by having 2 check points at the same address:

e.g.   cL 19F 12S0

                        cL 9F 12S0

MEMORY SPACE NEEDED FOR CODE 95

Code 95 itself occupies 57 memory positions. However, more
memory positions must be allowed after the last word of Code 95 to contain
the blocked orders, locations of numbers to be printed, and so on. Let "ℓ"
be the number of check-points (= the number of L's on your specification tape).
Allow 3 ℓ memory positions. Furthermore, allow one memory position for each
piece of information (word) you wish to have printed out, and one memory
position for each line feed character (each J on the specification tape) over
and above the automatic line feeds. Thus the total number of memory positions
needed is

Memory positions necessary $= 57 + 3\ell + s + j$

where "ℓ" is the number of L's on the specification tape, "s" is the number
of S's (not counting the second S in SS, however), and "j" is the number of
J's.

READING IN OF CODE 95

Code 95 is in two parts, both on the same tape. Read in
the program to be checked. Then read in Part I. When Part I is in, the
ILLIAC stops and the Specification Tape is read in. The ILLIAC stops again
and Part II is read in. The program then starts.

ILLIAC COPY OF CODE 95

The operator's copy uses a bootstrap input which places the
code at positions beginning with 900 and overwrites the Decimal Order Input.
If you have no program beyond 899, then you can use this and will have 67
locations for the list.

RT: 9/22/55.
DATE November 30, 1955
WRITTEN BY D.J. Wheeler
APPROVED BY

DJW:mge
Sept. 22, 1955

APPENDIX 12

THE COMBINED POST-MORTEM

Both the key characters F and L call into operation a single large
program known as the Combined Post-Mortem routine which is placed in the WM
after either of these key characters is encountered. The Combined Post-Mortem
reads data, via the tape reader, which specifies the exact type of post-mortem
that is desired and a memory address indicating the location of a block of ten
words in the memory to which the post-mortem is to be applied, or, in the case
of an address search, the address on which the search is to be applied. The
specific types of post-mortem which may be requested are:

      (1) Order Pairs

      (2) Decimal Integers

      (3) Decimal Fractions

      (4) Floating Point. Numbers

      (5) Sexadecimal Numbers

      (6) Address Search (WM only).

Memory Locations Available for Post-Mortem.* It should be obvious that
certain information in the memory will necessarily be lost whenever the Combined
Post-Mortem is called into operation. It is important that the user be aware of
the memory locations which can be post-mortemed and those which cannot. Since
the post-mortem always begins from a HOLD START, the contents of certain locations
in the memory are destroyed initially by the drum bootstrap and routines 1, 2, 3
and 4. The words in the memory which get overwritten are indicated in Table 1
of Appendix 10 "A Description of Routines Executed Subsequent to the Clear Start
and Preliminary to the Routine Selected by the Key Character".

     The WM post-mortem and the drum post-mortem treat the preservation
of the memory differently. If a WM post-mortem is requested, then a routine
is called into operation which preserves the WM, locations 20 through 3L5,
in drum locations 2FON through 31F1. The contents of the drum locations
2FON-31F1 are not preserved. Following this preservation

---

* All references to locations in the WM or drum are sexadecimal unless
  specified otherwise. Subscripts S and D are used to identify sexadecimal
  and decimal numbers respectively, whenever the base of any number
  is not obvious from the context.

of the WM a transfer back to routine 4 is made with a simulated key character
$k = F$ and routine 4 will be executed as if a drum post-mortem had been requested*.
On the other hand, if a drum post-mortem is requested, the the Combined Post-
Mortem is immediately read into the WM locations 20 through J6 from the drum
locations 670 through 726. The contents of the WM locations 20 - J6 <u>are not</u>
<u>preserved</u>. Thus, in a WM post-mortem the maximum amount of information in
the WM is preserved while in the drum post-mortem the maximum amount of
information on the drum is preserved.

The Combined Post-Mortem routine permits the user to run the post-
mortems in any desired order. However, it is clear from the above discussion
that the order of running the post-mortems will affect the memory locations
available for post-mortem. In Table 1** the memory locations available for
post-mortem are indicated for the two situations: the WM post-mortem is run
<u>first</u> and then drum and WM post-mortem follow in any order; the drum post-
mortem is run <u>first</u> and the drum and WM post-mortems follow in any order. The
locations indicated in Table 1 are available for post-mortem on <u>any</u> post-mortem
in the sequence of post-mortems which may follow the first.

<u>Format for the data tape</u>. In this discussion we will assume that the
characters on the data tape are indicated by c_0, c_1, c_2, ... Following the
key character F or L, three sexadecimal characters must appear on the tape
$(c_1 \ c_2 \ c_3)$. If the third character, c_3, is even (least significant binary
digit equals zero), then an address search is specified and three more sexadecimal characters will be read from the tape $(c_4 \ c_5 \ c_6)$ which specify the
search address. No other data is necessary for the address search post-mortem.
Returning to the three sexadecimal characters following the key character, if
c_3 is odd, then $c_1 \ c_2 \ c_3$ form the address of a transfer order entering a
subroutine to give one of post-mortems (1)-(5). In Table 2 the three characters,
for each type of post-mortem are listed.

---

* The routine "remembers" that a WM post-mortem was requested by the sign of a
certain word in the memory.

** Figures and Tables appear at the end of this appendix.

If the post-mortem desired is one of (1)-(5) then beginning with the character c_4 the tape is copied identically, with a line-feed and carriage return preceding the copy, until a one-hole delay character, say c_1, is read. The purpose of this operation is of course to print an appropriate heading.

At the completion of the copy tape operation a black switch (BS) STOP is encountered (21 02S). Following this stop the address of the block of storage on which the post-mortem is to be applied is read from the tape. There are two modes for the read-in of this data depending on whether a drum post-mortem or a WM post-mortem is desired. If a drum post-mortem is desired the address of the block on the drum is read in two stages. In the first stage the thousands portion of the address is specified and in the second stage the hundreds portion of the address is specified. Specifically, this read-in proceeds as follows:

(1) Read digits from tape as an integer until a space character is encountered. Thus, the sequence of digits 2, 0, 0, followed by a space would be read in as the integer two hundred.

(2) When the space character is encountered a BS STOP (34 02S) is obeyed.

(3) Resume read-in by putting the black switch to START. In this second stage the digits read in are converted as an integer and read-in continues until a character with the 5th hole punched, but not a space character, is encountered. Thus the sequence 3, 5, line feed, would be read in as the integer thirty-five.

(4) When the character with the 5th hole punched is encountered in step (3) the integer formed in step (3) is added to the integer in step (1). The result (which in the example cited above would be two hundred and thirty-five) is interpreted as the address of the block to be post-mortemed, divided by 10_D (thus in the current example the address of the desired block is two thousand three hundred and fifty). No stop is executed and the post-mortem proceeds immediately.

If a WM post-mortem is desired the read-in of the address proceeds in one stage starting at step (3) above and the register that would hold the integer from step (1) above is initially set to zero. It should be noted that it is the character terminating a sequence of digits read in which determines whether these digits form the most significant part (MSP) of the address (i.e. the thousands part) and that reading must continue to get the least significant part or whether these digits form the least significant part of the address (i.e. the hundreds part) and that they must be added to the MSP which has already been read.

The block to be post-mortemed is always assumed to contain just ten words, the address of the first word being read from the tape in the manner described above. After the ten words have been post-mortemed a BS STOP (30 029) is encountered. If the black switch is then set to START a new block address is read from the tape. The reading of this address proceeds in one or two stages depending on whether the digits are terminated by a space character or some other character with a 5th hole punch.

The library post-mortem tape contains the key character, transfer address, and heading for post-mortems (1)-(5). The tail of the tape contains all necessary block addresses. The block addresses are properly ordered so that consecutive blocks of ten words in storage will be processed without a STOP when the black switch is in the IGNORE position. The data for the drum post-mortem and WM post-mortem are contained on two separate library tapes.

For the address search post-mortem a special tape must be prepared. The leading character must be L (the key character designating a WM post-mortem). By convention the transfer address which must follow the L is OOK. Following the transfer address the search address is written as three tetrads. Thus, if the search address is 11_D, it must be written on the tape as OOS. The search address must follow immediately after the transfer address.

Output Format. Certain features of the output format which are common to the post-mortem routines (1)-(5) are discussed in this section.

Each post-mortem has a heading copied identically from the data tape,
as described earlier. Following this the address, divided by 10, of the block
to be post-mortemed is printed on a separate line, at the left of the page. On
the following lines the words printed from the memory as order pairs, or integers,
etc. are each preceeded by the least significant digit of the address. The
address digits are all printed as decimal numbers. Any word which is identically
zero is ignored by the post-mortem and thus does not appear in the post-mortem
output. Details of the output with examples follow.

Order Pairs. Words from the memory are printed on successive lines
as order pairs. The function digits are printed sexadecimally and addresses are
printed as unsigned decimal integers with zero suppression on all but the least
significant digit. P16 is used to print the address. If the right hand order is
identically zero it is not printed. An example of an output from the order-pair
post-mortem is shown in Figure 2. Figure 1 shows the relevant portion of the
memory as sexadecimal numbers at the time the results in Figure 2 were obtained.

Decimal Integers. Words from the memory are printed on successive
lines as decimal integers with + suppressed if the number is positive and zero
suppression. P16 is used for the printing. Using the data of Figure 1 the output
from a decimal integer post-mortem is shown in Figure 3. Notice that the word
80 000 00 000 in location 313 is given the correct integer representation, -2^{39}.

Decimal Fractions. Words from the memory are printed on successive
lines as twelve-place decimal fractions with + suppressed if the fraction is
positive. P16 is used for the printing. Using the data of Figure 1 the
output from a decimal fraction post-mortem is shown in Figure 4. Notice the
appearance of the word in location 313 when printed as a fraction. If we
regard K as the representation of 10_D then we see that -1 is represented
consistently.

Floating Point Numbers. Words from the memory are printed on successive
lines as floating point numbers. The floating point number is printed with the
fractional part first followed by the exponent, base 10_D. In the printing of the

fractional part, the entire word is treated as a fraction, thus the exponent acts like the least significant part of the fraction. The fraction is printed by P16 as a ten-place decimal fraction with + suppressed if the fraction is positive. The exponent is printed by P16 as a signed decimal integer with zero suppression on all but the least significant digit. Using the data of Figure 1 the output from a floating point post-mortem is shown in Figure 5. Notice the appearance of the word in location 313 when printed as a floating point number. The fractional part is the representation of minus one produced by P16 when a fraction print of less than 12 digits is requested.

Sexadecimal Numbers. Words from the memory are printed on successive lines as sexadecimal numbers. Using the data of Figure 1 the output from a sexadecimal post-mortem is shown in Figure 6.

Address Search. The general format of the address search post-mortem differs from that of the post-mortems discussed above. This post-mortem will not be headed by a title. The first line of output will contain the search address, printed as a sexadecimal number, followed by the sign =, followed by the search address, printed as a decimal integer.

The address of every instruction in the WM memory, locations 2-3L5, is examined and if the address of either the left instruction or right instruction or both of a word is equal to the search address, then the entire word is printed as an order pair on a distinct line. Just to the left of the order pair the memory location holding the order pair is printed as a decimal integer. Using the data of Figure 1 the output from an address search post-mortem with initial search address OOK and going back through search address 003 is shown in Figure 7.

Operating Procedure. The operation of the Combined Post-Mortem calls for a somewhat involved manipulation of the tapes and control switches.

There are essentially five distinct situations which should be cited in the procedures for the operation of the post-mortem. These procedures have been listed below for each of the five situations.

A. WM post-mortem and this is the first post-mortem to be executed.

(1) Place WM post-mortem library tape in reader in position to read data
for the desired post-mortem. (If an address search is desired follow
the procedure in (5) below.) These positions are marked on the tape
with the name of the post-mortem. The black switch should be set to
OBEY.

(2) Execute a HOLD START. A heading will be printed and a BS STOP
(21 02S) is reached.

(3) Position the tape to read the address of the block on which the
post-mortem is desired. The block addresses, divided by 10_D, are
on the tail of the tape.

(4) Begin the post-mortem with a BS START. If the black switch is in
the OBEY position a BS STOP (30 029) is reached after a blcok of
ten words has been post-mortemed. As long as the black switch is
in the IGNORE position consecutive blocks of ten words will be
post-mortemed without a STOP. To skip to some other block in the
memory return to step (3).

(5) For an address search proceed as follows. Prepare a tape with the
characters L O O K A_1 A_2 A_3, where the A_1 A_2 A_3 represents the three
sexadecimal characters of the search address. Any fifth hole characters
may precede the L.

(6) Place the tape in the reader and execute a HOLD START.

(7) If the black switch is in the OBEY position a BS STOP (24 06N) is
reached after a complete search of the memory. A subsequent BS START
will result in a new search with the search address reduced by 1. If
the black switch is in the IGNORE position successive searches will be
made with the search address decreased by 1 each time and with no
intermediate stop.

B. Drum post-mortem and this is the first post-mortem to be executed.

(1) Place the drum post-mortem library tape in the reader in position to read data for the desired post-mortem. These positions are marked on the tape with the name of the post-mortem. The black switch should be set to OBEY.

(2) Execute a HOLD START. A heading will be printed and a BS STOP (21 02S) is reached.

(3) Position the tape to read the thousands part of the address of the block on which the post-mortem is desired. These numbers, divided by 10_D, are located after the data for each post-mortem. (It is possible to "black switch through" these numbers until the desired one is reached.)

(4) Execute a BS START. A BS STOP (34 02S) is encountered.

(5) Position the tape to read the hundreds part of the address of the block on which the post-mortem is desired. These numbers, divided by 10_D, are located on the tail of the tape.

(6) Begin the post-mortem with a BS START. If the black switch is in the OBEY position a BS STOP (30 029) is reached after a block of ten words has been post-mortemed. As long as the black switch is in the IGNORE position consecutive blocks of ten words will be post-mortemed without a STOP.

(7) If a skip to some other block in the memory is desired then return to step three if the address of the new block has a different thousands part, otherwise return to step (5).

C. Drum post-mortem following any other post-mortem, WM or drum.

(1) Place the drum post-mortem library tape in the reader in position to read data for the desired post-mortem.

(2) If the previous post-mortem was not an address search, then execute a BS START, otherwise execute a SKIP START (white switch up and down). A heading will be printed and a BS STOP (21 02S) is reached. Proceed to step (3) in B above.

D. WM post-mortem following any other post-mortem and a WM post-mortem has already been run.

(1) Place the WM post-mortem library tape in the reader in position to read data for the desired post-mortem. (If an address search is desired follow the procedure in (3) below.)

(2) If the previous post-mortem was not an address search, then execute a BS START, otherwise execute a SKIP START (white switch up and down). A heading will be printed and a BS STOP (21 02S) is reached. Proceed to step (3) in A above.

(3) For an address search post-mortem proceed as follows. Prepare a tape as in step 5 of A.

(4) Place the tape in the reader. If the previous post-mortem was not an address search, then execute a BS START, otherwise execute a SKIP START. Proceed to step (7) of A.

E. WM post-mortem following a drum post-mortem and no WM post-mortem has yet been run.

(1) Procedure is identical to A above.

Restoration of the WM. At the completion of a post-mortem it is possible to restore locations 2-3L5 in the WM to their initial state, provided that they have been preserved with the WM post-mortem (Routine 5) as described earlier. This is accomplished as follows. When the post-mortem is complete insert a tape containing the following sequence of characters into the reader: L, 0, J, 1, 0, 1-hole delay, 0, line feeds. Begin restoration with a BS START. When restoration is complete a BS STOP (24 3LL) is encountered. Following this STOP any of the three possible starts, BS START, SKIP START, HOLD START, have the same effect as a HOLD START.

The Combined Post-Mortem has evolved from the work of many people, especially J. Fishel, R. Farrell, D. Gillies, D. Muller and J. Robertson. The present form of the Combined Post-Mortem is due to D. Gillies.

	WM Post-Mortem First		Drum Post-Mortem First	
	WM	Drum	WM	Drum
Sexadecimal	2-3L5	K00-2F0S	J7-3L5	K00-31F1
Decimal	2-1,013	2,560-11,787	215-1,013	2,560-12,769

Table 1

Memory Locations Available for Post-Mortem
as a Function of the Post-Mortem Run First.

Post Mortem (Drum or WM)	3 Tetrads following key character
Order Pairs	051
Decimal Integers	0SJ
Decimal Fractions	039
Floating Point Numbers	04S
Sexadecimal Numbers	059
Address Search (WM only)	00K*

Table 2

Tetrads Following the Key Character Specifying
Transfer to a Post-Mortem Subroutine.

---

* These tetrads are arbitrary so long as the least significant digit is even -
by convention 00K is used.

354

WM Address	Order Pair
12N	00 000
	00 00K
12J	L5 005
	40 064
12F	50 000
	22 135
12L	LL LLL
	LL LLL
130	40 000
	00 000
131	60 000
	00 000
132	00 000
	00 000
133	00 000
	00 000
134	70 000
	00 006
135	26 008
	40 008
136	L5 007
	66 003
137	74 000
	40 12J
138	36 12F
	24 12N
139	80 000
	00 C00
13K	00 000
	00 000

Figure 1 (Continued on the next page.)

WM Address	Order Pair
13S	00 000
	00 000
13N	00 000
	00 000
13J	00 000
	00 000
13F	00 000
	00 000
13L	00 000
	00 000

Figure 1

Contents of WM 12N-13L (300_D-319_D) at the time of the
post-mortems illustrated in Figs. 2-7.

```
        ORDER PAIRS
30
0 00     0 00   10
1 L5     5 40  100
2 50     0 22  309
3 LL4095 LL4095
4 40     0
5 60     0
8 70     0 00    6
9 26     8 40    8

31
0 L5     7 66    3
1 74     0 40  301
2 36   302 24  300
3 80     0
```

Figure 2

Output from fraction post-mortem on
blocks 300_D and 310_D of the WM.

```
        INTEGERS
30
0   10
1  -47239135132
2   343597523253
3  -1
4   274877906944
5   412316860416
8   481036337158
9   163217408008

31
0  -47236882429
1   498216468781
2   232245051692
3  -549755813888
```

Figure 3

Output from integer post-mortem on

blocks 300_D and 310_D of the WM.

```
        FRACTIONS
30
0   000000000018
1  -085927486238
2   625000253882
3  -000000000002
4   500000000000
5   750000000000
8   875000000011
9   296890735641

31
0  -085923388595
1   906250477385
2   422451288054
3  -+00000000001
```

Figure 4

Output from fraction post-mortem on

blocks 300_D and 310_D of the WM.

```
            FLOATING DECIMAL
         30
         0   0000000000 -54
         1  -0859274862 +36
         2   6250002539 -11
         3   0000000000 +63
         4   5000000000 -64
         5   7500000000 -64
         8   8750000000 -58
         9   2968907356 -56

         31
         0  -0859233886 -61
         1   2062504774 -19
         2   4224512881 -20
         3 -10000000000 -64
```

Figure 5

Output from floating point post-mortem on
blocks 300_D and 310_D of the WM.

```
            SEXADECIMAL
         30
         0 00000 0000+
         1 L5005 40064
         2 50000 22135
         3 LLLLL LLLLL
         4 40000 00000
         5 60000 00000
         8 70000 00006
         9 26008 40008

         31
         0 L5007 66003
         1 74000 4012J
         2 3612F 2412N
         3 80000 00000
```

Figure 6

Output from sexadecimal post-mortem
on blocks 300_D and 310_D of the WM.

```
00+=10
300  00    0 00   10

009=9

008=8
309   26   8 40    8

007=7
310  L5    7 66    3

006=6
308  70    0 00    6

005=5
301  L5    5 40  100

004=4

003=3
310  L5    7 66    3
```

Figure 7

Output from address search post-mortem with
initial search address OOK and final search address 003.

APPENDIX 13

THE COMPARISON POST-MORTEM

This diagnostic program provides a very effective means for locating a common type of coding blunder, namely, the alteration of a word which is supposed to remain unaltered during the running of a program. Such alterations, of course, result from an incorrect address on a store instruction. The inexperienced programmer will frequently use the order pair post-mortem to locate such blunders, however a little practice in using the comparison post-mortem will make evident its superiority in this area.

<u>USAGE</u>

Let us assume that a program on the ILLIAC has stopped for some unknown reason, presumably a coding error, and follow the action of a comparison post-mortem. The block on the drum holding the words of the present program as assembled by SADOI, specifically drum locations $11,758_D$ (2JFF) through $12,756_D$ (31J4), is examined. This block holds the words orginally assembled by SADOI into the Williams memory (WM) at locations 2 through 1000_D (3F8); provided of course this block on the drum was not overwritten by the program under diagnosis. Each word read from the drum is first tested to determine whether it is identically zero. If it is zero the next word in sequence is examined. If it is not zero, then it is compared with the word in the corresponding location of the (WM); the word from drum location Y is compared against the word in the WM location $Y - 11,756_D$. If the two words are different the word from the drum, the "BEFORE" word, and the word from the WM, the "AFTER" word, are printed. If they are identical no printing occurs and the program goes on to examine the next word on the drum. This process continues until all locations in the above indicated block have been examined. Thus it is seen that the words of the original program, except those identically equal to zero, are compared against their state at the time of the program stop and any difference results in a print-out of the BEFORE word and AFTER word. The BEFORE and AFTER words are printed as order pairs: sexadecimal function digits, decimal address. The print-out includes the WM address of the altered word.

At the completion of the comparison post-mortem, a symbolic address list is printed. This list contains all symbolic addresses and their WM decimal address assignments.

The short program below, designed to hang up on a zero left shift at location 106_D, will illustrate the type of output produced by the comparison post-mortem.

	00 100K	
(TEST)	L5 4 (TEST)	
	L4 4 (TEST)	
	40 4 (TEST)	
	L5 5 (TEST)	
	L4 4 (TEST)	
	40 5 (TEST)	
	26 (FAIL)	
	00 F	
	04 1F	by 1 (TEST)
	21 10F	
	00 F	by 2 (TEST)
	00 F	
(FAIL)	00 F	from
	00 F	3 (TEST)

Sample Program to Illustrate Comparison Post-Mortem Output.

The output from the comparison post mortem after the hang-up at 106_D is shown below.

```
COMPARISON POST MORTEM
  BEFORE        AFTER
104 04 001 21 010 08 002 42 020
106 FAIL
100 TEST
```

Notice that location 104_D which was altered by the program has its
BEFORE and AFTER words printed, but location 105_D which was also altered is
not similarly printed. The latter change is not printed because the BEFORE
word is identically zero and hence ignored by the comparison post-mortem.

The comparison post-mortem is commonly used together with the
address search post-mortem to locate coding blunders. Once the comparison
post-mortem has shown that a word has been altered that should not have
been altered, or has been altered improperly, then an address search on the
address of the altered word will usually produce the culprit instruction.

One can bypass the execution of the comparison post-mortem to
obtain only the symbolic address list print. The details for doing this are
given in the operators instructions at the end of this appendix.

LIMITATIONS ON USAGE

Since other post-mortem routines cause the BEFORE words on the drum
to be overwritten by the AFTER words in the WM it is essential that the comparison post mortem, if it is desired, be run before any other post-mortem.
After completion of the comparison post-mortem any other post-mortem may be
run.

It is clear from the earlier discussion that any words on the drum
in the block $11,758_D$ - $12,756_D$ which were altered by the program being
diagnosed will yield a meaningless comparison with the AFTER words.

The symbolic address list is stored on the drum in a block beginning
at $11,754_D$ and goes backwards, that is in the order of decreasing address
($11,754$; $11,753$; $11,752$ etc.). Consequently, if the program under diagnosis
has altered any word in the symbolic address list there will be a corresponding
error in the symbolic address list print.

The end constant determining the number of words in the symbolic
address list is never transferred to the drum by SADOI but remains in the right
address of 999_D in the WM. When the symbolic address list is printed by the
comparison post-mortem the number in the right address of 999_D is used to form
the printing end constant. There is a check to prohibit an almost infinite

amount of printing, should 999_D have been overwritten, such that no more than 325 words in the list will ever be printed. It is of course possible that 999_D was overwritten so as to make the symbolic address list appear shorter than it really is, in which case it is possible by appropriate switch operation (see operator's instructions, step 5) to cause the number of words in the list to be artificially set to 325. All of the symbolic addresses will then be printed at the start of the list and the remainder of the list will contain whatever gibberish was in the remainder of the 325 words. It is always assumed that there is at least one word in the list. This means that there will always be one word printed in the list whether or not the program actually contained a symbolic address. The address zero is printed as four spaces; the corresponding symbolic address is, of course, printed explicitly.

The comparison post-mortem causes the contents of the WM at locations 1001_D (3F9) - 1023_D (3LL), 0, and 1 to be destroyed. Thus, if a restore WM is executed at the completion of a comparison post-mortem, only locations 2 to 1,000 will be correctly restored.

Since SADOI only reads WM locations 2 - 998 on to the drum when it is called into operation it leaves the possibility that 999 and 1000 can cause a comparison post-mortem print-out if they are not initially cleared on the drum by some means.

FINAL STATE OF MACHINE

When the print of the symbolic address list is completed the contents of the WM block at 32_D (020) - 1000_D (3F8) is recorded on the drum block $11,788_D$ (2FON) - 12,756 (31J4). Then the combined post-mortem is read into the WM and the routine stops on 20 02N. At this point any of the combined post-mortem programs may be initiated with a BS START in the customary fashion.

COMPARISON POST-MORTEM

OPERATOR'S INSTRUCTIONS

1. Put tape in reader (1st character J) and begin with a HOLD START; a heading is now punched on the tape.

2. Now a BS STOP (24 002) occurs.

3. a) If a COMPARISON POST-MORTEM is desired, execute a BS START.

   b) If the COMPARISON POST-MORTEM is to be <u>suppressed</u> and only a SYMBOLIC ADDRESS LIST print is desired, then execute a SKIP START.

4. Now a BS STOP (24 014) occurs.

5. a) If the user has <u>not</u> overwritten location 999_D (3F7), then proceed with a BS START to print the SYMBOLIC ADDRESS LIST.

   b) If the user has overwritten location 999_D (3F7), then proceed with a SKIP START to print the SYMBOLIC ADDRESS LIST.

6. When the SYMBOLIC ADDRESS LIST printing is completed, a BS STOP 20 02N is encountered.

7. Now any POST-MORTEM (key character F or L) can be initiated with a BS START.

NOTES:

1. The COMPARISON POST-MORTEM must be run first before any other POST-MORTEM.

2. If step 5b is taken, then there will sometimes be gibberish printed at the end of the SYMBOLIC ADDRESS LIST.

ILLIAC ACTIVE PROGRAM LIBRARY INDEX⁺**

LABEL	SERIAL	DATE	TITLE
A1	63	12/29/55	Floating Decimal Arithmetic Routine (168) (DOI or SADOI)
A3	125	11/27/59	Convert a Number From Floating Decimal Representation to Normal Machine Form (27) (DOI or SADOI)
A4	87	10/28/58	1.7 Precision Floating Decimal (279) (DOI or SADOI)
A5	138	6/10/55	Complex Number Arithmetic (248) (DOI or SADOI)
A6	154	9/24/59	Floating Decimal Routine and Auxiliaries (See Description) (Separate Versions for DOI or SADOI)
A7	244	3/18/59	1.7 Precision Floating Binary Arithmetic and Double Precision Arithmetic With Floating Decimal Conversion (610) (DOI or SADOI)
D1	95	4/12/57	Check Point Routine (57+31+s+j(See Text)) (DOI or SADOI)
D4	70	9/12/58	Control Transfer Check (41) (DOI or SADOI)
E2	158	4/27/56	Integration by Simpson's Rule (Tabulated Values)(21)(DOI or SADOI)
E3	186	6/17/60	Integration by Simpson's Rule (Function Values)(38)(DOI or SADOI)
E4	193	8/7/59	Numerical Differentiation with Interpolation (103)(DOI or SADOI)
E5	195	7/20/59	Quadrature by Gauss' Method (18 + 2n) (DOI or SADOI)
F1	114	3/19/59	Solution of a System of Ordinary Differential Equations (41) (SADOI Only)
F2	115	1/23/59	Solution of a System of Differential Equations by Milne's Method (80-46) (SADOI Only)
F3	129	6/27/55	Integration of n Simultaneous 2nd Order Differential Equations with Initial Conditions Specified(Sub.39-Parameter Storage 1=40) (DOI or SADOI)
F5	229	9/22/58	Integration of a System of Ordinary Differential Equations up to a Specified Value of One Variable (60) (SADOI Only)
F6	239	4/10/59	Integration of a System of Ordinary Differential Equations with Automatic Control of Integration Interval (129) (SADOI Only)
FA1	122	12/9/59	Second Order Linear Differential Equation with Two Point Boundary Condition (101)(DOI Only)
FA2	203	7/20/59	Floating Decimal Solution of a System of Ordinary Differential Equations (See Description) (SADOI Only)
G1	78	3/19/59	LaPlace's Equation-Liebmann Method (5 thru 46) (DOI Only)
G2	98	4/10/59	Poisson's Equation-Liebmann-Frankel Method(6 thru 64)(DOI Only)
H1	71	1/23/59	Inverse Interpolation (33) (DOI or SADOI)
H2	72	1/23/59	A Search for the Real Roots of f(x) = 0 (80) (DOI or SADOI)
H3	80	12/16/58	Minimization of a Function of Two Variables (46) (DOI or SADOI)
H4	84	3/31/59	Minimization of a Function of Four Variables(75) (DOI or SADOI)
H5	85	3/5/59	Minimization of a Function of n Variables (89) (DOI or SADOI)
H6	86	7/22/59	Minimization of a Function of n Variables Treating One Variable at a Time (46) (DOI or SADOI)
I1	67	5/20/59	Interpolation (51) (DOI or SADOI)
J2	209	7/20/59	Roots of a Polynomial (Entire Program) (DOI Only)
J3	289	2/15/60	Roots of a Polynomial (85) (SADOI Only)*

⁺Number after title is number of words in Routine

* New additions to our Library
** Those routines compatible with both DOI and SADOI should have SADOI directives omitted when used with DOI.

ILLIAC ACTIVE PROGRAM LIBRARY INDEX**

LABEL	SERIAL	DATE	TITLE
K3	137	1/27/60	Least Squares (Entire Program) (DOI or SADOI)
K5	182	8/5/59	Autocorrelations (Entire Program) (DOI Only)
K6	185	7/22/59	Chi-Squared (23) (DOI or SADOI)
K8	189	11/27/59	Product Moment Correlations, Variance-Covariances, Means and Standard Deviation for Use with Magnetic Drum(Complete Program) (SADOI Only)
K9	190	9/12/58	Product Moment Correlation, Means, Standard Deviations, Variances in Logarithmic Scale (Entire Program) (DOI Only)
K10	191	9/13/58	Calculate Autocorrection of a Time Series (85) (DOI or SADOI)
K14	233	7/1/60	Multiple Regression Analysis with Transformations(Entire Program) (DOI)
K15	258	3/6/59	Analysis of Variance by Method of Fitting Constants(DOI or SADOI)
K16	263	1/13/60	Modified Multiple Regression Analysis (DOI Only) (Complete)
L3	100	5/20/59	Complete Linear Equation Solver (Complete Program) (DOI or SADOI)
L6	224	5/20/59	Solution of a Set of n Simultaneous Linear Algebraic Equations Using Magnetic Drum Storage (162) (DOI or SADOI)
L7	230	3/25/59	Automatic Linear Equation Solver With Programmed Checks and Calculation of Residues (Entire Program) (DOI or SADOI)
M4	136	10/13/55	Closed Eigenvalues and Eigenvectors (163) (DOI or SADOI)
M11	160	3/5/59	Matrix Multiplication (Closed) (77) (DOI or SADOI)
M12	173	12/3/58	Triangularization of a Matrix and its Determinant (Complete Program) (DOI Only)
M13	179	5/4/55	Complete Linear Matrix Equation Solver and General Matrix Inversion (Complete Program) (DOI Only)
M14	180	12/3/58	Linear Matrix Equation Solver and General Matrix Inversion (115) (DOI or SADOI)
M15	183	5/19/60	Linear Programming (Complete Program) (DOI or SADOI)
M17	197	11/9/55	Post Multiplication of a Matrix of its Transpose by a Vector (45) (DOI or SADOI)
M18	213	4/3/57	One-Step Automatic Eigenvalue-Eigenvector Program(Entire Program) (DOI)
M19	232	2/13/57	Solution of the Matrix Equation Ax=λBx where A+B are Symmetric and B is Positive Definite (Entire Program) (DOI or SADOI)
M20	234	1/23/59	Eigenvalues of a Symmetric Matrix by Given's Method (Entire Program) (SADOI Only)
M21	240	4/17/58	Matrix Multiplication (198) (SADOI Only)
M22	241	5/20/59	Eigenvalues and Eigenvectors of a Symmetric Matrix Using the Methods of Givens and Wilkinson (1054+data storage) (SADOI Only)
M23	246	11/21/58	Closed Eigenvectors and/or Eigenvalues by Jacobi Method(185) (DOI or SADOI)
M24	260	4/1/59	Complete Linear Matrix Equation Solver and General Matrix Inversion Routine Using Drum Storage (DOI Only)
M25	262	4/27/59	Eigenvalues and Eigenvectors of a Symmetric Matrix (SADOI Only)
M26	264	5/6/59	Eigenvalues and Eigenvectors of a Symmetric Matrix (SADOI Only)
M27	267	5/26/59	Linear Matrix Equation Solver and General Matrix Inversion Using Drum Storage (SADOI Only)
M28	270	9/28/59	Matrix Multiplication with or without rescaling(SADOI)*
MA1	104	6/4/58	Matrix Multiplication with Floating Decimal Auxiliary(21 or 26-See Description) (DOI or SADOI)

***Number after title is number of words in Routine
*   New Additions to our Library
** Those routines compatible with both DOI and SADOI should have SADOI directives omitted when used with DOI.

August 8, 1960

ILLIAC ACITVE PROGRAM LIBRARY INDEX**

LABEL	SERIAL	DATE	TITLE
N1	61	4/6/60	Input One Number from Tape, Integer or Fraction(19)(DOI or SADOI)
N2	88	7/7/55	Input a Sequence of Decimal Fractions (26)(DOI or SADOI)
N8	181	4/6/55	Read One Number from Tape as Integer or Fraction(22)(DOI or SADOI)
N12	225	10/29/58	Infraput (39) (DOI or SADOI)
N13	226	3/5/59	Input a Sequence of Fractions, all having the Same Number of Decimal Digits (21) (DOI or SADOI)
N14	227	3/4/59	Input a Sequence of Integers (18) (DOI or SADOI)
N15	271	11/3/59	Mixed Number Input (44)*
N16	281	1/20/60	Mixed Number Input (41) (DOI or SADOI)*
02	143	12/19/58	Routine to Plot Point and Axes (29) (SADOI Only)
03	147	6/4/58	Display Numbers and Letters on the Cathode Ray Tube(13+(See Text)) (DOI or SADOI)
04	161	9/12/58	Fast Fraction Display 4x6 Raster (68) (DOI or SADOI)
05	162	3/4/60	Fast Character Display 4x6 Raster(50 words for 0...9,+-)(SADOI)
06	177	3/11/54	Punch to Cathode Ray Tube Conversion Program(175+(See Des.))(DOI or SADOI)
07	245	11/18/58	Linear Interpolation for the Cathode Ray Tube (43) (DOI or SADOI)
P2	52	7/20/59	Print (A) with or without Sign to n Places as Determined by a Program Parameter (18) (DOI or SADOI)
P3	53	4/10/59	Print n Digits of an Integer with or without a Sign(20)(DOI or SADOI)
P4	55	1/23/59	Zero Suppression Integer Print (27) (DOI or SADOI)
P5	37	1/23/59	Print One Number in a Parameter Set Layout (24) (SADOI Only)
P12	194	12/29/59	Single Column Print (Revised) (13) (DOI or SADOI)
P13	204	12/3/58	Combined Integer Print (35) (DOI or SADOI)
P15	207	2/7/56	Multiple Precision Integer Conversion (32) (DOI or SADOI)
P16	214	3/9/59	Infraprint (56) (DOI or SADOI)
P17	242	4/22/58	Maximum Speed Fraction Print to Twelve or Fewer Places(59)(DOI or SADOI)
P19	252	1/15/59	Output for the Data Plotter (44) (DOI or SADOI)
R1	116	7/20/59	Square Root Routine (9) (DOI or SADOI)
R2	105	7/21/59	Integral Root A^1/P (24) (DOI or SADOI)
R3	106	9/28/59	Fractional Power Routine (18) (DOI or SADOI)
RA1	92	9/15/58	Floating Decimal Square Root Auxiliary (16) (DOI or SADOI)
S3	130	7/18/60	Logarithm (14) (DOI or SADOI)
S4	212	10/29/58	Exponential (21) (DOI or SADOI)
S5	231	10/29/58	1/32 Natural Logarithm (36) (DOI or SADOI)
SA2	127	6/5/58	Exponential Auxiliary for Floating Decimal (26) (DOI or SADOI)
SA3	155	1/23/59	Natural Logarithm (30) (DOI or SADOI)
T4	140	3/24/58	New Arctan X Routine (25) (DOI or SADOI)
T5	157	4/5/60	Sine Cosine (21) (DOI or SADOI)
T7	293	3/30/60	1/2 Sin X/X (37) (SADOI Only)*
TA1	126	6/5/58	Sine Auxiliary for Floating Decimal (26) (DOI or SADOI)
TA2	156	6/5/58	Arctan Auxiliary to the Floating Point Routine(48)(DOI or SADOI)
V1	82	7/21/59	Legendre Polynomials (8) (DOI or SADOI)
V2	120	9/23/55	Tchebyscheff Polynomials (15) (DOI or SADOI)
V4	178	4/4/55	Fourier Analysis (52) (DOI or SADOI)
V9	216	10/29/58	Generate 40-bit Random Numbers (27) (SADOI Only)

August 8, 1960

ILLIAC ACTIVE PROGRAM LIBRARY INDEX**

LABEL	SERIAL	DATE	TITLE
X1	218	3/17/59	Decimal Order Input (DOI) (25) (DOI Itself)
X3	222	10/15/56	Constant-Listing Auxiliary (21) (DOI Only)
X12	235	12/3/58	Symbolic Address Decimal Order Input (SADOI)(615)(SADOI Itself)
X16	284	1/12/60	"Current Floating Relativizer" SADOI Modification to be placed on Program Tape (Special)*
XA1	223	10/15/56	Constant Listing Auxiliary for Floating Decimal (18)(DOI Only)
Y1	199	7/29/60	Transfer Blocks of Words from the Memory to the Drum or from the Drum to the Memory (40) (DOI or SADOI)
Y5	291	3/10/60	Transfer Blocks of Words between the Drum and the Williams Memory (35)*

APPENDIX 15

ILLIAC LIBRARY DESCRIPTION OF N12:

INPUT DECIMAL INTEGERS AND FRACTIONS

LIBRARY ROUTINE N 12 - 225

By   Donald B. Gillies

TITLE	Infraput (D.O.I. or SADOI)
TYPE	Closed with one program parameter.
NUMBER OF WORDS	39
TEMPORARY STORAGE	0, 1, 2
ACCURACY	Up to 12 digit integers or fractions. Integers are exact; fractions are correctly rounded (error up to $\pm 2^{-40}$).
SPEED	Input time (4 ms per digit). This routine has an inner loop at $700\mathcal{M}$ sec. which makes it twice as fast, overall, as earlier input routines.
USE	To read a sequence of fractions into locations n, n+1, . . . enter with Q = 50 n

$$50\ q$$

To read a sequence of integers into locations, n, n+1, . . . enter with Q = 52 n

$$50\ q$$

Each number is punched with a sign (+ or -) followed by up to 12 decimal digits. Zero may be punched as + alone. A sequence is terminated by one of N,J,F,L. When one of these characters is encountered, control is transferred to the right hand side of q+1, with A = 0, 2^{-39}, 2.2^{-39}, 3.2^{-39} according as the termination was N,J,F,L. The left hand address of 21L relative to the subroutine at this time is n+k if k words have been read in to locations n, n+1, . . ., n+k-1.

RT: 10/8/59

DATE	January 29, 1957
CODED BY	D. B. Gillies
APPROVED BY	D. E. Muller

nj

LOCATION	ORDER		NOTES	N12
0	00 K(N12) K5 F			
	42 5L		Plant link and n	
1	46 21L			
	01 7F		Plant fraction/integer switch:	
2	L4 18L		set 16' as 17L if fractions (50 entry)	
	42 16L		19L if integers (52 entry)	
3	81 4F		read sign of first number of the sequence	
	LO 25L		$-1 + (s-10).2^{-39}$	
4	42 20L	←from 23'	set 20' as 0 or 1 for + or −	
	LO 38L		If instead of sign digit on N,J,F,L, A has	
5	50 26L		0,1,2,3, so obey link.	
	32 (link)F by 0'		Special word to Q: let g_i be the integer comprising $(q_1 q_2 q_3 q_4)$ of $2^{4+31} Q$ Then $N(g_i+24L) = \frac{1}{2} 10^i .2^{-39}$, a table.	
6	89 1F			
	22 9L		Enter digit loop with A = −1 (so $n_0 = 0$)	
7	10 3F			
	F4 F			
8	00 2F		$n_i = d_i -10 + 10(1+n_{i-1})$	
	F4 F			
9	00 1F			
	40 F		$-1 + 2^{-39} n_i$	
10	11 1F			
	80 4F			
11	LO 25L		$-1 + 2^{-39} (d_i -10)$	
	36 7L		loop if $d_i < 10$ (digit, not sign)	
12	40 2F		store $-1 + (s-10)2^{-39}$ (sign of next number)	
	01 4F		g_i (Q previously shifted 4+31 places left)	
13	L4 14L		g_i + 24L	
	42 15L		set addresses of $\frac{1}{2} 10^i .2^{-39}$	
14	42 17L			
	50 24L		waste (address used by 13)	
15	89 1F		−1	
	50 ( )F	by 13'		
16	L4 F		$n_i \cdot 2^{-39}$	
	26 (17 or 19)L by 2'		fraction/integer switch	

LOCATION	ORDER			NOTES	N2
17	SO F		Fraction	absolute value of fraction is	
	66 ( )F	By 14		$$\frac{2^{-39}\left(n_1 - \frac{1}{2}10^1 + 2^{-40}10^1\right)}{2^{-39}\left(\frac{1}{2}10^1\right)} \cdot \frac{1}{2} + \frac{1}{2} = \frac{n_1}{10^1} \text{ rounded.}$$	
18	10 1F		(From 16')		
	SJ 961L				
19	40 F		Integer	store positively in 0	
	L1 F				
20	40 1F			store negatively in 1	
	L5 (0 or 1)	by 4		correctly signed answer	
21	40 (n)F	by 1, 22'		store in sequence, and increase	
	L5 21L			address of store instruction by 1	
22	L4 L				
	46 21L				
23	L5 2F			$-1 + (s-10) \cdot 2^{-39}$	
	26 4L	→ 4		loop	
24	00 F			$\frac{1}{2}10^{12}$	
	00 500 000 000 000F				
25	80 F			$-1 + 10 \cdot 2^{-39}$	
	00 10F				
26	01 1229F			special constant for Q	
	59 3258F			during input loop	
27	00 F			$\frac{1}{2}10^3$	
	00 500 F				
28	00 F			$\frac{1}{2}10^1$	
	00 5F				
29	00 F			$\frac{1}{2}10^5$	
	00 50 000F				
30	00 F			$\frac{1}{2}10^2$	
	00 50 F				
31	00 F			$\frac{1}{2}10^7$	
	00 5000 000F				
32	00 F			$\frac{1}{2}10^{11}$	
	00 50 000 000 000F				
33	00 F			$\frac{1}{2}10^8$	
	00 50 000 000 F				
34	00 F			$\frac{1}{2}10^4$	
	00 5 000 F				

LOCATION	ORDER	NOTES
35	OO F	$\frac{1}{2} \; 10^9$
	OO 500 000 000 F	
36	OO F	$\frac{1}{2} \; 10^6$
	OO 500 000 F	
37	OO F	$\frac{1}{2} \; 10^{10}$
	OO 5 000 000 000F	
38	80 F	$-1 + 2.2^{-39}$
	OO 2F	

APPENDIX 16

ILLIAC LIBRARY DESCRIPTION OF P16:

PRINT DECIMAL INTEGERS AND FRACTIONS

LIBRARY ROUTINE   P 16 - 214

TITLE	Infraprint (DOI or SADOI)
TYPE	Closed with one program parameter
NUMBER OF WORDS	56
TEMPORARY STORAGE	0, 1, 2
ACCURACY	1 to 12 digit exactly rounded fractions or exact integers
SPEED	Punching time
USE	This INteger FRAction PRINT routine will print A to n-places (1 to 12) correctly rounded (n digits or spaces if the integer is less than 10^n, all digits if greater than 10^n), with (optional) decimal point anywhere, with non-significant zeros before the decimal point (whether this point is printed or not) replaced by spaces, sign before the first non-space character, with a - sign for a negative number and your choice of ÷, space, or delay character for a positive number, and no extra spaces.

If Q contains:	Then before going to the R.H. order at q+1:
50 nF	A is printed as an n-place fraction with a sign + or -,
50 qF	with no zero suppression.
52 nF	A is printed as an n-place integer with sign + or -
50 qF	with zero suppression on all but the last digit.
54 100p+nF	A is printed as an n-place fraction with sign + or -
50 qF	with a decimal point after p digits and zero suppression on the first p digits $0 \leq p \leq n$.
56 100p÷nF	A is printed as an n-place integer with sign + or -
50 qF	with a decimal point after p digits, and zero suppression before the decimal point. $0 \leq p \leq n$.

JO, J2, J4, J6 have the same effect as 50, 52, 54, 56 except that a space is printed instead of a + sign for positive numbers.

Entering the routine at the right hand order at 1 rather
than the left hand order at 0, with a J-type parameter
causes a delay character to be punched for the sign if
A is positive. This unsigned number entry omits the
sign of a positive number.

To obtain a space instead of a decimal point, change the
order pair at 51L (the 52nd word of the routine) to

$$92 \quad 963F$$
$$22 \quad 35L$$

To obtain unrounded fractions instead of rounded fractions,
change the order pair at 20L to

$$50 \quad 1F$$
$$75 \quad F$$

This routine does not print spaces after the number.

REMARKS

Fractions are converted to integers by a rounded
multiplication by 10^n. (The sign is the sign of the
rounded number so a small enough negative fraction is
printed as $+0$). The absolute value of the resulting
integer is taken, and converted to 12 decimal digits which
are omitted, replaced by spaces, or printed according to
the following rules:

1. The last digit is always printed.

2. The last n digits are always printed if 50 or J0
   parameter was specified.

3. All digits following a decimal point are printed.

4. The first non-zero digit is printed even if it
   occurs before the last n digits, and all subsequent
   digits are printed.

5. If no digits have been printed, zeros before the last
   n digits are omitted, and zeros during the last n
   places are replaced by spaces.

6. The sign is printed just before the first non-space character (which may be a digit or a point).

Thus all digits of an integer are printed, and if a fraction after correct rounding would equal 1 in absolute value, the fraction is printed to one more place. The number 1 to 3 places is 1000. The only exception is n = 12, when -1 is printed as

$$-+00000000000$$

meaning   -K00000000000

If integers or 12 place fractions are read back into the machine, the original numbers are recovered, without rounding - off error.

EXAMPLES

The numbers -.001, 1/2, .999, -1 would be printed via the following parameters as shown

50 2F:	J4 3F:	54 103F:	54 303F:
+00	-.001	-.01	-1.
+50	.500	+5.00	+500.
+100	.999	+9.99	+999.
-100	-1.000	-10.00	-1000.

The numbers 3×2^{-39}, -21×2^{-39}, 450×2^{-39}, 1364×2^{-39} would be printed via the following parameters as shown

52 1F:	J2 4F:	56 1F:	56 404F:
+3	3	+.3	+3.
-21	-21	-2.1	-21.
+450	450	+45.0	+450.
-1364	-1364	-136.4	-1364.

DATE June 19, 1956   rt: 3/9/59

PROGRAMMED BY   D. B. Gillies

APPROVED BY   J. P. Nash

lgr

LOCATION	ORDER			NOTES	
	00 K(P16)				P 16
0	40 F	←		Normal entry	
	L5 3L				
1	22 2L				
	40 F	←		Entry omitting space on positive number	
2	L5 8L	←			
	46 40L			Plant space or delay character	
3	K5 965F	by 0'		Plant order pair	
	40 2F				
4	42 42L			Plant link	
	49 1F			Set 1/2 in 1 (for $\frac{10^n}{2}$)	
5	00 7F				
	11 26F				
6	66 47L			$A = 2n \cdot 2^{-39}$ $Q = (2p + 1) \cdot 2^{-39}$	
	00 24F				
7	40 55L				
	10 4F				
8	SO 515F	by 2		$A = -2^{-14} + (n-p+3) \cdot 2^{-18} + \ldots + 4.2^{-33} + 3.2^{39}$	
	L4 54L			$55L = n \cdot 2^{-14}$	
9	22 13L				
	L1 2F	←		If integer, skip ($\frac{10^n}{2}$) calculation	
10	00 6F				
	36 13L				
11	50 1F			Calculate ($\frac{10^n}{2}$)	
	75 52L				
12	S4 642F			by 29'	
	40 1F				
13	L5 27L	←			
	L4 55L	←		Count down by 2^{-14}, up by 2^{-38}	
14	40 55L			[Produces finally	
	32 9L			$-2^{-14} + (n-p+3)2^{-18} + \ldots + 4 \cdot 2^{-33} + (n+3)2^{-39}$]	
15	L1 2F			If decimal point required leave counter	
	00 5F			intact.	
16	32 19L				
	00 1F			If no dec. pt. test no zero-suppression	
17	36 19L				
	50 55L			No zero suppression	

LOCATION	ORDER		NOTES
18	00 45F		
	42 55L		
19	47 55L	←	No decimal point
	19 1F	←	
20	50 1F		Rounded multiplication by 10^N or 1
	74 F		(with scaling factor 1/2)
21	32 27L	+→27	Test sign of rounded number
	00 1F		
22	40 F		If negative take the modulus
	L1 F		
23	40 F		And plant - sign
	L5 34L		
24	46 40L	←30	(Or + sign from 30L)
	50 53L	←29 sp	(or leave sign sp. or delay)
25	L5 F		
	32 30L	→30'	Test $1 \leq$ number < 2 (different round-off)
26	L1 33L		Negative round-off
	26 31L	→31	
27	LL 4064F		
	00 1F	←21	Store positive number
28	40 F		
	L1 2F		Print space or delay?
29	32 24L	→24'	
	L5 12L		Then plant + sign instead.
30	26 24L	→24	
	L5 33L	←25'	Positive round-off
31	74 F		Multiply by $2^{35}/10^{11} + (.2142)2^{-39}$
	36 33L	→33	Test size of multiplier
32	L4 53L		$1 \leq$ multiplier < 2 cause sign to have
	L4 53L		effect of +1 or -1 in multiplication.
33	10 35F	←31'	A = digit $\cdot 2^{-39}$ Q = fractional part.
	40 F	←49'	Plant both halves
34	85 706F	by 23'	of product
	40 1F		
35	L5 50L		
	L4 55L	←51'	Multiple (4-way) count

LOCATION	ORDER		NOTES
36	40 55L		
	36 39L		Prepare to print point?
37	00 29F		No
	36 39L		Prepare to print even non-significant zero?
38	L3 F		No
	36 41L	→ 41	This digit zero?
39	L3 2F	←	No
	36 41L	→ 41	have printed some digit already?
40	92 ( )F	by 2',24	Print sign
	41 2F		Record fact that all digits now to be printed
41	L5 55L	←38',39'	Print point?
	32 50L	→50'	
42	00 20F		Obey link?
	32 (link)F	by 4	
43	L3 2F		The result of these orders is negative if
	L4 F		no digit to be printed, and is that digit if print.
44	32 47L	→ 47'	Print digit?
	L5 55L		
45	00 35F		Don't print space
	32 48L	→48'	
46	92 96F		Print space
	22 48L	→48'	
47	00 F		
	00 100F	←44	Shift left 36
48	82 4F		Print
	50 52L	←45',46'	Multiply fraction by 10 to
49	70 1F		produce a digit in A, plus a
	22 33L	33'	fractional part in Q
50	03 2F		
	09 65F	41'	Print (.)and enter count loop in such
51	32 64F		a way as to inhibit further
	22 35L	35'	decimal pts.
52	00 F	10 2^{-39}	
	00 1oF		
53	28 4015F	$2^{35}/10^{11}$	Constants
	LN 755F		

378

LOCATION	ORDER		NOTES	P 16
54	LL 4071F	Count		
	90 1283F			
55	OO F		Intermediate storage for the	
	OO F		multiple count.	

APPENDIX 17

ILLIAC LIBRARY DESCRIPTION OF R1:

COMPUTE $\sqrt{a}$

LIBRARY ROUTINE R 1 - 116

TITLE	Square Root (DOI or SADOI)
TYPE	Closed
NUMBER OF WORDS	9
TEMPORARY STORAGE	0, 1, 2
ACCURACY	$\pm 2^{-39}$
DURATION	1.3 n milliseconds, where n is defined by

$$[(1 - \sqrt{a}) / (1 + \sqrt{a})]^{2n} < 2^{-39}$$

DESCRIPTION The argument a may consist of 39 digits or of 78 digits. The sign and 39 most significant digits should be in A but may be in address 1 if the routine is entered at the right hand side of the first word instead of at the normal left hand side. The 39 least significant digits (if any) must be in address 0.

The program uses Newton's method by means of the relations

$$x_0 = a/2 + 1/2$$

$$x_{n+1} = x_n + [a/x_n - x_n] / 2$$

and convergence is assumed to have occurred when

$$(a/x_n) - x_n = 2 (x_{n+1} - x_n) \geq 0.$$

NOTE The Illiac will stop if $a < 0$ or if $a = 1 - 2^{-39}$.

Rt: 7/20/59

DATE Oct. 23, 195? Rt. 3/18/58	
CODED BY D. J. Wheeler	
APPROVED BY J. P. Nash	

LOCATION	ORDER		NOTES	R 1
	00K (R1)			
0	40 1F		Store a	
	K5 F			
1	42 8L		Plant link	
	51 1F			
2	10 1F		$x_0 = a/2 + 1/2$	
	SJ F			
3	40 2F	From 7	to 2F	
	50 F			
4	L5 1F		a to A and Q	
	66 2F			
5	35 F			
	L0 2F		$x_{n+1} - x_n$ to A	
6	10 1F			
	36 8L		End test	
7	L4 2F			
	26 5L		Re-enter loop	
8	L5 2F		$\sqrt{a}$ to A	
	22 F	by 1	Link	

APPENDIX 18

ILLIAC LIBRARY DESCRIPTION OF S4:

COMPUTE e^x

LIBRARY ROUTINE **8 4 - 212**

TITLE	Exponential (D.O.I. or SADOI)
TYPE	Closed, standard entry
NUMBER OF WORDS	21
TEMPORARY STORAGE	0, 1, 2
ACCURACY	Maximum error: 5×10^{-12} (see description)
DURATION	11.3 m seconds (max) (see description)
DESCRIPTION	This routine replaces x, the contents of A before entry by e^x. The quantity x is in the range $-1 < x < 0$. The computation is performed by evaluating a continued fraction expansion for e^x.

The expansion used[1] is:

(1) $$\frac{e^x}{2} = 1/2 + (x/4) \left(\frac{1}{1/2 - x/2 + F/2} \right) \quad \text{where}$$

(2) $$F = \cfrac{\frac{x^2}{4 \cdot 16}}{\frac{3}{16} + \cfrac{\frac{x^2}{4 \cdot 16 \cdot 16}}{\frac{5}{16} + \cfrac{\frac{x^2}{4 \cdot 16 \cdot 16}}{\frac{7}{16} + \cdot \cdot \cdot}}}$$

---

[1] N. Macon, "On the Computation of Exponential and Hyperbolic Function Using Continued Fractions", Jour. ACM, pp 262 - 267, October 1955.

This routine is so written that the first 5 terms of
F (eq. 2) are used in computing e^x. It is possible
to modify this, however, by changing the first digit in
instruction 17L, [i.e. the 5 in 58F 00F] to 4, 3, or 2.
The smaller the number used in place of 5, the shorter
the duration of the computation but the greater the
error. A simplified version of the dependency of
speed and accuracy is given by the tables below:

TABLE I

Digit	Max. Error	Duration
5	5×10^{-12}	11.3 m sec.
4	5×10^{-9}	9.7 m sec.
3	5×10^{-6}	8.1 m sec.
2	5×10^{-5}	6.5 m sec.

for $-1 < x < 0$.

It should be noted that the error increases with x
approaching -1. Thus for x in the range
$-1/2 \leq x < 0$ we have the following table:

TABLE II

Digit	Max. Error	Duration
5	5×10^{-12}	Speed same as Table I.
4	5×10^{-11}	
3	5×10^{-10}	
2	5×10^{-8}	

DATE 4/26/56 RT: 10/29/58

PROGRAMMED BY Jack Goldberg

APPROVED BY J. P. Nash

lgr

LOCATION	ORDER	NOTES	8 4
	00 K(84)		
0	40 F	Set Exit	
	K5 F		
1	42 16L		
	L5 F		
2	10 2F	Form x/2	
	50 F		
3	40 F	Form $x^2/4$	
	7J F		
4	40 1F		
	41 2F		
5	L5 17I		
	40 19L		
6	50 2F		
	S5 F		
7	10 3F	Compute F	
	L4 19L		
8	40 20L		
	L5 1F		
9	10 5F		
	66 20L		
10	L5 19L	Test for end of F	
	L0 18L	compulation.	
11	40 19L		
	L0 18L		
12	32 6L	$1/2 - x/2$	
	L9 F		
13	84 F	$1/2 - x/2 + F/2$	
	40 20L		
14	50 2F		
	L5 F		
15	66 20L	$\dfrac{x/4}{1/2 - x/2 + F/2} + 1/2$	
	SJ F		
16	00 1F	e^x	
	22 F		

LOCATION	ORDER		NOTES
17	58 F		Constant = 11/16
	00 F		
18	10 F		Constant = 1/16
	00 F		
19	00 F		
	00 F		Temporary locations
20	00 F		
	00 F		

APPENDIX 19

ILLIAC LIBRARY DESCRIPTION OF T5:

COMPUTE SIN-COS

LIBRARY ROUTINE T5 - 157

TITLE	Sine-Cosine Routine (D.O.I or SADOI)
TYPE	Closed
NUMBER OF WORDS	21
TEMPORARY STORAGE	0, 1, 2
DURATION	9 milliseconds
ACCURACY	2^{-38}
DESCRIPTION	Given Θ/π in A, the routine places $(1/2)$ sin Θ in A when a standard entry is used.
REMARKS	(1) If A contains $1/2 \pm \Theta/\pi$, the quantity $1/2$ cos Θ will be obtained.
	(2) If Θ/π overflows in A from left shifts or addition the result is unaffected because sin $(\Theta + 2n \pi) =$ sin Θ.
EXAMPLES	(1) If memory location q contains Θ/π, $(1/2)$ cos Θ may be obtained with the entry

	LJ q
p	50 p
p + 1	26 -

(2) To find sin 3.82 radians when memory location q contains 0.382 and memory location r contains $10/4\pi$, we proceed as follows, ignoring the overflow in A.

	50 q
p - 1	
	75 r
	00 2F
r	
	50 p
p + 1	26 -

METHOD	(1) Given Θ in radians we evaluate sin $(\Theta/2)$ by a Tchebyscheff polynomial expansion to the Taylor series expansion of the sine function, using Library routine KA-1.

(2) If Θ is scaled so that $-1 \leq 2^{-n}\Theta < 1$, we form
$2^n (2^{-n}\Theta/\pi = \Theta/\pi \pmod 2)) = \Theta'/\pi$.

(3) Using the identity $\sin a = \sin (\pi - a)$ we obtain
Θ'' with $-1/2 \leq \Theta''/\pi < 1/2$ such that $\sin \Theta'' = \sin \Theta'$
$= \sin \Theta$.

ERROR ANALYSIS   (1) In word 4 we develop $-4 (\Theta/\pi)^2$. Consider
$|\Theta/\pi| < 1/2$. This quantity possesses up to 38 significant binary digits. We
form $(\Theta/\pi)^2 < 1/4$ and shift left twice, introducing thereby at most an error
of 2^{-39}, since q_1 contains a significant binary digit.

      (2) We next develop the polynomial:

$$1/2 \sin \Theta = \Theta/\pi \, [a_{13}(2\Theta/\pi)^{12} + a_{11}(2\Theta/\pi)^{10} +$$

$$a_9(2\Theta/\pi)^8 + a_7(2\Theta/\pi)^6 + a_5(2\Theta/\pi)^4 +$$

$$a_3(2\Theta/\pi)^2 + a_1]$$

This is accomplished by the recursion relation:

$$S_0 = 0$$

$$S_{i+1} = (2\Theta/\pi)^2 S_i + a_j \quad \begin{matrix}(i=0,1,2,\ldots7)\\(j=12,11,9,\ldots1)\end{matrix}$$

At each one of these steps we introduce a round-off
error due to the multiplication. Letting $(2\Theta/\pi)^2 = x$, we obtain:

$$1/2 \sin \Theta = [a_{13}x^6 + a_{11}x^5 + a_9x^4 + a_7x^3 + a_5x^2 + a_3x + a_1$$

$$+ 2^{-40}(x^5 + x^4 + x^3 + x^2 + x + 1) \Theta/\pi + 2^{-40}]$$

Since x cannot exceed 1 and $|\Theta/\pi| < 1/2$ we have as error
$3.2^{-40} + 2^{-40}$. The maximum total generated error is therefore 2^{-38}.

      (3) There will also be developed a propogated error due
to the inaccuracy of the quantity $4(\Theta/\pi)^2$. We will admit only the error resulting from the term $a_3(2\Theta/\pi)^2$ in equation (1) due to the relative small contribu-
tions propagated by the other terms.

Thus:

$$a_3(2\Theta/\pi)^2 = .4[4\ \Theta^2/\pi^2 \pm 2^{-39}] = .4(2\Theta/\pi)^2 \pm (.4)2^{-39}.$$

The propagated error is therefore: $(.4)2^{-39}$

(4) The total maximum error is therefore:

$$2^{-38} + (.4)2^{-39} = (2 + .4)\ 2^{-39} = (2.4)2^{-39}$$

(5) A sample of calculations for the sine of a number of arguments was found to be in error at most 3×10^{-12} which is less than the maximum error indicated above.

(6) Finally, we consider the case $|\Theta/\pi| = 1/2$. The error was found experimentally to be less than 2^{-39}.

DATE 11/29/54 RT: 4/5/60	
PROGRAMMED BY Werner L. Frank	
APPROVED BY J. P. Nash	

ns

LOCATION	ORDER		NOTES
0	00 F(T5)		Store θ/π
	40 F		
	K5 14L		
1	42 12L		Plant link
	L9 F		$1/2 - \theta/\pi$
2	40 F		
	LS F		$1/2 - |1/2 - \theta/\pi| = \theta'/\pi$
3	40 F		
	50 F		$-1/2 = \theta'/\pi < 1/2$
4	71 F		
	00 2F		$-4\,(\theta'/\pi)^2$
5	40 1F		
	L5 L		
6	42 7L		
	50 13L		
7	79 1F		$-4\,a_n(\theta'/\pi)^2 + a_{n+1}$
	L4 (14)L	6,9'	
8	40 2F		
	50 2F		
9	F5 7L		
	42 7L		
10	L0 20L		Test
	36 7L		
11	LJ 9L		Prepare round off
	74 F		$1/4 \sin \theta$
12	00 1F		$1/2 \sin \theta$
	22 ( ) F	1	
13	00 F		
	00 27232J		$a_{13} = .27232 \times 10^{-7}$
14	NO F		
	00 499998202409J		$a_{11} = .1797591 \times 10^{-5}$
15	00 F		
	00 80219199J		$a_9 = .80219199 \times 10^{-4}$

LOCATION	ORDER	NOTES	**T5**
16	NO F		
	00 497659123501J	$a_7 = .2340876499 \times 10^{-2}$	
17	00 F		
	00 39846313004J	$a_5 = .39846313004 \times 10^{-1}$	
18	NO F		
	00 177017951058J	$a_3 = - .785398163397$	
19	40 F		
	00 285398163397J	$a_1 = .785398163397$	
20	L9 1F	End constant	
	L4 20L		

APPENDIX 20

ILLIAC LIBRARY DESCRIPTION

OF Y5: DRUM TRANSFER

LIBRARY ROUTINE _ Y ₅ - 291

TITLE: Transfer Blocks of Words between the Drum and the Williams Memory.

TYPE: Closed subroutine with 3 program parameters.

NUMBER OF WORDS: 35

TEMPORARY STORAGE: 0

DURATION: 10 + 1.3r milliseconds to record or play back, where r is the number of words transferred.

DESCRIPTION: The entries to this routine are identical to those used by routine Y 1 - 199.

The entry

```
        p       JO n
                50 p
        p + 1   26 --
                00 q
        p + 2   00 r
```

will cause the block of r words starting at location n in the Williams Memory to be recorded on the drum starting at drum location q. A sum check constant will be recorded at q + r. Control will be returned to the right hand side of p + 2.

The entry

```
        p       50 n
                50 p
        p + 1   26 --
                00 q
        p + 2   00 r
```

will cause the block of r words starting at drum location q to be placed in the williams memory starting at drum location n. A sum check constant must be in q + r on the drum. This sum check constant will be compared with the sum calculated from the words played back from

the drum, and if the two do not agree, a second attempt
will be made to play back the desired words. If the sum
checking again fails, an error will be indicated by
the machine stopping on an FF OLO on the left hand side
of word 33 relative to the routine. At this point it is
possible to execute a white switch start which will
cause two more attempts to play back the desired words.
If the sum check constant agrees with the calculated sum,
control will be returned to the right hand side of $p + 2$.

WARNING: This routine cannot be used for the playback of words
recorded by routine Y 1, nor can it be used to record
words which will later be played back by routine Y 1, since
the two routines do not store the same quantities on the drum.
It is also not practical to use the drum post mortem
routine for printing words which have been recorded by
this routine, as the successive differences of words are
recorded rather than the words themselves.

NOTE 1: The contents of the accumulator after a sum check failure
are not related to the actual error and will have the form
K1***00000.

NOTE 2: It should be noted that Y 5 is shorter (35 versus 40 words)
than Y 1. In addition Y 5 provides the same speed on record
as on playback (10 + 1.3r ms.) whereas Y 1 requires
(10 + 1.8r ms.) on record. These improvements are achieved
through the storage of differences which allows the additional
sum checking loop on the record option to be eliminated.

DATE March 10, 1960
PROGRAMMED BY B.D. Elliott
APPROVED BY J.N.Snyder

ns

LOCATION	ORDER	NOTES	Y 5
	00K(Y5)		
0	K5 F		
	42 3L		
1	F5 3L		
	42 5L		
2	42 31L		
	00 19F		
3	42 24L	Set up	
	L5 F		
4	L6 34L		
	40 26L		
5	41 F		
	L5 F		
6	10 20F		
	L4 26L		
7	40 29L		
	K1 F	$q_0 = 1$ for record	
8	36 20L		
	L3 34L	Set switch for two playbacks	
9	40 34L		
	41 F	Reenter for second trial	
10	L5 24L		
	42 14L	Set up playback	
11	L5 26L		
	40 13L		
12	L0 29L		
	36 29L		
13	85 11F		
	00 F		
14	L4 F		
	40 F	Playback	
15	40 F		
	F5 14L		
16	42 14L		
	F5 13L		
17	22 11L		

LOCATION	ORDER	NOTES	Y 5
	F1 F		
18	86 11F	Record check	
	00 F		
19	23 31L		
	00 F		
20	19 6F		
	L4 29L		
21	40 18L	Set up recording	
	19 6F		
22	L4 26L		
	40 26L		
23	L0 18L		
	32 17L		
24	50 F		
	L5 F		
25	40 F		
	S0 F	Record	
26	86 11F		
	00 F	During playback is $\begin{matrix} 85 \ 11F \\ 00 \ nF \end{matrix}$	
27	F5 24L		
	42 24L		
28	F5 26L		
	22 22L		
29	85 11F		
	00 F		
30	L4 F	Check playback for error	
	40 F		
31	F3 F		
	32 F	Link	
32	L1 34L		
	36 9L	Check for two attempts	
33	FF 240F		
	26 9L	White switch fot two more attempts	
34	K0 4085L	Constant for forming drum orders	
	0C F	Also used as binary switch	

ILLIAC LIBRARY DESCRIPTION OF F1: SOLUTION OF A SYSTEM

OF ORDINARY DIFFERENTIAL EQUATIONS

ILLINOIS CODE F 1 - 114

TITLE	Solution of a System of Ordinary Differential Equations
	(Originally Code 27) (SADOI Only)
TYPE	Closed - with one program parameter

Location	Program	
p	00 mF	
	50 pF	The first word of
p+1	26 xF	Routine F 1 - 114
		is at x.

NUMBER OF WORDS   41

TEMPORARY STORAGE   0, 1, 2, 3

PARAMETERS   The locations 3 to 7 must contain the following parameters

before and during the input of this subroutine.

STORAGE LOCATIONS	CONTENTS	USE
3	00F 00 aF	$N(a + i)$ are the variables y_i ($i = 0$, 1, ..., n - 1) Originally the initial values are placed here.
4	00F 00 bF	$N(b + i)$ are the scaled derivatives, $2^m hy_i'$ ($= 2^m hf_i$), ($i = 0, 1, 2, ..., n - 1$), calculated by the auxiliary subroutine. $b > a + n-1$
5	00F 00 cF	Locations $c + i$, ($i = 0, 1, ..., n-1$) are used as temporary storage for this subroutine. These locations must be cleared to zero before this integration subroutine is entered for the first time. $c > b + n-1.$
6	00F 00 nF	n is the number of differential equations to be solved.
7	00F 00 dF	d is the location of the first word of the auxiliary subroutine.

DURATION	$T = 7 + n(15 + 0.1m) + 4t$ ms where

T = time in milliseconds to perform one step of integration.

t = time in milliseconds for the auxiliary subroutine.

DESCRIPTION   This subroutine will handle a set of n simultaneous first order ordinary differential equations, in which each derivative is expressed explicitly in terms of the variables

$$y_0' = f_0 (y_0, y_1, \ldots, y_{n-1})$$
$$y_1' = f_1 (y_0, y_1, \ldots, y_{n-1})$$
$$y_{n-1}' = f_{n-1} (y_0, y_1, \ldots, y_{n-1})$$

Any differential equation or set of differential equations to be solved must first be expressed in the above form before this subroutine can be applied. For example, the second order differential equation

$$y'' = w^2 y$$

must be written as two first order differential equations

$$y_0' = wy_1 \qquad\qquad y_1' = wy_0$$

where $y_1 = y$ and $y_0 = y'/w$.

Each time this subroutine is called into use, it will carry out one integration step of length h. Each of the integrals y_i (i = 0, 1, 2, ..., n-1) is replaced by its value at the end of a step of length h. In doing so, this subroutine employs an auxiliary closed subroutine which evaluates the functions $f_0, f_1, f_2, \ldots, f_{n-1}$ from the given values of y_i. The coder must write this auxiliary subroutine for his individual problem since it defines the equations being solved and, this depends entirely on his specific problem.

The purpose of the auxiliary subroutine is to calculate and store in locations b + i, (i = 0, 1, 2, ..., n-1), the quantities hf_i multiplied by a suitable scale factor 2^m. h is the increment of the independent variable and m is a positive integer to be chosen as large as possible without having any of the quantities $2^m hf_i$ exceed capacity anywhere throughout the range of integration. The factor 2^m is introduced to increase the accuracy of the integration subroutine. The variables, y_i, must all be scaled so that they are less than one throughout the range of integration before they are used in the auxiliary subroutine. Also for maximum accuracy, one should store $2^m h$ instead of just h. This auxiliary subroutine must be located in a sequence of locations beginning with location d, where d is defined by the parameter S7. In integrating over one step, the integration subroutine will call in the auxiliary subroutine four times.

This integration subroutine requires 3n arbitrary storage locations. The n consecutive locations a + i, (i = 0, 1, 2, ..., n-1; a arbitrary), are used to store the variables y_i. It is in these locations that the initial values are to be placed. It is also in these locations that the final results are found. The n consecutive locations b + i, (i = 0, 1, 2, ..., n-1; b > a + n-1), are used to store the scaled derivatives, $2^m h_y'$ ($= 2^m h f_i$), which are calculated by the auxiliary subroutine. The n consecutive locations c + i (i = 0, 1, 2, ..., n-1; c > b + n-1) are used for temporary storage by the integration subroutine. These locations will hold the quantities $2^m q_i$ (See page 7). The numbers left in these locations at the end of an integration step are $3 \cdot 2^m$ times the roundoff errors of the quantities y_i. These numbers are taken into account during the following step and serve to prevent the rapid accumulation of roundoff errors. As a result the effective numerical accuracy is m digits more than the capacity of the storage locations. Therefore, it is important that the locations c + i, (i = 0, 1, 2, ..., n-1) be cleared to zero before the integration subroutine is entered. Otherwise, this integration subroutine will add spurious corrections to the variables. Thus before the

integration subroutine can be entered, the main routine
must clear the temporary storage locations $c + i$ to zero
and set the initial values of the variables y_i in locations
$a + i$.

SUMMARY

Supposing that, in the course of his routine, a coder
has to solve a set of differential equations over a specified
range given the initial value of the independent variable,
a possible procedure would be the following:

(1) Reduce the given set of differential equations to a
set of n first order differential equations.

(2) Calculate the initial values of the dependent
variables, y_i.

(3) Scale all the functions so that all the values y_i
are less than one throughout the range of integration.

(4) Choose a proper value of h (See note I).

(5) Choose m properly.

(6) Determine the parameters to be placed in S3 - S7,
observing that $a < b < c$.

(7) Write an auxiliary subroutine which evaluates the
functions $2^m h f_i$ and stores them in locations $b + i$.

(8) Make certain that the main routine sets the scaled
initial values in locations $a + i$, and clears the temporary
storage locations $c + i$ to zero before the integration
subroutine is entered.

With respect to the solution of a set of differential
equations, a program can be broken up into four parts:

(1) Locations 3 through 7 which contain the parameters,

(2) The main routine,

(3) The integration subroutine (Code F 1 - 114)

(4) The auxiliary subroutine.

THE INDEPENDENT VARIABLE

If the independent variable x occurs in the functions f_i or if it is required during an integration as an index, then it must be obtained by integrating the equation $x' = 1$. The independent variable x is then treated as an additional dependent variable, for which the auxiliary subroutine has to provide the quantity $2^m hx' = 2^m h$. However, this latter quantity may be planted at the beginning of the integration in the appropriate location (e.g. in location b) and left there, so that the auxiliary subroutine is relieved of the task. If the independent variable does not appear in any of the f_i's but is merely wanted for indication purposes, it is quicker to use a simple counter in the main routine.

NOTES.

I) Accuracy: The truncation error in one step is of the order of h^5. Ordinarily, that is for a small set of well behaved equations, its magnitude is about $10^{-2} h^5$; for large sets or difficult equations it may be greater. Over the range of integration this error will amount to about $h^4/100$. Roundoff errors accumulate at a rate corresponding to the keeping of $(39 + m)$ binary digits. The choice of the length of the increment h is governed largely by the accuracy desired. An increase in the length of h will result in a decrease in accuracy and in operating time. Likewise, a decrease in the length of h will result in an increase in both accuracy and operating time. However, no further increase in accuracy can be gained by choosing $h < 2^{-8}$ because of the introduced truncation error. But, if the functions are very sensitive to variations in y_i, or if the number of equations is very large, smaller steps will probably be necessary with, of course, a corresponding increase in the time required. Now, the process used in the integration subroutine is a fourth order one. Thus, 1/15 of the following difference,

   (the value of y_e calculated using an interval of length h)

   -(the value of y_e calculated using an interval of length 2h)

is an approximation of the error.

II) Adjustment of the increment h: There exist essentially two ways of adjusting the increment

a) One may double or halve the increment by varying the value of m in the main routine. This may be done over the complete range of integration or just over part of it. When only the parameter 00 mF in the link between the main routine and the auxiliary subroutine is changed to 00 (m+1)F and the auxiliary subroutine is unaltered, the length of the increment is halved. Likewise, when only the parameter 00 mF is changed to 00 (m-1)F the length of the increment is doubled. The auxiliary subroutine is not altered since $2^m h = 2^{m+1} h/2$. If one adjusts the increment over the complete range, adjusting only the value of m is sufficient. However, if one wishes to adjust the length of the increment within the range of integration, one must also adjust all the quantities in locations c + i. Otherwise, one will introduce roundoff errors in y_i of the magnitude,

   2 (old value of h - new value of h) x 2^{-40}.

Now by also doubling the quantities in c + i when one halves the increment one will introduce no roundoff error. Similarly, by halving the quantities in c + i when one doubles the length of the increment, one will introduce no roundoff error. If one clears the locations c + i, one introduces roundoff errors of magnitude 2^{-40}.

b) One may alter the length of the increment in any ratio by adjusting the scaling factor $2^m h$ in the auxiliary subroutine. Here also one may adjust the length of the increment within the range of integration. Now it is not necessary to adjust the quantities in $c + i$. If, however, $2^m h$ becomes small, then roundoff errors are introduced by inaccuracies in the auxiliary subroutine. Thus one should not keep $2^m h$ small when integrating over large ranges unless the loss of accuracy and time does not matter.

III) Often it is desired to evaluate functions involving expressions like $\sin x$ or $J_m(x)$. These expressions can be evaluated by solving extra distinct differential equations along with the desired ones. For example,

$$d^2/dx^2 \; (\sin x)/2 = -(\sin x)/2.$$

Thus we can evaluate $(\sin x)/2$ by using the extra pair of equations

$$y'_{n+1} = 2^m h y_n \qquad\qquad y'_n = -2^m h y_{n+1}$$

and suitable initial conditions.

METHOD USED FOR INTEGRATION IN THE ROUTINE

Given a set of differential equations,

$$y'_i = f_i \; (y_0, y_1, y_2, \ldots, y_{n-1}), \quad (i = 0, 1, 2, \ldots, n-1)$$

The process used in the integration is defined by the following equations

$$k_{ij} = 2^m h f_i \; (y_{0j}, \; y_{1j}, \; \ldots, \; y_{n-1 \, j})$$

$$r_{i,j+1} = (A_{j+1} + 1) \; (k_{i,j} - B_j \, q_{i,j})$$

$$y_{i,j+1} = y_{i,j} + 2^{-m} \, r_{i,j+1}$$

$$q_{i,j+1} = q_{ij} + 3r_{i,j} + (C_j - 1) \, k_{i,j+1}$$

with the following table of values

j	A_{j+1}	B_j	C_j
0	$-1/2$	2	$1/2$
1	$-(1/2)^{1/2}$	1	$(1/2)^{1/2}$
2	$(1/2)^{1/2}$	1	$-(1/2)^{1/2}$
3	$-5/6$	2	$1/2$

Of the double subscripts used in the above equations, the first subscript, i, indicates which variable is being considered, and the second subscript, j, indicate which of the four parts of one step is being performed. The auxiliary subroutine evaluates the quantities $k_{i,j}$. In the above equations, only the quantities $q_{i,4}$ and $y_{i,4}$ are carried over from step to step. The quantities $r_{i,j}$ are calculated in the course of one step; they are not carried directly from step to step. When $j = 4$, we replace it by zero, increase i by 1, and terminate the step.

For one step, the sequence of operations is as follows:

$j = 0$ $i = 0, 1, 2, \ldots, n-1$
$j = 1$ $i = 0, 1, 2, \ldots, n-1$
$j = 2$ $i = 0, 1, 2, \ldots, n-1$
$j = 3$ $i = 0, 1, 2, \ldots, n-1$

REFERENCES

Gill, S., "A Process for the Step-by-Step Integration of Differential Equations in an Automatic Digital Computing Machine", Proceedings of the Cambridge Philosophical Society, vol. 47 (1951) pp. 96 - 108.

Wilkes, M. V., Wheeler, D.J., and Gill, S., The Preparations of Programs for an Electronic Digital Computer Addison-Wesley Press, Inc. Cambridge, Mass., (1951) pp. 32-33, 56-57, 86-87, 132-134.

DATE October 27, 1953 Rt. 3/19/59
CODED BY   D.J. Wheeler
REVISED BY   R. Polivka
APPROVED BY J.P. Nash

LOCATION	ORDER	NOTES	F 1
	00 K(F1)		
	00 S3		
	00 g4		
	00 S5		
	00 86		
	01 29K		
0	L5 5F		
	L4 6F		
1	00 20F		
	46 571F		
2	L5 4F		
	L0 3F		
3	42 573F		
	00 20F		
4	46 573F		
	L5 5F		
5	L0 4F		
	42 574F		
6	00 20F		
	46 574F		
7	26 93F		
	00 F		
8	64 F	c+n	
	00 33L		
9	80 S3	a	
	00 S3	a	
10	00 F	b–a	
	00 F	b–a	
11	00 F	c–b	
	00 F	c–b	
12	26 1469N		
	01 K		
0	S5 F	Set shift addresses	
	46 8L	= m	
1	46 11L		
	L4 3L		

LOCATION	ORDER		NOTES	**F1**
2	42 22L		Set link address	
	22 21L			
3	L5 $(q_{i,j})$F	From 21		
	40 1F	By 20		
4	L5 $(k_{i,j})$F	By 18		
	40 F			
5	L0 (1)F	By 23		
	L0 1F		$(k_{i,j} - B_j \, q_{ij})$	
6	40 3F			
	50 (A_j)F	By 24		
7	7J 3F			
	L4 3F		$(k_{ij} - B_j \, q_{ij}) \, (A_j + 1) \, 2^{-m}$	
8	10 (m)F	By 0		
	40 3F			
9	L4 (y_{ij})F	By 17		
	40 $(y_{i,j+1})$F	By 17	Step y_i	
10	L5 3F			
	50 2F		Form $r_{i,j+1}$	
11	00 (m)F	By 1		
	40 3F			
12	50 (C_j)F	By 25		
	7J F		$C_j \, k_{ij} - k_{ij}$	
13	L0 F			
	L4 1F			
14	L4 3F			
	L4 3F		$q_{ij} + 3 \, r_{i,j+1}$	
15	L4 3F			
	40 $(q_{i,j+1})$F	By 19		
16	L5 9L			
	L4 13L			
17	42 9L			
	46 9L		Increase all addresses depending	
18	L4 39L			
	46 4L		on i by 1	

LOCATION	ORDER		NOTES	F1
19	L4 40L			
	42 15L			
20	46 3L		until i = n	
	L0 37L			
21	36 3L			
	L5 (33)L	By 22,		
22	42 21L	From 2'	Increase j from 0 to 3 and then leave	
	32 ( )F	By 2	by link	
23	46 5L			
	10 10F		Adjust addresses which depend on j	
24	L4 18L			
	42 6L			
25	46 12L			
	50 25L		Call in auxiliary subroutine	
26	26 S7			
	41 2F		Clear 2F so that it can be used as zero.	
27	L5 38L			
	26 17L		Start new i cycle.	
28	40 F			
	00 F	1/2	C_0, C_3	
29	NO F			
	00 F	-1/2	A_0	
30	40 F			
	00 2071 0678 1186 J		$1/\sqrt{2}$ C_1, A_2	
31	80 F			
	00 2928 9321 8814 J		$-1/\sqrt{2}$ A_1, C_2	
32	80 F			
	00 1666 6666 6667 J		$-5/6$ A_3	
33	LJ 1025F	-11, 1		
	06 1058L	25,34L	Expressed in units of 2^{-9}, 2^{-19}, 2^{-29}, 2^{-39}.	
34	LJ 3074F	-9 2	Addresses used to set addresses to refer to	
	06 3107L	27, 35L	the constants A_j, C_j and make the address in	
35	LF 2F	-8, 2	5L, 1 or 2 according as B_j 2 or 1, and to	
	06 2084L	26, 36L	stop the address in 21, dependent on j, and	
36	LJ 1025F	-11, 1	to stop when positive.	
	07 37L	28, 37L		
	0141K			

APPENDIX 22

ILLIAC LIBRARY DESCRIPTION OF E3:

INTEGRATION BY SIMPSON'S RULE (FUNCTION VALUES)

LIBRARY ROUTINE E 3 ⊢ 186

TITLE:	Integration by Simpson's Rule (Function Values) (SADOI or DOI)
TYPE:	Closed
NUMBER OF WORDS:	38
TEMPORARY STORAGE:	Location O
ACCURACY:	$\pm 2^{-39}$ + truncation error
DURATION:	$3 + (4 + d)n$ milliseconds where d is the number of milliseconds required to evaluate f with the auxiliary routine.
DESCRIPTION:	This routine computes $\frac{1}{b-a} \int_a^b f(x)dx$ by using the approximation

$$\frac{1}{b-a} \int_a^b f(x)dx \approx \frac{1}{3n} (f_0 + 4f_1 + 2f_2 + \ldots + f_n)$$

where $f_i = f(\frac{\lfloor b - a \rfloor}{n} i + a)$ is the value of $f(x)$

calculated by an auxiliary routine at an odd number $n + 1$ of equally spaced points $a + \frac{b - a}{n} i$, $i = 0, 1, 2, \ldots, n$, where $b > a$.

ENTRY:	Place a in location O and b in A and enter with

q	50 pF
	50 qF
q + 1	26 --
	00 nF

where p is the location of the closed auxiliary subroutine which calculates $f(x)$.

AUXILIARY SUBROUTINE:	The auxiliary subroutine placed at p must be a closed routine which takes x from A and places $f(x)$ in A.
RESULT:	Control is returned to the left side of q + 2 with the result in A and Q.
NOTE:	If $f(x)$ is tabulated use Library Routine E 2.

DATE June 2, 1955   RT: 6/17/60

CODED BY L. Isaacson

APPROVED BY J. P. Nash

nj

LOCATION	ORDER	NOTES	E 3
	00 K(E3)		
0	L0 F		
	40 31L	b - a	
1	L5 F	Store a	
	40 32L		
2	41 33L	Clear counter	
	K5 6F		
3	42 5L	Plant q + 1	
	L4 28L		
4	42 27L	Plant link	
	46 10L		
5	46 18L		
	L5 ( )F		
6	L0 30L		
	40 35L	n	
7	L4 35L		
	L4 35L		
8	40 34L	3n	
	41 36L		
9	L5 32L		
	50 9L		
10	26 ( )F	p	
	40 37L		
11	F5 33L		
	40 33L	Step m	
12	F0 35L	Test (m + 1 - n)	
	32 24L		
13	50 31L		
	75 33L		
14	10 1F		
	32 15L		
15	L4 33L		
	S5 35L		
16	S5 F		
	S4 F		

LOCATION	ORDER	NOTES
17	L4 32L	$a + \frac{m}{n}(b - c)$
	50 17L	
18	26 ( )F	
	40 F	
19	50 29L	
	L5 37L	
20	74 F	
	L4 36L	
21	40 36L	
	S5 F	
22	40 37L	
	L5 2L	
23	L0 29L	Binary switch
	42 29L	
24	26 11L	
	50 F	
25	L5 37L	
	70 28L	
26	L4 36L	
	66 34L	
27	S5 F	
	26 ( )F	Link
28	00 F	
	00 1F	
29	00 F	
	00 4F	
30	26 L	
	00 F	
31	00 F	$b - a$
	00 F	
32	00 F	a
	00 F	
33	00 F	m
	00 F	

408

LOCATION	ORDER	NOTES	E 3
34	00 F		
	00 F	$3n$	
35	00 F		
	00 F	n	
36	00 F		
	00 F		
37	00 F		
	00 F	$f(x)$	

APPENDIX 23

ILLIAC LIBRARY DESCRIPTION OF A1:

FLOATING DECIMAL ARITHMETIC ROUTINE

LIBRARY ROUTINE A 1 - 63

TITLE	Floating Decimal Arithmetic Routine
TYPE	Interpretive routine with 18 interpretive orders, entered as a closed routine, left by an 8J interpretive order.
NUMBER OF WORDS	168
PURPOSE	This routine manipulates numbers in the floating decimal form,

that is numbers which are represented as A x 10^P. It is of the interpretive type. This means that it selects parameters called <u>interpretive orders</u> which are written by the user one at a time and performs a calculation corresponding to each interpretive order. Interpretive orders carry out normal arithmetic operations such as addition and multiplication and some red tape operations such as counting and address changing.

In general, one will use this routine to do computations which do not require the full speed of the computer but which are too time consuming to be done by hand. It is especially effective for problems with scaling difficulties. In a sense one may think of the floating decimal routine as converting the Illiac to a medium speed floating decimal computer having a very convenient order code.

ACCURACY   About 9 decimals

TEMPORARY STORAGE 0, 1, 2

PRESET PARAMETERS S3 is used to specify two locations of non-temporary storage, S3 and 1S3, which are used for the floating decimal accumulator.

METHOD OF USE   The floating decimal routine is entered as a standard subroutine. Following the entry, i.e. after the transfer of control to the subroutine, one begins writing interpretive orders. These orders each occupy one half word and consist of a pair of function digits followed by a single address. They therefore have the same form as standard machine orders and may be read by the Decimal Order Input with full use of the conventional terminating symbols.

The first of the two function digits of an interpretive order describes the group characteristics of the order and may take values 0, 1,..., 8. Normal arithmetic interpretive orders have this digit equal to 8. The second of the two function digits describes the type of interpretive order.

<u>INTERPRETIVE ORDER LIST WITH FIRST FUNCTION DIGIT b = 8</u>

Let F be the floating decimal number in the floating accumulator and let F(n) be the floating decimal number in location n.

80 N Replace F by F - F(n).

81 n Replace F by -F(n).

82 n Transfer control to the right hand interpretive order in n if $F \geq 0$.

83 n Transfer control to the left hand interpretive order in n if $F \geq 0$.

84 n Replace F by F + F(n).

85 n Replace F by F(n).

86 n Replace F by F/F(n).

87 n Replace F by F x F(n).

88 0 Replace F by one number read from the input tape punched as sign, any number of decimal digits, sign, and two decimal digits to represent the exponent. For example, $.8971 \times 10^{10}$ would be punched as + 8971 + 10.

89 n Punch or print F as a sign, n decimal digits, sign, two decimal digits to represent the exponent and two spaces. This print out may be re-read by this routine. After F has been punched or printed it may not remain in the floating accumulator unmodified. n can take values 2 to 9.

8K n Replace F by n if $0 \leq n < 200$

8S n Replace F(n) by F.

8N n Replace F by $|F| - |F(n)|$.

8J n Transfer control to the ordinary Illiac order on the left hand side of n. This used to escape from the floating decimal subroutine.

8F n Give a carriage return and line feed and start a new block of printing having n columns. This order is only obeyed <u>once</u> for a particular block of printing. At this time a counter is set up which will cause a carriage return and line feed to occur automatically from then on after every set of n numbers that is printed.

INTERPRETIVE ORDERS WITH b $\neq$ 8. If the first function digit of an interpretive order is 0, 1,...,7 it will refer to one of a set of control registers or b-registers in the floating decimal routine which are similarly numbered. These registers are used for counting the number of passages through loops or cycles and for advancing addresses on successive passages. For this purpose a particular b-registers which may be used in a particular cycle contains two counting indice g_b and c_b. These are both integers in the range 0 to 1023. The index c_b is used for counting purposes to determine the number of passages through a loop. The index g_b is used for advancing the addresses of interpretive arithmetic orders. Although the interpretive order with first function digit b is not actually altered in the memory it is obeyed as if g_b were added to its address. The index g_b is increased by one upon each passage through the cycle. The multiplicity of b-registers allows one to program many loops within loops.

ORDER LIST WITH n $\neq$ 8

b0 n	Replace F by F - $F(n+g_b)$
b1 n	Replace F by $-F(n+g_b)$
b2 n	Replace g_b, c_b by g_b + 1, c_b + 1.
b3 n	Then transfer control to the right hand (if b2 n) or left hand interpretive (if b3 n) order in n if c_b+1 is negative. This transfer is used at the end of a loop.
b4 n	Replace F by F + $F(n + g_b)$
b5 n	Replace F by $F(n + g_b)$
b6 n	Replace F by $F/F(n+g_b)$
b7 n	Replace F by F x $F(n+g_b)$
bK n	Replace g_b, c_b by 0, -n. This interpretive order is used for preparing to cycle around a loop n times.
bS n	Replace $F(n + g_b)$ by F
bN n	Replace F by $|F| - |F(n+g_b)|$
bL n	Replace g_b, c_b by g_b + n, c_b. This interpretive order is used when one wishes to step addresses by some increment other than +1 in a loop. If one places bL 1022 in a loop the effect will be to decrease addresses by one on each passage. bL 1 will increase them by 2 etc.
8L n	Replace g_b c_b by n, c_b, where b is the last b-register referred to by some previous interpretive order.

DURATION OF INDIVIDUAL INTERPRETIVE ORDERS

8N 80 84	5 milliseconds + m x (3/2). Where m is the number of shifts required to convert A, p back to standard form.
81 85	2 milliseconds
82 83	3 milliseconds
87	5 milliseconds
86	6 millisecons
8K	3 milliseconds
88	3 milliseconds
8F	3 milliseconds
8L	2 milliseconds
8J	3 milliseconds

When an interpretive order is preceeded by $b \neq 8$, add one millisecond to the above times.

When one wishes to repeat a cycle of interpretive orders n times the interpretive order bK n may be written before entering the loop to set the counter c_b to -η. The interpretive orders in the loop will be obeyed n times if the loop is terminated with a b2 or b3 interpretive order to transfer control to the beginning of the loop. This transfer of control interpretive order will be obeyed n-1 times and disobeyed the nth time.

The following examples illustrate the construction of such loops.

EXAMPLE 1   Calculate x^{10} where $x = F(4)$

0	8K 1F	Set $F = 1$
	2K 10F	Set to cycle 10 times
1	87 4F	$c_2 = -10$
	23 1L	Transfer control to 1 relative 9 times.

EXAMPLE 2   Replace $F(100 + i)$ by $F(200 + i) + F(300 + i), i = 0,1,\ldots,9$

6	OK 10F	$g_0 = 0$, $c_0 = -10$
	05 200F	$F = F(200 + g_0)$
7	04 300F	$F = F(200 + g_0) + F(300 + g_0)$
	OS 100F	$F(100 + g_0) + F(200 + g_0) + F(300 + g_0)$
8	02 6L	increase g_0 by 1, transfer control 9 times to 6 relative.

EXAMPLE 3   Evaluate $\sum\limits_{i=0}^{19} a_i \, x^{19-i}$, where $a_i = F(100 + i)$, $x = F(10)$. The operations

form $(((a_0 x + a_1) \, x + a_2) \, x + a_3) \, x + \; \text{---}$

2	8K F	Clear F
	OK 20F	Prepare to cycle 20 times
3	87 10F	multiply by x
	04 100F	add $F(100 + g_0)$
4	03 3L	

EXAMPLE 4   Print 10 numbers each with 5 decimal figures in a block of 3 columns from 100 to 109.

22	8F 3F	Start block with 3 columns
	OK 10F	
23	05 100F	Print 10 numbers
	89 5F	
24	03 23L	

EXAMPLE 5   Place the number $F(200 + i)$ in $300 + 2i$ for $i = 0,1,\ldots,24$.

5	OK 25F	$g_0 = g_1 = 0$
	1K F	$c_0 = -25$
6	05 200F	
	1S 300 F	
7	1L 2F	advance g_1 by 2
	03 6L	

__EXAMPLE 6__   Place the number $F(200 + i)$ in $300 - i$ for $i = 0,1,...,24$

5	OK 25F	
	1K F	
6	05 200F	
	1S 300F	
7	1L 1023F	reduce g_1 by 1
	03 6L	increase g_0 and c_0 by 1

__Use of Auxiliary Routines.__ It is often convenient to be able to
leave the floating decimal routine so as to modify interpretive orders or to
perform calculations which may be done more effectively outside of floating point.
To leave the floating decimal routine one uses an 8J n order. (All standard
floating decimal auxiliaries are entered in this way.) To return to floating decimal
one should transfer control to the left hand side of word 29 of the floating decimal
routine. The interpretive order following the 8J n order which was last obeyed will
then be obeyed and so on. In this way it is not necessary to plant a link in auxiliary subroutines. One may, in fact, think of the 8J n order as a subroutine order.
In case any changes are made in the floating decimal accumulator while outside the
floating decimal routine, control should be returned to the left hand side of word
19 rather than 29 so that this number may be standardized before reentry.

__Handling of Numbers__ Each number is represented in the form $A \times 10^p$
where $1 > |A| \geq 1/10$, and $64 > p \geq -64$. In a single register of the memory the
number A is placed in the 33 most significant binary digits $(a_0, a_1, ..., a_{32})$
in the same way as an ordinary fraction is placed in the entire register. An
accuracy of between 8 and 9 decimal digits is therefore achieved. The exponent
p is stored as the integer $p + 64$ in the 7 least significant digits of the same
register. For convenience the floating decimal accumulator uses two registers
S3 and 1S3 for holding the number $A \times 10^p$. The fraction $A/2$ is in S3 and the
integer $p + 64$ is in 1S3.

The only exeption to the above rules is the number zero which can-
not, of course, be represented as $A \times 10^p$ with $|A| \geq 10$. For this reason zero is
handled in a special way. It is represented as a number with $A = 0$ and $p = -64$.

This representation happens to correspond exactly with the ordinary machine representation of zero.

After each arithmetic interpretive order is obeyed the number in the floating decimal accumulator is standardized, i.e. the number of S3 representing $A/2$ is adjusted so $1 > |A| \geq 1/10$ and p is changed accordingly. To accomplish this control is transferred to word 19 in the floating decimal routine after each arithmetic order.

If an interpretive store order is attempted when F has an exponent greater than 63 the machine will stop on the order 34 p at location p, where p is word 72 of the routine.

Important Words in the Routine. Word 2 in the floating decimal routine determines the location of the current interpretive order. When obeying the left hand interpretive order in location n this word is 50 nF S5 20F and when obeying the right hand interpretive order in location n it is L5 nF 00 20F. Other words of interest are the b-registers which start at word 158 (for g_0 and c_0) and go to 165 (g_7 and c_7). These register hold g_b and c_b in the form

$$80\ g_b F\ 00\ (2048 + c_b)\ F.$$

Warning When the same number is continually added to a sum, such as when an argument is being increased, the error can be quite large, because it is additive over a decade. For example, if we increase 10 to 100 by units we can get a maximum error of 90×2^{-33} because the errors all have the same sign. If we increase 10^3 to 10^4 we can have a maximum error of $9,000 \times 2^{-33}$. This can easily be prevented by writing an auxiliary subroutine to stabilize the fractional part of F, i.e. to replace it by the nearest multiple of say 10^{-7}. Such a subroutine could be as follows

m	50 S3	
	7J m+3F	A contains nearest multiple of 10^{-7}
m + 1	50 1F	Location 1 contains zero
	66 m+3F	converts to fraction again
m + 2	S5 F	
	22 s+18F	return to 18th order of Routine A-1
m + 3	00 F	
	00 20,000,000F	$2 \times 10^7 \times 2^{-39}$

RT: 8/3/60

DATE November 18, 1953

BY David J Wheeler   APPROVED BY J. P. Nash

APPENDIX 24

ILLIAC LIBRARY DESCRIPTION OF A6:

FLOATING DECIMAL ROUTINE AND AUXILIARIES

Library Routine   A 6 - 154

TITLE:	Floating Decimal Routine and Auxiliaries (SADOI and DOI - Separate Version for Each)
TEMPORARY STORAGE:	0, 1, 2 and space 557 - 1023 used by routines.
PURPOSE:	To make available on a single tape Library Routine A 1 and its auxiliaries for use with a set of interpretive orders.
ENTRY:	Two methods of entry are possible:

(1) If the set of interpretive orders has no directive, entry to Library Routine A 1 consists simply of transferring control to the left hand side of fixed location 428 by the order 26 428N. In this case the interpretive orders will be read in and stored in locations starting at 430; the control transfer will then cause the interpretive orders to be obeyed in the order in which they occur.

(2) If the programmer wishes to place his interpretive orders elsewhere in the memory, he must precede them by a directive and the standard entry use of Library Routine A 1.

DESCRIPTION OF THE PROGRAM

The following routines are included: A 1, A 3, RA 1, TA 1, SA 2, TA 2, SA 3. These are stored in locations defined by parameters S 3 - SK. (See below.) The constant-listing auxiliary XA 1 is placed in locations beginning at 944 and the sum check at 902.

The parameters S 3 through SK are preset by the program and need not concern the programmer. For entry to auxiliaries, refer to the corresponding routines. Space available for the programmer depends on the entry. If the entry is made by method (1), interpretive orders will occupy locations starting at 430 and locations up to 556 are available for them.

So the programmer can use locations unoccupied by
interpretive orders together with locations from
3 to 429 for any purpose he wishes. By the other
method of entry, locations 3 to 556 are completely at
the programmer's disposal.

ACCURACY

All routines have the same accuracy, for a given number,
as the floating decimal routine.

PRESET PARAMETERS

Parameter	Address	Referring To
S3, 1S3	557, 558	Floating accumulator
S4	559	Library Routine A 1 Floating Decimal
S5	727	Library Routine A 3 Number Conversion Routine
S6	754	Library Routine RA 1 Square Root Auxiliary
S7	770	Library Routine TA 1 Sine Auxiliary
S8	796	Library Routine SA2 Exponential Auxiliary
S9	822	Library Routine SA 3 Natural Logarithm Auxiliary
SK	852	Library Routine TA 2 Arc Tangent Auxiliary

THE SADOI-DRUM VERSION OF A 6

Like other subroutines on the drum, A6 is called for
by a modified directive, (A6) 00nK. Regardless of the
value of n the subroutines comprising A6 are stored
in the same locations indicated previously for the
Tape-D. O. I. version of A6.

When A6 is called, SADOI automatically presets the
parameters in 3 to 10, and the subroutines comprising
A6 are then inserted, followed by the two words

428 22 428F
    50 428F
429 26 S4
    83 430F

The computer then stops on a 2410J (sexadecimal) order.
It should be noted that the drum version of A6 does
not contain XA 1, the Constant Listing Auxiliary.
A choice is then available:

(1) White switch over the 2410J order. The assembled
program is then placed in Williams Memory and a drum
bootstrap start begins automatically. When the white
switch is used and the first character on the tape is
"0" the D.O.I. is placed in 999-1023 of the Williams
Memory and tape input is resumed. This choice permits
use of the Constant Listing Auxiliary (Routine XA 1)
which will work only with D.O.I. and not with SADOI.
It (Routine XA 1) should be placed on the tape so that
it will be read in by the D.O.I. after use of the
white switch. (See B below)

(2) Black switch to execute the 2410J order. SADOI
automatically receives the directive 00 430K. Tape
input begins and words of the program are stored,
beginning at 430, until a new directive is received.

A. Normally, for use with the black switch
when the XA 1 is not desired, the program tape is
made up in the following manner:

      J

    Title

    1-hole delay

    KOK (to obtain SADOI)

    (A6) 00 K

    Program (with or without directive)

    24 999N

    26 428N A1 will begin interpreting at 430.

B. Make up of the program tape for use with the
white switch when the Constant Listing Auxiliary is
desired.

      J

    Title

    1-hole delay

    KOK

    (A6) 00 K

Directive   (preferably 00 944K)

Constant Listing Auxiliary

Directive   (preferably 00 430K)

Program

24 999N) With 00 430K directive. If other directive
26 428N) is used a new entry to A 1 must be written
so it will begin interpreting properly.

USE OF LIBRARY ROUTINE D1 (95)

Locations from 900 onwards are available for the use
of Library Routine D 1. It may be used by blocking
orders in Library Routine A 1. If the fourth word
(namely, 562) of A 1 is blocked, D 1 will print before
each interpretive order is obeyed. The location of
this interpretive order is given by the left hand
address in location 561. The floating accumulator
(557, 558) may be printed at this time. The interpretive
order being obeyed appears on the left hand side of
the accumulator. A typical specification might therefore
be:

562 L Blocking order to 562

100 K Print 100 times

561 S6 Print location of interpretive order

900 S0 Print interpretive order being obeyed

557 S5 Print floating accumulator

558 SN Contents

428 N6 Start program (first method of entry)

Rt: 9/24/59

DATE 11/11/54

REVISED WRITEUP 10/14/58

PROGRAMMED BY D.J.Wheeler

REVISED BY Lily Seshu

APPROVED BY J.P.Nash

REVISED BY R. Flenner

APPROVED BY J.N.Snyder

lgr

www.ingramcontent.com/pod-product-compliance
Lightning Source LLC
LaVergne TN
LVHW012206040326
832903LV00003B/162